The Hindu Sufis of South Asia

The Hindu Sufis of South Asia

*Partition, Shrine Culture and
the Sindhis in India*

Michel Boivin

I.B. TAURIS
LONDON • NEW YORK • OXFORD • NEW DELHI • SYDNEY

I.B. TAURIS
Bloomsbury Publishing Plc
50 Bedford Square, London, WC1B 3DP, UK
1385 Broadway, New York, NY 10018, USA

BLOOMSBURY, I.B. TAURIS and the Diana logo are trademarks of
Bloomsbury Publishing Plc

First published in Great Britain 2019

Copyright © Michel Boivin 2019

Cover design: Adriana Brioso
Cover image: Mumbai, 2017. Courtesy of the Author.

A catalogue record for this book is available from the British Library.

A catalog record for this book is available from the Library of Congress.

ISBN: 978-0-7556-4369-1
eISBN: 978-1-7883-1956-0
ePDF: 978-1-7883-1957-7

Series: Library of Islamic South Asia

Typeset by Deanta Global Publishing Services, Chennai, India

To find out more about our authors and books visit www.bloomsbury.com and
sign up for our newsletters.

پاونا پگِتُ گِیَني، آچارَجُ آوتوتُ

Contents

List of Illustrations   ix

Acknowledgements   x

Table of annexes   xii

Introduction   1

  Mapping the issue: From Sindh to the Sindhicate area   1

  Sufism and the Sufi culture of Sindh   4

  The Sufi and Hindu encounter as an issue in social sciences   7

  Hinduism and Sufism in the Sindhicate area   14

1 The religious market in Sindh on the eve of partition   23

  Social structure and religious belonging in colonial Sindh   25

  The Amils, the intelligentsia and the objectification of Sufism   30

  The recomposition of the religious scene and the *darbar* culture   37

  The birth of a middle class and the emergence of Hindu Sufi paths   41

  Partition in Sindh   48

  Conclusion   50

2 The new settlement and the making of the *darbars*   53

  Building the *darbars* in India   54

  Authority, the legitimization process and succession   59

  Naming the shrine in India as a first step   64

  Sacralizing the new territory   66

  Conclusion   71

3 Sufi poetry and the production of the mystical space   73

  Bhakti and Vedanta   74

  The classical Sufi corpus   77

  The modern Sufi corpus   82

  The vernacular ideology of the *wahdat-e wujud*   86

  Hindu references in the Sufi poetry   91

  Conclusion   95

4   Alternative Sufi structures as networking India and beyond   99
     The *darbar* and its extensions   100
     The *samadhi* as an alternative Sufi structure   104
     The Sufi *mandir* and the pilgrimage to Bijapur   110
     Mulchand Kafi   111
     Conclusion   114

5   Rituals as connecting spaces and community   117
     Iconography as an idiom of transference   118
     Initiation and meditation   123
     Daily rituals and informal Sufi practices   127
     Annual fairs: From *urs* to *versi*   131
     The 'Darazi *satsangs*'   137
     Conclusion   139

6   The transmission of the Sufi legacy in India   141
     Ram Panjwani (1911–87) and the challenge of post-partition
          transmission   142
     Non-poetic chains for the transmission of Sufism   149
     Other networks of transmission   156
     The role of the diaspora in the transmission of the Sufi legacy   157
     Conclusion   160

7   The Sufi paths and the Hindus of Sindh in Pakistan   163
     Sindhi encounters between Sufism and Hinduism   164
     The Hindus and the Sehwan system   166
     The 'Hindu *dargah*' of Tando Ahmad Khan   171
     Neither Hindu nor Muslim: The Sufi-related cults of the Sindhi Dalits 174
     Conclusion   179

General conclusion   183

Notes   195
Glossary   205
Annexes   208
     1. Abstracts of Sufi poetry in Sindhi and English translation   208
     2. Hindu Sufis' *silsilas* in Sindh   214
Bibliography   216
Index   226

Illustrations

Figures

All images belong to the author.

1.1   Three Hindu Sufis with their Muslim *murshid*s. (a) Qutub Ali Shah, (b) Rochaldas, (c) Rakhiyyal Shah, (d) Mulchand Faqir, (e) Sakhi Qabul Muhammad II and (f) Nimano Faqir 45

2.1   Sufi seats from Sindh in India 56

2.2   Hindu Sufi figures and their Sufi connections in Sindh 63

2.3   Lal Shahbaz Qalandar's *alam* in Rochaldas's *darbar* 68

2.4   External view of two Indian *darbar*s, Haridwar and Vadodara. (a) The Dada Sain Kuthir, Haridwar, 2012 and (b) The Nimanal Sangam, Vadodara, 2012 70

4.1   Shoba, the *gaddi nashin*'s sister, unveiling Nimano's picture, Mumbai 103

4.2   Mulchand's tomb in Sehwan Sharif 113

5.1   Iconographical agency in the Mulchand and Rochaldas's *samadhis*. (a) *Mulchand's altar, Dada Sain Kuthir, Haridwar, 2012 and (b) Rochaldas's darbar, Ulhasnagar, 2012* 121

5.2   Two *mehndi*s in Ulhasnagar (India) and Sehwan Sharif (Pakistan). (a) Damodar's *mehndi* procession at Rochaldas's *darbar*, Ulhasnagar, 2012 and (b) Ramchand's *dastarbandi* before the *mehndi* procession in Sehwan Sharif, 2011 136

7.1   Asan Gul, a Hindu *sajjada nashin* in Sehwan Sharif 169

7.2   Map of the Hindu *dargah*, Tando Ahmad Khan 172

7.3   Pithoro Pir's tomb with the *Om* 177

Table

5.1   Daily programme of Rochaldas's *versi* in 2012 133

Acknowledgements

This study is the result of some years being spent here and there in *darbar*s, talking or observing or translating. Nonetheless, all of the material presented here is not wholly new, meaning unpublished, as various pieces of this study have been presented elsewhere in the time leading up to this publication. Some parts have already been published, in English and in French (see Bibliography), and others presented in conferences or workshops, but these various pieces are now brought together in full, and introduced within this new, and more complete, shape and frame.

I would like to warmly thank all my Sufi *dust*s for the time and data they have shared with me. As has been the case with much of my other research devoted to Sindh studies, two generations of the Gidwani family from Pune have been keen to share their interests and knowledge of Sufism from Sindh, as well as many other skills regarding the Sindhi language, and different scripts. Also, I must thank Dada Ishwar Balani (1920–2004), the founder of the Sindhi Community House in London, who pushed me into the world of the Hindu Sufis when he gave me books on Sindhi Sufism in India, back when we met in London in 2002.

I am unable to show how grateful I am to the many Hindu Sufs I have met, and worked with. In Ulhasnagar, Damodar and Pritam Mansharamani, as well as Daulatram Motwani, Soni Katharia, Jaichand Sharma and Mira Rajani. In Pimpri, my thanks go to Isha Pohani, Gehimal Motwani's daughter. In Mumbai, Dadi Dhan Samtani (d. 2014), Devi Naik, Daulat Kesvani and Dhuru Sipahimalani, with his sister Vina, similarly welcomed my research on the Hindu Sufs, and fnally I must here thank Shoba Vaswani. In Vadodara, Murli Kanunga and Suresh Advani, as well as Kamla, whose full name I do not know, and in Delhi and Haridwar, Basant Jethwani and his wife Sonu.

This study was also a golden opportunity for me to observe that the sacrosaint 'social networks' were not always unuseful, since it is thanks to the internet that I was in touch with Manu Bhatia, who made me familiar with Isarlal's *kalam*, which he had published with his cousin Lachhman Bhatia.

Regarding the translations included here in the text, I am most grateful for the help provided by a number of friends, mostly belonging to the Gidwani family from Pune and the Matlani family from Mumbai-Ulhasnagar. Nonetheless, I am the only one responsible for translations when the name of the author is given after a quotation. When it is not the name of an author given, this signifies that I am using another translation, and in this case, this is the name of the translator which is provided. As it will be noted, there is no attempt to provide any academic transliteration.

Table of annexes

1   Abstracts of Sufi poetry   208
    Dalpat Sufi   208
    Qutub Ali Shah   210
    Dadi Ganga   211
    Nimano Faqir   212
    Gehimal Motwani   213

2. Hindu Sufis' *silsilas* in Sindh   214

Introduction

Mapping the issue: From Sindh to the Sindhicate area

In 2004, while I was in London for a research programme on Sindhi material, I was told there was a 'Sindhi Community House' in the northern part of the city. Thus, I went to Cricklewood, the area where it was located, and I was welcomed by the *shewadaris*, the attendants who were in charge of the centre.[1] After some time, I met Dada Ishwar Balani (1920–2004), the founder of the centre. He showed me the library and told me I could take all the books I wanted. Among them, I was attracted by the English title of a small volume published in 1997 by S. L. Gajwani: *Sindhi Sufi Literature in Independent India* (Gajwani 1997). This book contained a list of books published by Sindhis, especially Hindu Sindhis, on Sufism. The main part of it had been published in post-partition India in the Sindhi language, and this book offered clear evidence that the Sindhi Sufi tradition was still well alive among the Hindu Sindhis of India, exactly half a century after partition. For me, this find was the equivalent of discovering a new world.

As I had been working on Sindh studies for years, I was well aware that the Sindhi Hindus of Sindh had gone to Sufi shrines, and that they shared their passion for Sufi poetry with Muslim Sindhis and others, especially through Shah Abd al-Latif's *Shah jo Risalo*. But I had totally ignored the fact that the Sindhi Hindus of India were still linked with Sufi traditions from Sindh. I had totally ignored the fact that the Hindu Sindhis who had fled Pakistan from 1947 onwards had 'transferred' to India not only their Hindu cults but also their Sufi cults. Later on, it took me some years to see how Sufi traditions were still permeating the life of a number of Hindu Sindhis of India. In 2011, I went to Ulhasnagar in Maharashtra for another research project, but I also took this opportunity to pay a visit to some places related to the Sufism of Sindh in India. Gajwani, the author of the small book, was a follower of Sain Rochaldas, whose shrine or *darbar* was well known in Shantinagar, an area located in

Ulhasnagar. In a few months, I went on to become familiar with at least three main Sufi-related paths among the Sindhi Hindus of India, and a number of minor ones.

As an anthropologist, my interest is to understand how, in the early twenty-first century, a number of people in India claiming to be Hindu still maintain a tradition in which the Sufi elements – usually associated with Islam – are playing a leading part in structuring it, if they are not the core of the tradition itself, and furthermore, I am talking about a tradition with permanent links with Pakistan. In addressing this issue, observation of rituals and interviews with people must obviously be completed and enmeshed in a work on written sources, because, as we shall see, Sufi poetry plays a cardinal role in the setting. The written corpus is mostly made of Sufi poetry in Sindhi, most of it recently published in post-partition India. Another related issue to address is the significance of the Sufi legacy for the Hindu Sindhi community of India. In other words, what did it really mean for them to involve the Sufi legacy in the process of renewing the Hindu Sindhi identity in a brand new environment? And, in more demographic terms, what is the weight and influence of the Sindhi Hindu Sufis in the Indian communities of Sindhi Hindus? As well as in the diaspora?

By the way, it is a worthwhile question to wonder whether the Sindhis of India are a part of a larger diaspora,[2] though the question goes far beyond the scope of this study. Given the question's relation to the work at hand, however, I feel I should note here that I have no problem in considering that they are since they have been compelled to leave their ancestral home, and thus they don't have a 'national' or 'nation-like' territory. Nonetheless, I believe the issue is more complex. As a matter of fact, the region they are coming from belongs to a territory that is a part of their same cultural unit, despite an obvious element of diversity, and the question also arises because they have built in India a genuine community which is known as such, despite their lack of territory. But finally, it is a highly political matter, related mostly to nineteenth-century theories on the nation-states.

Notwithstanding, I locate the Sindhi diaspora as being made up of the Sindhi people who live in Asian countries outside of South Asia as well as in Europe, Africa and America. Interestingly, a number of excellent studies have already been devoted to the Sindhi diaspora settled in different countries, especially in the South and Far East Asia. Consequently, one can count three different spaces in which Sindhi-speaking people are living: in Pakistan, in India and as diaspora. The first two spaces are nation-states, and the rest of the people are scattered in many other nation-states.

Due to this specific situation, I shall use the neologism 'Sindhicate area' – as drawn upon Marshall Hodgson's notions of 'Islamicate' and also 'Persaniate'.[3] In selecting the term 'Sindhicate' instead of 'Sindh', 'Sindhi world' or 'Sindhi area', I want to highlight that, beyond religious associations, be they Muslim, Hindu, Sikh, Christian and so on, this area has produced a shared culture using historical references, a lexicon and a symbolic discourse – in brief, integrating a number of elements which are usually seen as making a distinct culture – despite the territorial discontinuity of the Sindhicate area. Briefly put, this study is thus connected to issues going beyond the Sindhicate area and culture, since it is related to nation-state borders, relations between centre and periphery, the making of a community and the construction of a tradition in a twenty-first-century environment.

Among other aims, this study also works to underscore how the transformation of community and tradition is attached to authority, and especially to those who are in charge; therefore, it will also question the ways through which authority is legitimized and thus acknowledged and accepted by followers, as well as challenged. Beyond authority, this study addresses the issue of the social construction and the interplay between dominating groups and allegedly dominated groups: How is Sufism entangled in this complex process? Is Sufism producing a distinct community, in being able to spread new types of relationships between groups and individuals?

Finally, this study will address the issue of overlapping of religion and society in the modern world, and in a fresh way that will give further insight into the topic at hand. It will illustrate that the closed categories adopted as universal, but which were built by the West at a time when it was the dominating power(s) all over the world, were challenged through the building of new agencies, implementing new processes of confrontation and transaction between different groups of people. In many cases, as it will be argued, religion was more a referential idiom to legitimize the access to power of new groups. Notwithstanding, this point does not mean that religion is to be reduced to a form of power: this study focuses on the management of religious cults and it does not directly interfere with matters related to the individual or collective faith of the believers.

Sufism and the Sufi culture of Sindh

For years, my research has focused on *Sindh ji sufyani saqafat*, the Sufi culture of Sindh (Boivin 2016). The use of this expression indicates that it is more a matter of taking an interest in the social and cultural productions of Sufism, rather than addressing a more theological understanding of Sufism itself.[4] Clifford Geertz rightly pointed out the culture 'as consisting not so much in customs and institutions as in the sorts of interpretations the members of a society apply to their experience, the constructions they put upon the events through which they live' (Geertz 1968: 90). The object of this study is the Sufi culture of Sindh, rather than an essentialized form of Sufism. It is based on a number of cultural expressions such as literature, music and art, but it also includes other fields such as rituals and artefacts. This culture has been called Sufi culture because it is inspired largely by Sufism, even when it is produced by non-Muslims. The Sufi culture puts forward the idea that the quest for the divine is the same in all religions. The representation of the divine is similar: it is the ultimate reality and at the same time its presence is everywhere. As early as the nineteenth century, the British quickly realized that Sufism permeated local cultures, especially through devotional poetry.

While it resulted from a process of vernacularization,[5] it is necessary to analyse the Sufi culture of Sindh and to understand why and how it constituted the dominant form of the episteme of the region at the turn of the nineteenth and twentieth centuries. The historical context is fundamental: it is dominated by British colonization. In terms of agents, this emergence has in fact been based on an often-desired and planned interaction between new local elites and colonial administrators, as early as the middle of the nineteenth century. In terms of corpus, it has promoted, in addition to 'classical'[6] poetry, through the canonization of *Shah jo Risalo* by Shah Abd al-Latif, new sciences, new literary forms and, in short, a new approach to knowledge.

In this 'social architecture of knowledge', to quote Michel de Certeau (Certeau 1990: 141–64), 'secondary' corpuses have been rejected from the construction of a modern literary reference, although based on their content and expression they are part of this culture. This is because the producers did not, however, enter into the social representation promoted by the British, and often guided by the Muslim and above all the Hindu elites. They belonged to declassified communities, meaning they were within groups standing at the edges of their society. Because of their social marginalization, they were not entitled to produce cultural items to be consumed by the whole society. Also, this is because, following the Western representation of the time, the dominant knowledge of these groups was related to magic in opposition to Sufi poetry that was raising a mystical goal, the union of the soul with God. Another literary category was also dismissed, albeit to a lesser degree: that which Pakistani and Indian scholars still call 'folkloric'. These are largely oral-based corpuses, and it was only after the partition that Nabi Bakhsh Baloch made a gigantic undertaking to measure their scale and impact (Baloch 1959, 1964, 1985–7, 1992).

All in all, another main issue to be addressed here is the nature of the group made up by the Hindu Sufis and their followers. In the introduction to the book, *Literary Cultures in History: Reconstructions from South Asia*, published in 2003, Sheldon Pollock develops the concept of 'sociotextual community'. This denomination refers to 'the community for which literature is produced, in which it circulates, and which derives a part of its own understanding as a community of the action of hearing, reading, performing, reproducing and circulating literary texts' (Pollock 2003: 27). In her book on the social space of language, and acknowledging her debt to Pollock, Farina Mir refers to the concept of 'Punjabi literary formation', which she describes as 'a group made up of members who share practices, production, circulation, performance, reading and reception of Punjabi literary texts' (Mir 2010: 97). The present study takes up some of the objectives assigned by Pollock when he seeks to explore, for example, 'the relations that existed between literature and the simultaneous categories of oral, written and printed cultures' (Pollock 2003: 15). But I will emphasize the role played by the agents operating this Sufi culture at the centre of the study, and I will also highlight the relationship they built with their followers, their masters and their rivals in the religious market, in scrutinizing what all these networks tell us about their social milieu.

Regarding Mir's assertion, it seems difficult in the case of the Sindhicate area to draw on a unified and harmonized society, even if a number of cultural products are obviously shared. The Sufi culture of Sindh was nonetheless the most shared product, but this does not prevent the society from being highly fragmented. Consequently, I will follow Pierre Bourdieu when he speaks of a cultural product as resulting from

> the struggle between those who, because of the dominant (temporal) position they occupy in the field ... are committed to conservation, that is to say, the defense of routine and routinization, banality and banalization, in a word, of the established symbolic order, and those who are prone to breaking hereticism, criticizing established forms, the subversion of the models in force, and the return to the purity of the origins (Bourdieu 1992: 340).

While the poetry was and still is the core of the Sufi culture, this study does not stop at the analysis of the construction and reinvention of the literary corpus. It attends to the fact that other productions beyond those in the literary field alone are to be erected into objects of analysis. Let us quote for example the ritual field, also explored by Pierre Bourdieu from a re-reading of Max Weber. Bourdieu focuses his approach on the 'social function of ritual and ... the social significance of the line, of the limit, whose ritual permits passage, transgression' (Bourdieu 1987: 206). As a result, it seems more appropriate to speak in this work of 'Sufi sociocultural communities'. A Sufi sociocultural community is a community for which poetry is produced, and by which it is consumed, and in which a number of symbolic products are circulating throughout an array of rituals. These are the basic elements that construct the Sufi sociocultural community.

Finally, this study will also seek to deconstruct the notion of the Sufi culture of Sindh by decentring the analysis in the direction of sociocultural communities that hardly enter the spectrum of the usual analysed objects. In the context of the Sindhicate area, and South Asia in general, they include both cultural expressions catalogued as folkloric and socially marginalized groups. In short, I will temporarily designate them as 'outcasts', although the expression formerly formulated by the British seems more pertinent, that of their being 'neither Muslim nor Hindu'. As early as 1851, Richard Burton pointed out that certain populations of Sindh could not be considered a Muslim or a Hindu

(Burton 1851: 307, 323). I shall devote a part of the last chapter of this study to this neglected topic.

The use of a double negation to designate a group is interesting, but it also raises the following questions: Does this mean that there is no correct category to designate the group? And why not build an ad hoc category? What is at stake in this aporia? Five years after Burton's publication, Stanley N. Raikes, another British officer, spoke of populations that are not recognized by Muslims or Hindus (Raikes 1856: 4). The most amazing point is that, coincidentally, the category of 'neither...nor' met the credo of the Sufis of Sindh, whose works known as *kalam*s constituted the foundations of Sufi culture. As stated by Dalpat Sufi, or Sachal Sarmast, hereafter Sachal, the true Sufi is beyond religion, hence the formula *hindu momin nahyan*, to quote Nimano Faqir, one of the Hindu Sufi figures under study (Nimano Faqir 1997: 284), for which 'neither...nor' is the exact English translation.

In concluding his book on caste production by the colonial administration, Nicholas Dirks quotes Kancha Ilaiah's words: 'I was not born a Hindu for the simple reason that my parents did not know that they were Hindus' (Dirks 2001: 297). More than any other object of study, the Sufi culture of Sindh leads one to question the social and religious representations that were, almost or remotely, fabricated by the colonial administration. Indeed, what is the significance of these designations when – as at Sehwan Sharif, for example – a Hindu disciple of Lal Shahbaz Qalandar initiates Muslims to the path (*tariqa*) of Qalandariyya shahbaziyya? In India, the Sufi heritage from Sindh was perpetuated by the Hindus who emigrated from 1947 onwards. They have edited and published heretofore unpublished texts. These texts remain alive specifically because they form the basis of prayers and rituals. These same Hindu Sufis also composed *kalam*s.

The Sufi and Hindu encounter as an issue in social sciences

The history of the studies devoted to encounters between Islam and Hinduism is not that long. In 1970, Simon Dibgy, while speaking of 'Encounterings with jogis in Indian Sufi hagiography' in a seminar at SOAS, was interested in encounters before the Mughal period, namely during the thirteenth to

sixteenth centuries. He focused on Persian sources like *tazkiras* (hagiographical
life narratives of Sufi saints) and *malfuzats* (dialogues between a Sufi Master
and his disciples), and started with observing that the sources on the relations
between Muslims and non-Muslims were 'disappointingly little'. However,
in the Persian sources, the main Hindu figure is the *jogi*. The term 'jogi' is
usually employed for the Nathpanthis, a Shivaite school of renunciants who
were the followers of Gorakhnath.[7] The Sufis asked the following questions:
Can a non-Muslim receive God's favours? May a non-Muslim be close to
God? They provided answers through a number of anecdotes which were
classified by Digby into five groups: voluntary conversions of *jogis* followed
by their attainment of a high level in the Sufi path; magic contests leading
to subjugation and conversion of the *jogis*; the same, but with a regional
significance; and refusal of a proffered gift, by which a *shaykh* demonstrates
his superiority over a *jogi*.

In the conclusion, Digby employs the word 'influence' for stating that,
mainly because of the opacity of sources, it is difficult to sustain the most
common idea according to which Indian Sufis were much influenced by
Indian traditions. For him, the translation of two literary works provides
evidence enough to illustrate the 'Yogic influence', and he thus claims that
the Persian sources 'often conceal a much Indianised situation'. The use of the
word 'influence' for speaking of the encounter between Islam and Hinduism
was vividly criticized. Carl Ernst, in his book on the islamization of yoga,
pointed out that the use of such a word, if not the notion itself, implies the idea
of the superiority of one religion over another. Non-Christian religions were
'hybrids composed of various "Oriental" influences, that was the testimony to
their dependent and inferior nature' (Ernst 2016: 189).

Such a statement leading us to speak in terms of influence is often based on
another prerequisite: what Sheldon Pollock calls the 'ideology of antiquity'. He
explains: 'The more archaic a text, the purer it is thought to be, and the more
recent, the more derivative and even mongrel' (Pollock 2003: 4). Another
point he criticizes is related to the relation of central centres of learning, most
often called imperial centres, and regional centres of learning. Once again, it
is necessary to quote him, as he rightly pointed out that, in the second half
of the nineteenth century, 'regional literatures [were] seen increasingly as
subordinate to a so-called "Indian Literature"' (Pollock 2003: 6).

The most innovative approach to the issue of encounters between Islam and Hinduism was expressed by Tony Stewart. He claimed to 'reconceive the nature of the religious encounter that characterizes the region in this pre- and early colonial period' (Stewart 2001: 261). For him, the encounter emphasizes the local, the creative efforts of individuals trying to make sense of an environment that does not always cooperate. He states that 'translation in this context defines a way that religious practitioners seek "equivalence" among their counterparts'. Enduring frameworks of religious organizations and interpretation eventually grounded traditions as we understand them today in their regional forms. Finally, Stewart concludes that 'the search for equivalence in the encounter of religions – when understood through the translation models we have characterized as literal, refractive, dynamic, and metaphoric – is an attempt to be understood, to make oneself understood in a language not always one's own' (Stewart 2001: 263).

Addressing the issue of encounters between Islam and Hinduism in Sindh requires us to turn back to the relationship the so-called Muslims had with Islam, or in other words, to look at what it meant to be Muslim. Historical sources provide evidence that, before the eighteenth century, the people who identified themselves as Muslims were few: probably, this is related to the fact that the denomination of Muslims was restricted to the sayyids and their dependents. The sayyids were the alleged descendants of Prophet Muhammad, and this genealogy provided them with a legitimacy to occupy a dominant position in their local society. But even among those who claimed a Muslim identity, the main issue was: How to be a good Muslim when you are not an Arabic speaker? How to enforce a correct understanding of what Islam is when you cannot read the original text of the Quran? Moreover, how to understand notions and concepts that are outside of the scope of your cultural framework?

In the early eighteenth century, a number of treatises were written in Sindh by Naqshbandi scholars from Lowari Sharif, a village close to Badin in Southern Sindh. The main author was Makhdum Muhammad Hashim (1692–1762), who was *qazi* in Thatta. With other Naqshbandi Sufis, he provided evidence that the Muslim Sindhis did not know the Quran, and, consequently, they first wrote paraphrasings of the Arabic text, and finally a Sindhi translation of the Arabic Quran, with glosses to explain the words or the ideas behind the literal text. Also, in these treatises, they explained how to be a good Muslim: the importance of the canonical prayer (*namaz*), how to perform it properly, and so on. They condemned some rituals, especially coined as Hindu or Shia, as non-Islamic.

Manuscripts and early lithographed books provide evidence that the religious culture of Sindh had been vernacularized: what does this mean, though? Borrowing from Sheldon Pollock's work, vernacularization is here understood to be a process through which the local literati, especially Sindhi poets, appropriate notions or concepts coming from other linguistic and cultural areas (Pollock 2006: 23). Pollock was, however, working in a very different context in terms of time since he is a specialist of Sanskrit literature in medieval India. It must be understood that the process of vernacularization sometimes occurs in different ways and phases. In Sindh, the first phase was usually a linguistic translation, which means, in this case, the translation of a word from a foreign language. In the present case, it was a translation from Arabic and Persian into Sindhi. The next step is the translation of a notion or concept, which implies a slight change in its meaning since the notion or concept is recast into the local milieu. Still another step is the incorporation of local motifs and local figures.

In Sindh, one can identify several historical steps in the long-term process of vernacularization. The first step can be identified as the Ismaili step, since the Ismailis were the main agents of vernacularization and used Sindhi for writing their devotional poetry known as *ginan*. The main intention of the Ismaili *pirs* was to present arguments for demonstrating the homology between Ismaili and Hindu concepts, and the foremost role of the *Imam* as saviour. From the thirteenth century onward, the second step was that of classical Sufism, the main features of which were the incorporation of *desi* (local) literary motifs, the figure of the *jogi* as a symbol of Sufism, and the vital role played by music in the mystical quest. Be they Ismaili or Sohrawardi, the agents' goals were similar: to gain followers of a *pir* rather than to convert individuals to Islam. The third and last step was the colonial step. The main change was that, because of a number of new factors (including the census), the people had more and more to identify themselves according to their affiliation to 'great religions' – primarily Islam or Hinduism. Before, they had not identified themselves through a religious persuasion, but according to their locality, caste and ethnicity.

Thus, the final identification of the Indians with a 'great religion' was the result on the long-term process, and for centuries, the purity of a religion, that is to say it could not share anything with another religion, was not an issue. On the contrary, there was an old tradition of scholars attempting to find bridges between their own religion and others', and the first endeavours were implemented in the field of literature. Scholars used to look for similarities into two traditions that are in contact. In the Islamic context, there was Nasir-e Khusraw (1004–74), who tried to bridge Islamic tradition and Greek philosophy. In the Indian context, there was Shah Jahan's son and heir, Prince Dara Shikoh (1615–59), who is the author of an emblematic work: the *Majma' al-bahrayn* (or, the confluence of the two oceans). He was probably the first to face the challenge of selecting similarities between Sufism and Hinduism in depth. While writing in Persian, and being a herald of the Akbarian persuasion in Delhi,[8] Dara Shikoh's work was to reach the courtly elite of the Mughal Empire. Then in the nineteenth century, many British authors underscored what they called the 'syncretism' prevailing in a number of religious communities of India. Usually, the word 'syncretism' was used as a derogatory word for depicting a religious system without consistency, made of mixed elements that were motley. A syncretist religion could not be a true religion, or a good religion. And most of the time, the British identified those syncretist religions among the low classes: the impure religion was forcibly that of low classes, which were themselves impure.

Turning back to the Sindhicate area, the encounters between Islam and Hinduism probably started throughout Ismailism, a Shia branch of Islam. Among the 'translating' persuasions of India, the Ismaili literature was the most investigated, surely because of the standards of the highly educated community since most of the scholars in this field are themselves Ismaili. However, since the head of the Ismaili is a Muslim, Shah Karim al-Husayni (better known as Aga Khan IV), the literature of the Ismailis went through a process of islamization which led to the withdrawal of Hindu references from the corpus, be they names of gods, elements of the technical lexicon such as *avatar*, references to Hindu fairs, and so on. Interestingly, in some parts of India, especially Gujarat, some segments of the community were submitted to a hinduization process through which all of the so-called Islamic elements were suppressed. Once again, it will be worthwhile to keep this process in mind when we turn to the Hindu Sufis of Sindh. In this respect, one can quote the case of Imam Shah's cult. In Pirana, a place located close to Ahmedabad, the *dargah* of Imam Shah is now under Hindu control, and the official narrative does not mention that he was an Ismaili Shia preacher. The shared devotional literature is also 'hinduized' through the substitution of Arabic words for Sanskrit ones.[9]

In recent years, the encounter between Sufism and Hinduism has also attracted scholars in anthropology. In the 2000s, a number of studies underscored that the Sufi *dargah*s in South Asia were important places of 'encountering' between Islam and Hinduism. But what does that mean, exactly? Most of the time, this assumption was related to the fact that Hindus used to go to a Sufi *dargah* as a pilgrimage. It is noteworthy that, even if in most of the case studies Sufism was involved, some Muslim sanctuaries were originated in other Muslim traditions, such as the Shia tradition. Carla Bellamy's research is devoted to Hussein Tikri, a sanctuary created by a Shia Khoja from Bombay. Interestingly, while the place is not used as a Shia place by the majority of the users, all the *dargah*s are devoted to Shia figures (Bellamy 2011).

Regarding the encountering of Sufism and Hinduism, a groundbreaking study was published by Thomas Dahnhardt in 2002. In the preface, he himself introduces his study as 'an attempt to delineate the meeting of two different esoteric currents in a cross-cultural encounter between Islam and Hinduism in the Indian Subcontinent from the second half of the last century down to the present' (Dahnhardt 2002: vii). Dahnhardt's work is of special interest for a number of reasons, and not only because, obviously, his study is the most thorough analysis of a Hindu branch in a Sufi *tariqa*. Although mainly based on the study of writings, it provides a remarkable view of a meeting between Islam and Hinduism in colonial India. Furthermore, the Hindu Sufis he is scrutinizing belong to the same generation as the Hindu Sindhi Sufis who are the core of the present work. Of course, this is not a mere coincidence. Other interesting connections can be found as pertaining to a given Hindu milieu related to educated middle classes.

Therefore, it is worthwhile here to provide a survey of the main results found by Dahnhardt. In terms of figures, the first Hindu to have been initiated in the Naqshbandi *tariqa* is Mahatma Ramchandraji Maharaj (1873–1931). He belonged to the Saksena, a subcaste of the Kayasht community, whose members had for centuries served in the administrative and military service of Muslim-ruling dynasties, especially the Mughals (Dahnhardt 2002: 197). Interestingly, after 1857 and at the end of the Mughal Empire, many Kayasht migrated to work in the Princely States, including the Khairpur emirate in Sindh. Although Pandit Brahmashankar Mishra (1861–1907), another prominent member, spent years in Karachi and Hyderabad, no formal relation between Sindh and the Hindu branch of the Naqshbandiyya has been found.

Two other features of interest have been identified by Dahnhardt: the Hindu sectarian background of the Hindu Naqshbandis and the role played by the technical lexicon for bridging their Hindu background and the Sufi affiliation. While Ramachandra's family was embedded into a Ramaite devotional tradition, the background of the majority of the Hindu Sufis included the Kabirpanth and the Nanakpanth. Nonetheless, the technical lexicon built by Ramachandra and his doctrinal elaboration were that of the Vedanta. Dahnhardt observes that 'the technical vocabulary can vary quite unpredictably from an author to another, work to work and even passage to passage' (Dahnhardt 2002: 382). Last but not least, Dahnhardt refers many times to a process of the hinduization of the Naqshbandiyya, both in terms of the doctrinal background and the methodology. As will be discussed in the following chapters, these elements were broadly shared by the Hindu Sufis of Sindh.

Still, the Hindu Naqshbandis keep some characteristics in contrast to the Hindu Sufis of Sindh. For example, the non-Kayasht Hindu Naqshbandis were Brahmans who could be former members of the Arya Samaj. Nonetheless, the main difference between these two Hindu Sufi paths is the role given to poetry. Among the Hindu Naqshbandis, Sufi poetry is not the core of the Sufi tradition while, with the Sindhi Hindu Sufis, poetry, as we shall see in Chapter 3, plays a tremendous role: it is relevant to claim that Sufi poetry is the backbone of Sufism in Sindh, including for the Hindu Sufis. Thus, this point will drive us to examine the specific history of Sindh, or, in other words, to understand how Sufi poetry came to shape the core of the culture in Sindh. But before we get to that point, it is necessary to understand how the relations between Sufism and Hinduism were approached by academic studies in the Sindhicate area.

Hinduism and Sufism in the Sindhicate area

My intention here is to briefly introduce how the scholars addressed the issue of the relations between Sufism and Hinduism in the context of the Sindhicate area. One of the pioneering works is the dissertation submitted to the University of Bombay in 1932 by N. J. Narsain. She clearly states that the integration of Sufism inside of the religious environment of the Hindu Sindhis dates back to the nineteenth century, and that the main actors involved were the Amils, the literary class. Narsain challenges Weber's theory when she claims that the Sufi cults fitted well into the way of life of the Amils (Narsain 1932: 73–5). I refer here to the well-known theory of Max Weber, according to which the *guru*, a term he coined as the 'living saviour', is worshipped by the non-literate middle classes in India. This signifies that these groups need to have a direct intercessor since they have no direct access to the sacred scriptures. In the context of Sindh, the Sufi Master shares many features with what Weber names a *guru*, but his followers, the Amils, belong to the literate class (Weber 1958: 334).

We cannot find any new relevant study after this until 2005, when Anita Raina Thapan published a paper titled 'Sufism and Sikhism'. Yet, she did not focus only on Sufism, as her main objective was to understand the dynamics of tradition and change in the beliefs and practices of Sindhi Hindus (Thapan 2005). While many scholars have only referred to the custom among the Hindus to visit Sufi shrines, she is perhaps the first to ask directly: what does it mean for a Hindu to be a Sufi? To answer this question, she investigated three Sufi lineages in India and rightly observed that the spiritual masters (*sajjada nashin* or *pir*) are still in Sindh, Pakistan. They are the *sajjada nashin* of Daraza, of Tando Jahaniya and of Jhok Sharif. At each of them, a great Sufi poet is attached: Sachal Sarmast, Qutub Ali Shah and Nasir Faqir (Thapan 2005: 210–11).

For the author, 'A Hindu who calls himself a Sufi was normally one who had taken initiation from a Sufi pir.' She also clearly states, apparently according to interviews, that 'Hindu disciples of Sufi pirs did not represent the majority' (Thapan 2005: 213). Among a number of other convincing achievements, Thapar proposed a tentative typology of the Hindu Sufis among the Sindhis. She mentions four categories: the disciples of Muslim *pir*s in Sindh; the disciples of Hindu masters initiated by a Sufi *pir* in Pakistan; the disciples of the successors of the previous categories; and Hindu Sufis who had become disciples of Sufi saints in India (Thapan 2005: 219). Thapar's categories deserve discussion.

As a kind of conclusion, she explains in a tautological assertion how Sufism was introduced among the Hindu Sindhis as follows: 'This cultural dimension was intrinsic to the Sindhi heritage' (Thapan 2005: 220). In the wake of Thapar's culturalist approach, Rita Kothari uses the concept of translation to explain how Sufism was a part of the religious legacy of the Hindu Sindhis. For her, 'translation constitutes un/willing movement from origins, a movement that leads to an experience for the original that is both rupturing and enriching' (Kothari 2009: 119). The process of translation prevents the fixing of any identity, and is rather based on constant hybridizing which leads to tolerance. Under these circumstances, Sufism became 'one of the chief markers of a "Sindhi" identity' (Kothari 2009: 120).

With a diversity of qualifiers for religious identities – such as *hybrid*, *syncretic*, *fuzzy*, *eclectic*, or *fluid* – Kothari finds explanations in the localization of Sindh as a frontier. This means there was a permanent influx of migrants. For her, another key reason involved here is that Sindh was localized far from the main imperial centres. She also confessed that the relation to Sufism is diminishing in post-partition Sindhi generations of India. Nevertheless, it is possible to see its remnants in the generation that crossed the border (Kothari 2009: 124). Through the concept of translation, or more exactly of being-in-translation, Kothari balances her ideas here against other concepts, especially those of indigenization and vernacularization. However, she mostly sticks to a literary tradition that is based on what she names 'non-textualized' versions of Hinduism and Islam.

In 2008, Steven Ramey was the first to devote a whole academic study to the issue of the religion of the Hindu Sindhis. For him, their religious identity is a blend of Hindu, Sikh and Sufi elements. He disputes the use of the word 'syncretism', that is, he adds, mostly used for them. Hence, he proposes that 'analyzing the syncretic references within the Sindhi Hindu representations highlights further the choices that Sindhi Hindus make and the continuing influence of the dominant understandings on them' (Ramey 2008: 7). In fact, Ramsey is more interested in labelling the 'syncretism' of the Sindhi Hindus instead of identifying the role played by Sufism in their religious beliefs and practices. Furthermore, Ramey does not address the issue in the more relevant way when he puts in the title: Hindu, Sikh or Sufi.

I argue that the whole religious system of the Hindu Sindhis was mostly constructed – up to recent years, and is still in some cases, including the Hindu Sindhi Sufis – against this 'or', as well as against any 'and'. Because, for them, it was a system, so that they did not take the issue of their religion, their beliefs as well as their practices, as being this or that, or this and that. This understanding is what I call the organic theory, since the Sufism as practised by the Hindu Sindhis is a religious system organized of its own, as a separate and distinct entity. Nonetheless, Ramey tries to argue in his conclusion that the Sindhi religious construction adds a new layer to the issue of syncretism, since it allows for not conceiving their system as a homogenized religion (Ramey 2008: 190). Going further on, I would argue that, once again, scholars are facing the paucity of technical terminology, since regarding the religious field, the common vocabulary has been mainly borrowed, or coined, from a Christian environment.

Studying the encounters between Islam and Hinduism, and surely those among other religions, is to observe very complex processes involving not only religious matters but also primarily social factors, as well as political and economic considerations. The elaboration of an organic tradition results from a body of elements, which have ultimately been aggregated through different historical circumstances. It is the final aim of the present study: to uncover the various and numerous factors that allow for and prevent the formation of an organic tradition.

On the chapters

The book is divided into seven chapters, out of which six are devoted to India, and to diaspora to a lesser extent, and one, the last one, to Pakistan. In the first chapter, the distinct religious context of the region of Sindh will be depicted. It is a fact that Sindh, because of its geographical location both as an isolated and a buffer zone, has hosted many unorthodox versions of normative religions, especially Hinduism and Islam. This plays out as a breeding ground for new religious elaborations that flourished especially in the nineteenth century. The chapter will provide a survey of the religious market in colonial Sindh, coupled with the impact of British colonization on the socio-economic structures of Sindh. I will show that one of the main consequences of the reframing of knowledge as implemented by the British was a new reading of the Sufi legacy, for which the Theosophical Society provided the ideological infrastructure. New social agents acted as the main agents in this renewal of the Sufi legacy, and they belonged to an intelligentsia and a middle class that emerged following the socio-economic impact of colonization, as well as the spread of British education. The main result was the emergence of the *darbar* culture, a trans-religious denomination of a new religiosity where the Sindhis – whether Muslim, Hindu or Sikh – could perform their religious duties by rooting them on an individual conviction, allowing them to match up with modernity as defined by the colonial power. Finally, the chapter will introduce the Sufi masters under study, as well as the tradition they have developed in Pakistan and in India, and also in the diaspora.

These Hindu Sufis shared a number of features. First, the three main Sufi masters belong to the same generation: a generation born in pre-partition India, who could have migrated after independence. They belonged to different Sufi traditions and, furthermore, since they were Hindu, their families also belonged to different Hindu-related traditions. I shall underscore the regional factor as a key factor, referring to the role played by the locality – not only the part of Sindh where they were born but also the village, the town or city, which had its own 'personality' framed throughout the centuries. For example, to be born in Sehwan Sharif, in central Sindh where Vicholi was spoken (a Sindhi dialect which was officially proclaimed to be the official Sindhi language by the British), was different from being born in Hyderabad, this being the late capital of the independent Sindh before the British conquest.

Still another experience was to be born in Shikarpur or in Rohri, which was another story entirely. Shikarpur, the northern city of Sindh where the Northern dialect of Sindhi known as Utradi or Siraiki was spoken, was a hub of international commerce at this time. It was the core of merchant networks that allowed them to control commerce between Central Asia and overseas countries. Here, the *baniya*s were the dominant group. Contrary to the Amils, they tended to belong to non-literate groups, and their religious inclination was mostly towards the Nanakpanth. Nonetheless, the triangle of Rohri-Sukkur-Shikarpur, on both sides of the Indus River, was the locale for an amazingly rich dialogue between different creeds. It suffices to quote some remarkable sanctuaries such as Khwaja Khizr, on an island, Sadh Bela, on another island, and the *dargah* of Sachal Sarmast. Last but not least, the *amirs* of Khairpur were themselves staunch Shia Muslims, and they built beautiful *imambaras* in the nineteenth century, but it did not prevent them from being generous patrons for all of the religious buildings as, for instance, the famous Udasi temple in Sadh Bela which was created thanks to a gift of land.

The second chapter will centre on the partition, followed by the migration of the Hindu Sindhis to India. These dramatic changes in the lives of the Hindu Sindhis will be scrutinized to analyse how Sufi *darbars* were created in India. Broadly put, the main aim here will be to decipher the impact of partition and migration on the traditional structures of Sufism, such as authority, legitimacy and succession. While the Hindu Sufis were in touch with their Muslim masters, now settled in Pakistan, they had also to deal with a brand new environment, dominated by non-Sindhi Hindus. In this process, the key event would be the construction of a physical space, a *darbar*, along with its naming. It will be obvious from this discussion that the different Sufi Hindu traditions deal with specific, separate conditions. The built construction of such a space is the first step leading to the making of the mystical space.

In point of fact, to build a physical structure was a necessary process for not only enacting the Sufi cults but also appropriating the new soil. The second step here was the creation of a mystical environment. Therefore, the third chapter will scrutinize how several Sufi poetry corpuses were involved in the process, all expressed in Sindhi language, knowing that every corpus plays out a specific function at a specific level. The shaping of an 'imaginal' space gives birth to a possibility for the Hindu Sindhis to perform Sufi rituals. This chapter will also disentangle the different layers on which this Sufi legacy was acting, and how this interplay makes it possible for the devotees to cumulate their Hindu affiliation, and their Sindhi belonging, with a Sufi-expressed universal brotherhood, itself matching with the new Western ideologies present following the Industrial Revolution. Here, the Sufi poetry is reinforced by the iconography in implementing the mystical space.

The articulation between the spaces, physical and mystical, and the community of followers is completed through the performance of the rituals. These issues will be addressed in the fourth chapter. Furthermore, the rituals were the channels through which a connection between the followers and the masters –the ones in India as well as the ones who stayed in Pakistan – was re-enacted. They will be studied in the fourth chapter. The fifth chapter will analyse how the Hindu Sindhis of India who did not strictly belong to a Sufi path negotiated with the Sufi culture of Sindh. It will deal with issues such as the extent to which Sufism still permeates the life of the Hindu Sindhis of India as well as with the process through which the Sufis' culture of Sindh became more and more challenged in a growing hinduized India. It is also worth noting that broader issues will be addressed here in reference to the Sindhi identity of India. For example, a primary question of concern is related to the use of the Sindhi language among the new generation of Sindhis, in India as well as in the diaspora. In this context, the challenge of the transmission of the Sufi legacy also concerns other fields of the Sindhi identity.

The sixth and last chapter will move the reader from India to Pakistan in order to establish the ways through which the Hindu Sindhis connect with the Sufi paths in Sindh. For the purposes of a brief depiction, different case studies will be selected to highlight the diversity of the approaches the Hindu Sindhis of Sindh apply to Sufism. I shall depict a variety of situations involving different categories of Hindus. While some traditions can extend ancient negotiations between dominant and dominated groups, it is clear that new negotiations are also at work. The issue is thus to know whether these new negotiations are a clue of the vitality of Sufism in the Sindhi culture of Sindh, or, in a more pragmatic way, evidence of the capacity for flexibility of dominant Hindu groups, such as the Lohanas. Also, this chapter will allow space for evaluation of the impact of the dominant religion in updating the dynamics of a minor religious tradition.

Throughout this study, great attention is given to what Michel Foucault calls the conditions of possibility, which can explain why and how a tradition has developed in a given way and not in others. In this study, the Hindu Sufi traditions are understood to have been greatly affected by a main historical event: partition. After the British left India, a new country was created for the Muslims and known as Pakistan. The questions to be addressed, then, involve:

how have the Hindu Sufis negotiated with partition, an event that followed
a previous communalization of the identities in South Asia? They all had to
face a new environment: India. From a Muslim-dominated region, they had
to deal anew with a country where the large majority of the population was
Hindu. While through the late census in Sindh, they identified more and
more as Hindu, they quickly realized that what they call Hinduism was not
considered as such by some peoples in the new regions they were to settle,
mostly Gujarat and Maharashtra. Obviously, this new situation forced them
to renegotiate their relation to Sufism, and to construct a new bridge between
their Sufi legacy and the religion that was now a kind of normative Hinduism.

Different answers were found to the challenge. But, often, the tool of
renegotiation was transacted throughout space and territory. This means that
not only settlement could be renegotiated but also that space itself was devoted
to the sanctuaries. The organization of the space was nonetheless constructed
in relation to the specific components of a given tradition. Seventy years
after partition, a period when processes of 'solidification' – and sometimes
radicalization – of religious identities were at work, both Hindu and Islamic,
it could sound reductive to speak of a hinduization process since, once again,
a single term overshadows the many micro-processes involved. But on the
other hand, it is relevant to speak of hinduization since this term implies a
reduction of Sufi referents, both in terms of rituals and devotional poetry.
Here again, notable differences have to be highlighted between the Hindu Sufi
traditions under study. Showing them in comparison will be highly productive
in illustrating out the numerous factors involved in such complex dynamics.

It is not an exaggeration to say this study addresses the issue of the survival
of the Sufi legacy among the Hindu Sindhis of India. Beyond the Islamic
origin of Sufism, which is very negatively appreciated in a BJP-ruled India,
the transmission of Hindu Sufism meets other expectations – first, that of
the transmission of Sindhi language. Since the 1950s when Ram Panjwani
published Sufi anthologies in Sindhi, and printed in Arabic-Sindhi script, the
new generations, especially the third one after the migrants,[10] have lost their
link with the Sufi devotional literature in Sindhi. As of today, I have never
yet met a third-generation individual who can read Arabic-Sindhi script, an
alphabet in which the near total of Sufi devotional literature is printed. This
said, such a situation was already experimented upon in the Western diaspora

and, for example, an American Sindhi started to use the Latin alphabet for printing this poetry.

I am not inclined to think things were better 'before'. Here, 'before' would mean before partition. Because we all know that the human mind has a natural tendency to forget the bad in the past, and to remember only the good. Maybe this instinct is related to something like a remnant of a survival instinct. Nonetheless, beyond the rational argumentation, it is difficult not to think that the Sufi legacy of the Hindu Sindhis is vanishing. Except for some monuments such as the *Shah jo Risalo* by the Sufi Shah Abd al-Latif, what will be left of the wonderful Sufi poetry in Sindhi among the new generations? Thus, though pretentious it may be, my warmest wish is that this modest work might make this encounter between some Sindhi Hindu *panth*s, and the Nanakpanth with Sufism, unforgettable. Notwithstanding, I have some reason to think this study will not be an epitaph-like endeavour. Since I am writing these lines seventy years after partition and migration, and because of the many interactions I have had with them, my hope is carved in the third generation – namely the grandchildren of the migrant Sindhis.

1

The religious market in Sindh
on the eve of partition

This chapter aims to introduce the Hindu Sufi figures who founded the three paths which are the main topic under study. Interestingly, Rochaldas, Mulchand Faqir and Nimano Faqir were all born during the climax of British colonization, and they passed away in the first years of the independence of India and Pakistan. As we saw in the Introduction, while the Hindu–Muslim encounter has existed for centuries in South Asia, the main purpose here is to decipher the process through which a shared Sufi culture, and not Sufism, was built mostly during the second half of the nineteenth century, thus developing exactly at that time when the three Sufi figures noted above were born. To this end, this chapter will start with an examination of the possibility of a shared culture. It is usually claimed that a group of Hindu scribes of Sindh, the Amils, played a primary role in the spread of Sufism among the Hindus of Sindh. While I shall examine this theory, I am more interested in understanding why some Hindus became disciples of Sufi masters rather than followers of Hindu gurus, especially since many Hindu *darbar*s were created during that period of colonial Sindh. I shall also look at providing a tentative typology of the Hindus who were followers of Sufi *pir*s in terms of both caste and class.

This said, where it is not possible to provide details about the social milieu in terms of castes, I argue that these figures belonged to the same social milieu pertaining to the new middle class that was mostly working in British administration. Frequently, the claim arises that there was no caste system in Sindh, or at least not so rigid a caste system as seen in other parts of India, because of the very small number of Brahmans. Indeed, it is possible that Sindh hosted a specific social fabric, but even this point is not to underrate another main actor: the colonial power, which directly and indirectly operated a deep renewal of the social fabric, in Sindh and of course everywhere else in India. This point is fundamental to understanding the formation and the spread of modern Sufi paths among the Hindu Sindhis. This point is worth noting although it is beyond the scope of the present study, as it would have required an examination of the economic forces at work since, in Europe, the social fabric was totally renewed by the Industrial Revolution. Nevertheless, a brief survey of the birth and spread of new dominant economic groups will be provided.

However, the Sufi culture which was born in the nineteenth century was always associated with a place. In South Asia, the Sufi sanctuary was centred at the tomb of the Sufi saint, and it was mostly known as the *dargah* from a Persian word, with the meaning of *threshold*. In Sindh, another Persian word was mostly used, that of *darbar*, or court. Of course, one can find many other words for a sacred place, but the term *darbar* was used by different religions, including the Sikhs.[1] In South Asia, it referred first to the court of the king, and through a symbolic interpretation, it was the court of God. In Sindh, the *darbar* was the sacred territory in which the Sufi culture was at work. It was therefore a public culture, shared with the public, and an open space. All through this study, I argue that Sindh hosted a specific shared religious culture resulting from a process of vernacularization, which is not contradictory of the fact that some of its features can also be found in neighbouring provinces. This '*darbar* culture' operated through different dynamics, implementing different kinds of encounters between Hinduism and Sufism.

Beyond the issue of castes and classes, there is additionally that of regional belonging. One can deduce that Sufism had already permeated the religious life of different categories, not to say different castes, of the Hindus. Nonetheless, British colonization affected the socio-economic structures as well as the relation the Sindhis had with their religious beliefs. The main result was the spread of intelligentsia from 1850 onwards, with an emerging middle class made up of civil servants working in the colonial administration, and also lawyers and doctors. Combined with the growth of the Theosophical Society, the intelligentsia produced a new reading of Sufism, where cultural patterns were dominant, and embodied in the Sufi poetry.

Another result was a renewal of the religiosity among the Sindhis, whether they were Muslim, Sikh or Hindu. The religiosity was increasingly expressed and performed in a peculiar site: the *darbar*. This encompassing denomination was used by the Sikhs, the Muslims and the Hindus. Many new *darbars* were founded and the oldest ones were renovated; as such, they shared a basic set-up in which the personal relation between the spiritual Master and his disciple was at the core of the religiosity – and it was a perfect fit for the busy schedule of the emerging middle classes. The main question involved here is why different Sindhis select a Sufi *darbar*, a Nanakpanthi *darbar* or a Daryapanthi *darbar*. I shall try to solve this question through examining the life of the three Hindu Sufis and the nature of the paths they founded.

Social structure and religious belonging in colonial Sindh

Sindh's population statistics are not available in the first census of 1872. The population was 2,333,527 million. Sindh had 1,718,688 Muslims, 393,092 Hindus, 5,034 Christians and 86,663 persons put in a category titled 'Other castes such as Sikhs, Parsis, Jews, etc.' (Hughes 1876: 878). Two remarks are necessary from the outset. On the one hand, there are three explicitly named religions: Islam, Hinduism and Christianity. Their nominal designation implies that they are regarded as major religious institutions. The last section also contains religions considered to be minor. Moreover, they are called castes. Rather than seeing confusion in labelling a religion a caste, we must understand that 'caste' as a term had already established itself as an inescapable paradigm for categorizing any human group in the Indian context.

How was the society of Sindh organized in 1843? Before discussing the question of affiliation in a section devoted to religion, I should note that the discussion will be based initially on what the British considered the Muslim populations.[2] As played out elsewhere in the Indian subcontinent, the Muslim society of Sindh was segmented according to ethnic criteria that distinguished the Ashrafs and the Ajlafs.[3] Given the political domination of the Talpurs, the Baluchis were at the top of local society. Since the eighteenth century, they provided the bulk of the troops of the Kalhoras, who had ruled Sindh before them. Once in power, they reinforced their rule by distributing *jagir* to clan chiefs. Their domination was consequently doubled in power, with their being both warriors and landowners. The second dominant group of Muslim society was the Sayyids. Their superiority was due to the fact that they were recognized as the direct descendants of the prophet of Islam, Muhammad. This status conferred on them from the outset a sacredness, and hence an innate religious authority. They were the most prestigious group of the Ashrafs, and the British soon saw them as equivalents of the Brahmans.

In Sindh, the Sayyids had two characteristics. The majority of them were landowners (*zamindar*), but they were also *pir*. They were responsible for managing the sanctuaries where the Muslim saints were buried. We are talking about material management as well as charismatic management. The *pir*s of Sindh play the role of mediators between the tribes, and between the rulers and the governed, as well. The power of the *pir* was reinforced in the eighteenth century when the Kalhora developed the irrigation system. The *pir* had created a new system of social relations that, although inspired by the tribal system, was based more on association than on blood ties (Ansari 1992: 28–9). There was in fact a close intertwining between tribal power, feudal power and charismatic power that reflected the region's turbulent history. Let us take the example of the Jats, who are settled in the Indus delta.

The *malik* of the Jats was not a Jat, but a Baluch. It was, however, he who exercised the power of chief over the tribe. But although the Jats did not regard him as a *pir*, he was for many of his dependents more than a tribal chief: he was also a spiritual leader (Westphal-Hellbusch and Westphal 1964: 22). Moreover, the *malik* exercised a feudal power over those of the Jats who resided on his *jagir*. Apart from a few groups of Afghans and Pathans in the northwest, the bulk of the Muslims were Sindhis, most of whom were landless farmers (*hari*). There were also traders and craftsmen. Although trade was dominated by the Hindus, three Muslim groups carried out this activity: the Memon, the Khojah and the Bohrah.

Finally, at the bottom of the social hierarchy, there were excluded groups that could almost be said to reproduce the situation of the Hindu untouchables. These groups were specialized in degrading tasks that had to do with dirt or with death. The Shikaris, for example, although Muslims, were not allowed to enter a mosque without submitting to a purification ritual (Burton 1851: 308). Slaves of African origin known as Shidi could, despite their status, gain access to high positions. The general who commanded the troops of the Mir of Mirpur Khas at the battle of Dabbo was a Shidi. His heroic resistance to the British and his final sacrifice are still celebrated today.

In the Hindu society of Sindh, the British knowledge is often limited to mercantile castes from which two points arose: the absence of a real system of castes and the small role played by the Brahmans. The most numerous Brahmans belonged to the caste of Saraswat Brahmans. They accepted food from the Lohanas, for whom they were the spiritual guides. The Saraswat ate meat and drank alcohol (Aitken 1907: 182–3). The Lohanas, who represented half of the total Hindu population, were specialized in wholesale and retail trade. The British sources traditionally divided them into two groups: the Amils, who finally created a new caste, and to whom I shall return, and the Bhaibands. The Bhaibands made up the majority of the Lohanas, who were specialized in any form of commerce. In Eastern Sindh, the Rajput had retained their feudal prerogatives under the Talpur, and the British had reinstated them in exchange for their loyalty. Other groups of Hindu traders, such as the Bhatias, were much less numerous than the Lohanas.

Contrary to popular belief, there were many untouchables in Sindh. They lived outside of the villages and their members were never permitted to enter the houses of the village (Thakur 1959: 70). From the beginning of the nineteenth century onwards, British travellers reported the presence of untouchables like Bhils or Kohlis. Another important untouchable group was made of the Menghwar, mostly settled around Umerkot. Part of their devotional literature was and still is in Sindhi. On the other hand, it is certain whether these populations were established in the east of the province, which is none other than the ultimate extension of the great Thar Desert. The first census reports that many would have migrated from Gujarat or Rajasthan between 1843 and 1872. On the other hand, what is certainly true is that the majority of these untouchables worked in agriculture. There is hardly any trace of untouchables in records of crafts. Rumour has it that the Hindu untouchable artisans all converted to Islam, and it is true that crafts were largely in the hands of Muslims.

The *panchayat* system prevailed among the Hindus of Sindh. In rural Sindh, the *panchayat* of the Lohanas could have authority over other castes which, because of their small number, had none. This was the case, for example, with the Sonaros (or the Brahmans). In a similar way, when the Brahmans were few in number, they constituted a 'territorial unit' – with the Jajiks and Bhats governed by a council known as *mastan* (Thakur 1959: 73). The functions of the *panchayat* were social and religious. For example, the *panchayat* fixed the taxes relative to marriages and other rites of passage. On the other hand, it had to provide for the maintenance of the temple, pay the wages of the Brahmans and give alms to religious orders. It also had the power to punish the offenders for his injunctions until they were excommunicated (Thakur 1959: 74–5).

Before 1843, Muslims were divided between being Sunnis and Shiites. The Sunnis were in the majority, but the sovereigns, the Talpur, were themselves Shiites. But beyond the affiliation to one of two main Islamic religious branches, the real issue is to know what was the relationship between the Muslims and the canonical sources of Islam, that is, the Arabic language. Richard Burton (1821–90) laconically asserted that Arabic was known only to Muslim scholars, as Sanskrit was to Hindu scholars (Burton 1851: 58). Arabic was taught in the *madrasats*, which were to form different categories of professional religious agents such as *qazi*, *mufti* and *faqih*. Teaching was divided into religious sciences (*manqullat*) and rational sciences (*maqallat*). At the end of the seventeenth century, there were 400 *madrasats* in just the city of Thattah, which was comparable to the major cities of Iraq (Burton 1851: 341).

The manuscripts of the India Office Library, the majority of which do not go back beyond the eighteenth century, supplement this information. We can cite, for example, the *Fara'iz al-islam*, a treatise which was composed in Arabic by Makhdum Muhammad Hashim, then translated by the author into Sindhi in 1731 (Blumhardt, 1905: 35).[4] This text is a manual on the Muslim faith that describes the faith's most important ceremonies. Other manuscripts are treatises in which Quranic verses are written in Arabic and then commented on in Sindhi. Another manuscript titled *Muqaddimat al-Salat* was composed by a Sufi Naqshbandi, Mian Abu'l Hasan (1711). He exposed for the first time in Sindhi the questions relating to the ritual practices and the fundamental duties of Islam in relation to fighting emotional devotion. Mian Abu'l Hasan concentrated on religious education related to the fundamental duties of Islam, and he opposed emotional devotion (Blumhardt 1905: 37; Schimmel 1974: 18).

On the other hand, other manuscripts composed in Sindhi refer to the prophet, his miracles and his birth or his marriage. Finally, several manuscripts are devoted to the martyrdom of Hasan and Husayn or to the members of Husayn's family, as for example Ali Akbar (Blumhardt 1905: 37–9). A special mention must be made of the treaty composed by Husayn Va'iz Kashefi (d. 1505) with the title of *Rauzat al-Shahid*. This is an eighteenth-century manuscript where the text is translated into versified Sindhi. This treatise is considered to be a synthesis of the *maqtal nama*, the accounts of the revenge of the martyrs of Karbala under the direction of Muhammad al-Hanafiyya.

Two lessons can be drawn from these elements. On the one hand, there are treatises whose goal is to determine orthodoxy and orthopraxis from Arab sources. The use of Arabic sources works as de facto authentication of true Islam. These texts, however, are either translated into Sindhi or commented on in Sindhi. The Naqshbandis of Sindh followed the reforming enterprise led by Shah Waliullah in Delhi, who has translated the Quran into Urdu. This Islamic renewal is to be placed in the more general context of the decline of the Mughal Empire. As a matter of fact, while the Muslim power was weakened, the Naqshbandis thought one of the main factors was that the Indian Muslims, including the Mughals, did not practise the authentic Islam. They had incorporated many non-Islamic practices and beliefs, and there was therefore a huge need to go back to the sacred scriptures of Islam, such as the Quran. The second category of the manuscripts of the India Office Library provides a particular track: devotional literature of Shiite origin (*marsiya*). It is noteworthy that, in Sindh, this devotional poetry is cherished by both Muslims and Hindus, the latter being performers as well as authors. The other important element of religious knowledge includes a set of practices and beliefs related to magic and divination.

Among the Hindus, it is necessary to distinguish three categories of cults: those participated in by the Hindus of the mercantile castes like the Lohanas, those participated in by the Rajputs and finally those participated in by the untouchables. Among the Lohanas and related mercantile groups, two main cults were followed: the Nanakpanth and the Daryapanth. The Daryapanth is in all probability the oldest of the two. It is based on the deification of the Indus River. According to tradition, Udero Lal emerged from the river to help the Hindus persecuted by a Muslim ruler in the mid-tenth century. The Daryapanth was managed by a priestly caste, the Thakurs. Most of the rituals were related to changes in the level of the Indus during a given year. Although there are several temples dedicated to Udero Lal, the main centre of the Daryapanth is in Udero Lal, the name given to the village which houses a vast sanctuary dating back to the seventeenth century. The Nanakpanth would have been initiated later. It is possible that the Aroras imported this cult from Punjab during their migrations in Sindh in the eighteenth century. The Nanakpanth is a form of Sikhism that does not recognize the authority of the Khalsa. Additionally, the Lohana practised animal sacrifices on several occasions. One of them was the celebration of Navratri, the festival of Bhavani, a figure of the goddess; a kid or a he-goat was then sacrificed. The second occasion was the festival of Khetrapal, a disciple of Shiva: a kid or a he-goat was sacrificed to the *dargah* of a *pir* in this case (Thakur 1959: 158 and 175).

The Rajputs did not practise in either the Nanakpanth or the Daryapanth. They were, as elsewhere, devotees of Shiva and Devi. The untouchables venerated Devi as well as a specific category of divinities that Christopher Fuller described as 'divinized heroes' (Fuller 1992: 49–50). In Sindh, the most popular deified heroes were Rama Pir (Ramdeo or Ramdev), Pithoro Pir, Pabuji and Guga Pir. The organization of their respective cults could reproduce the relations of domination between Rajput and the other castes. In the case of Pithoro Pir, for example, worship was in the hands of the Pithoropirpotas, who were a section of the Rajputs claiming to be the descendants of Pithoro Pir. The main body of their disciples is Menghwar (Boivin 2010).

The Amils, the intelligentsia and the objectification of Sufism

Knowing the flexibility of religious identity, at least in relation to some sections of the Sindhi population, it is obvious that many Sindhis did not identify themselves as being members of a normative religion, especially Islam and Hinduism. Nonetheless, it is well documented that a major shift occurred in the nineteenth century regarding the relation of people to their religions, as well as in relation to their representation and understanding of the same. Sindh, like most of the regions of India, was subject to this change at different levels and extents. Regarding the topic under study, we shall focus on the change in the representation of Sufism that occurred in the last quarter of the nineteenth century. A surge of new representation of Sufism resulted from the birth and growth of a new elite, the intelligentsia, which operated a process of objectification of the Sufi legacy in Sindh. Throughout this process, Sufism was gradually transformed into an autonomous system of values, which can be described, interpreted and distinguished from the other systems by the believers. Furthermore, the implementation of this process was reinforced by the spread of new Western spiritualities, especially that of the Theosophical Society.

The impact of British colonization on the Indian subcontinent has been studied at length. Nonetheless, the complex process through which new classes appeared in peripheral regions like Sindh has not yet gotten such attention. An exception is related to the case of the domination of new Hindu groups in the rural areas of Sindh, as their domination over local society has been well studied (Cheesman 1997). After the growth of new emporium in Sindh, especially Karachi, the Lohanas took benefit of the extension of the commercial networks throughout the British colonial empire all over the world. These benefits allowed them to invest in the agricultural lands, mainly cotton, and they became powerful landowners, locally known as *zamindars*, at the end of the nineteenth century. The impact of British colonization on Sindhi society was nevertheless not restricted to the growth of mercantile castes. British policy regarding the Sindhi language also had a strong impact, as can be seen by looking to the second half of nineteenth century when a new intellectual class was born – the intelligentsia.[5]

Outside of the realm of religion, a Hindu group known as the Amils was to play a role in the field of knowledge, although they did not belong to a religious community of specialists. Originating from the mainstream caste of the Lohanas, they specialized in administration service, probably from the eighteenth century onwards. During the Talpur rule (1783–1843), they reinforced their influence to the point where they almost monopolized the function of *kardar*. In a given district, the *kardar* exercised almost royalty-level powers since he was collecting taxes and dispensing justice. Only the army was not under his control. The Amils emerged as a new elite through a process which is still not known, probably in early eighteenth century. However, when the British conquered Sindh, they had already formed a separate social class which was itself divided into a number of subgroups. When Persian as official language was given up in the 1850s, Sindhi and English were the two languages used in the administration. The Amils kept the same administrative role and they were at the vanguard in the huge campaign of translation launched by Sir Bartle Frere (1815–84), the commissioner in Sindh.

In the first phase of the building of the intelligentsia, the Amils were thus the core. During the Raj, the Amils were largely employed by the British for the translation of English texts into Sindhi, to be used in newly created schools. One of the most productive was Nandirani Merani, an Amil from Sehwan Sharif who translated many books on different matters such as history, geography and so on. And while the Amils were the bulk of the literati in Sindh, they were also instrumental in incorporating Sufism in the religiosity of the local Hindus. S. J. Narsain clearly states that Sufism entered into the life of the Amils. She comments that this faith was 'more successfully suited to their ideals and thoughts, and were more adaptable to their ways of life'.[6]

According to her, it is through Sufi poetry that 'the teachings of Sufism have imperceptibly and almost unconsciously glided into the life of the Amil community' (Narsain 1932: 73–4). The Amils who had studied in British schools were followed by other groups from non-dominant backgrounds whose members did not belong to the traditional elite of Sindh. At the same time, it is interesting to observe that works published in the second half of the nineteenth century could be the result of cooperation between a Hindu and a Muslim. Beyond the Sufi culture of Sindh, the new elite was also open and attracted by both different Indian reformists, and new Western spiritual movements which were spreading in the Indian subcontinent at the same period.

Due to colonization, both the Muslims and the Hindus re-evaluated their religious legacies and, for different and sometimes opposite reasons, they were convinced their religions were to be reformed. Although this usually meant 'purified' from alien accretions, the suppression of superstitious or magic-like beliefs and practices implemented a rationalizing process of the religious traditions. The 'dis-enchanting' result was not the disappearance of religion, but rather a new discourse on what was religion. Among the Hindus, a primary trend was for them to reshape Hinduism as a universal religion for a new humanity, as expressed by charismatic leaders like Rama Krishna (1836–86) and his follower Vivekananda (1863–1902). Among the Muslims, the discourse was centred on establishing the existence of a homogeneous Muslim community in India, which would itself be a part of the Ummah, the universal Muslim community.

Beyond the impact of colonial rule on local society, it is important to point out the role played by Christian missionaries in organizing intellectual debates in Karachi. One of the most influential priests in this respect was Reverend Bambridge, who was the head of the Church Missionary Mission. In August of 1885, he started the 'Literary Society' for 'English-speaking educated Indians'. The main objective of the society was the 'intellectual and moral improvement of its members', and there were 74 Europeans and 207 Indian members (Gidumal 1932: 290). Among them, six Indians, five Hindus and one Muslim graduated from a university. The majority of the graduated Indians were Hindu, and then Parsi and Muslim. A number of lectures were proposed on topics such as the prevention of child marriage and the remarriage of widows. The lectures were published in the *Sindh Times*, edited by Hiranand Shahani, this being the official journal of the Sindh Sabha. The lectures organized by Reverend Bambridge mirrored the interest in comparative religions that was developing in the West. In Sindh, the lectures led to a revival of religious and theological studies.

A number of hints clearly show that the new elite of Sindhi literati was attracted by the many recent spiritual movements coming from Europe. The first to reach Sindh was that of Freemasonry, since the conqueror and first governor of Sindh, Sir Charles Napier, built a Masonic lodge in 1843 in Karachi. Three other lodges were founded in the following years, along with, in 1873, an association for the relief of distressed widows and orphans (Hughes 1872: 385). Social issues were thus incorporated into the area's practice of Freemasonry. Other kinds of spirituality were often related to occultist or esoteric traditions, as well as nurtured by new lectures on Oriental philosophies.

Other spiritual movements aimed to work for the building of a fraternal humanity. One of the most influential was the Theosophical Society. It was founded in New York City in 1875, with the motto 'There is no Religion higher than Truth'. The main objective of the society was to build a universal brotherhood rooted in a universal wisdom. Helena Blavatsky (1831–91) was the main actor in spreading the ideology of the Theosophical Society. She believed that Hinduism was the closest religious tradition to the original wisdom of humanity. Another leading figure of the Theosophical Society was Annie Besant (1847–1933).

A Marxist and a feminist in the first part of her life, Besant met Helena Blavatsky in 1890 and became a member of the Theosophical Society. In 1893, she visited India for the first time and quickly became interested in education.

Consequently, she created the Central Hindu College in 1898. In 1907, she became president of the Theosophical Society. Besant was very active in Indian politics and she also became a member of the Indian National Congress. In 1916, she created with Tilak the Home Rule League and then was eventually arrested by the British in 1917, and freed after a few months. She became president of the Congress for a year. Besant published many books, including a translation of the Bhagavad Gita. One of her last publications was *The Life and Teaching of Muhammad* (1932).

In Karachi, the Theosophical Society was founded in 1896 after Annie Besant visited this city as well as Hyderabad, where she delivered a number of lectures. After Annie Besant's visit, Dhunjishaw, Jamshed Nusserwanji and Dayaram Jethmal decided to create a branch in Karachi. In the first years of its presence, the Parsis were the most active members, but the society attracted other gentlemen belonging to different creeds. According to Aitken, who published his *Gazetteer* in 1907, the Karachi branch had forty members (Aitken 1907: 167). They started by meeting in the new Dayaram Jethmal Science College. Later on, an Englishman donated his residence to the Society. Jamshed Nusserwanji then decided to build a new building with an auditorium, a library and a lecture room.[7] A Montessori school, one of the earliest in the city of Karachi, was opened on the building's third floor.

Many members of the intelligentsia were attracted by the work of the Theosophical Society. In his autobiography, Sadhu Vaswani clearly alluded to the impact Annie Besant had on the Sindhi literati. He also added that she was known in Sindh as Basanti Devi – an interesting pun with her name, Besant, and the festival of Basant, that of the Spring. Like many young intellectuals, Vaswani was keen to attend Annie Besant's lectures. According to him, her speeches were attracting people 'like a magnet'. He confessed that, in Hyderabad, her speech was about Hindu religion (Sadhu Vaswani 2001: 31). Later on, the society invited him to England and organized a number of meetings in different cities (Sadhu Vaswani 2001: 125).

The process of the objectification of Sufism can be divided into several historical phases related to colonization. The beginning of the process is undoubtedly related to the advent of the printing press (Boivin 2014). In Sindh, a printing press was brought to Karachi in the 1850s, but the main event in relation to Sufism came with the printing in 1866 of the *Shah jo Risalo*, the poetry composed by the Sufi poet Shah Abd al-Latif (d. 1752). The second phase was that of the rationalization of the poetry through the implementation of an analysis of the technical lexicon, initiated by Hindu literati in the 1890s, and the third phase came when the Sindhi literati took interest in the Sufi poet's life rather than the poetry alone. All of these elements combined provided an objectification of Sufism.

A main actor in the objectification of Sufism was Jethmal Parsram (1886–1947). Jethmal Parsram was a prolific author and trained as a journalist. In 1914, he established the Sindh Sahitiyya Society. He was also a staunch Theosophist, and the printing house he founded in Hyderabad was named Blavatsky Printing. Parsram translated into Sindhi many famous Theosophical books, including in 1925 *Shabd anahat* from *The Voice of Silence* by Helena Blavatsky, and five works by Annie Besant – for example, *Upanishad Gyan* from *Wisdom of the Upanishad*. Another Besant book he translated under the title of *Jagat ja netaun*, or 'The Ethics of Purity', is noteworthy here since the author introduced the different *satgurus*, the 'true guides', who came to deliver their messages at different times. They are Manu, Zarathustra, Buddha, Krishna, Jesus and Muhammad (Belani 1990: 82–4).

The first books authored by Parsram himself were nevertheless devoted to Shah Abd al-Latif's work, but not to his poetry. He was more interested in teasing out the moral values of the folktales (*akhaniyyun*) used by Shah Abd al-Latif. After publishing two books on the topic, he wrote another book on Sachal Sarmast in 1922,[8] and finally a biography of Shah Abd al-Latif in 1926. Meanwhile, in 1921, he had published with Lilaram Premchand a book named *Sufi sagora* which can be seen as the first attempt at locating Sindhi Sufism in the wake of acknowledging Sufism at large (Premchand and Parsram 1921). This work is introduced as a history of what the authors call *Sufi math*, or namely, the Sufi religion. It can be seen as an attempt to state that Sufism is a distinct religion in itself. A portion of the work is also devoted to the life of Shah Abd al-Latif, and probably borrowed from Parsram's own publication on the same topic. Another chapter is on Jalal al-Din Rumi.

This said, Parsram's main contribution to the field was his *Sind and its Sufis* published in English in 1924, three years after the previous manuscript. It was the first book devoted to Sufism of Sindh ever published in English. After the first section on historical contextualization, the second is on Sufi culture in

Sindh, the third one on Lal Shahbaz Qalandar and the last on 'three great Sufi teachers', who are Shah Inayat, Shah Abd al-Latif and Sachal Sarmast (Boivin 2016). The small book is a perfect summary of how the new middle class of Sindhis represented Sufism. Interestingly, it was published by the Theosophical Society in Madras, where the headquarters of the organization was and is located. Like Mirza Qalich Beg (1853–1929), another important Sindhi literati, and maybe even more so than him, Parsram read Sufism through the lens of Theosophy since he spoke in his book of 'what the Sufi calls Tasawwuf or Theosophy' (Parsram 1924: 127).

Parsram is one of the first Sindhi literati to speak of the Sufi culture of Sindh. He started out by summarizing the many religions that have flourished in Sindh, like Buddhism, Jainism and Hinduism. More recently, he added, two other religions had become dominant: Sikhism and Sufism. The mysticism of the Sufis of Sindh contains, in his words, 'the threads of both Indo-Aryan Sanatana Dharma and the Arabic-Persian mystic culture. In fact, there is hardly a country in the whole of Asia, including India, in which the mystic thought of two great civilizations, the Indian and the Arabic-Iranian, is seen as in so beautiful a union as in Sind.' Interestingly, Parsram spoke of the Amils as the main actors involved since they 'are the main supporters and advisers of both the devotees of the Sufi pirs and [the] holders of the Gadi' (Parsram 1924: 83–4).

In the portion of the work devoted to Lal Shahbaz Qalandar, Parsram provided a summary of what he called the mystic doctrine of Sind. He explained that Sufi poetry is a powerful tool unifying all the classes of society. Although the book was written for a large English-speaking audience, he also gave technical explanations – for example, detailing why the Sufis used the word 'All is he', or *hama ust* in Persian, or 'Unicity', *vahiadaoo* in Sindhi, as the *ism-e azam*, meaning the expression/word on which meditation is performed. It is for him the exact equivalent of the *mantra* of the Vedantists (Parsram 1924: 119–20). He added that Shah Abd al-Latif himself referred to the 'one curved word', namely *om*. He provided a translation of Shah Latif's quotation, according to which *om* is as light in the darkness, and that the Sufi has to keep *mim* (m) in his mind, and place *alif* (a) before.[9] Parsram finally explained that, through meditation on this word, the Sufi achieves identification of the universal soul with the individual soul.

However, the most significant point about Parsram is how he was able to bridge Theosophy's ideal with the Sufi culture of Sindh. According to the society, there was once a universal wisdom, a kind of primordial wisdom through which humanity could reach immortality. It was lost many centuries ago, except for in a remote area Blavatsly usually located in Tibet. She claimed to have met the last masters of this lost wisdom. In his book, Parsram claimed that the universal wisdom is kept in Sindh, in Hinglaj to be exact, which is a pilgrimage centre located in the Sindhi-speaking area of Baluchistan. He added that he had met a very old Sufi who claimed to be a recipient of their teaching, as Shah Latif had been before him. This figure was Qutub Ali Shah, and according to Parsram, 'Kutub Shah used to say at this place there existed no difference whatever between Islam and Hinduism' (Parsram 1924: 81).

The recomposition of the religious scene and the *darbar* culture

In her book published in 2011, Carla Bellamy claimed that *dargah* culture is 'neither Islamic nor Islamicate', and that it is 'a distinct (religious) culture and particularly South Asian' (Bellamy 201: 19). Before addressing the issue of the possible 'distinctiveness' of the *dargah* culture, though, it is necessary to examine what I name *darbar* culture, and to try to provide a kind of typology in the context of the Sindhicate area. There are four categories of worship that are shared here to varying degrees. First, certain Sufi cults are practised by Muslims and Hindus. Usually, they worship a Sufi saint who is buried in a *dargah*. Known as *ziyarat*, both Hindus and Muslims bring textiles to put on the tomb, or they only touch and kiss the tomb for obtaining blessings from the buried saint. This is the case of the visit to the *dargah* by the great mystic poet Shah Abd al-Latif. The second case is when the place of worship is divided, but where the saint in focus is venerated under two different names by the Hindus and the Muslims. In Sehwan Sharif, for example, there is only one place of worship but the saint is denominated Lal Shahbaz Qalandar by Muslims and Raja Bharthari (or Raja Vir) by Hindus.

Third, we have the case where, although there is a single sanctuary, the Hindus worship the saint with a specific name and in a specific chapel, while the Muslims give him another name and worship him in another chapel. In Udero Lal, for example, to which I shall return, the Hindus venerate Udero Lal in a chapel of the sanctuary, and the Muslims worship Shaykh Tahir in another chapel of the same sanctuary (Boivin and Rajpal 2018). Finally, there are also saints of Muslim origin who are massively venerated by the Hindus, and only marginally by the Muslims. This is the case, for example, with Pithoro Pir. The guardians of Pithoro Pir's *darbar* are Hindu Rajputs, and they recognize that Pithoro Pir was a Muslim Sufi initiated by Bahauddin Zakariyya, a famous Sufi Master of the Sohrawardiyya.

This typology finally reveals a complex religious situation. It can be observed that these cults are generally linked to Sufis, which at least means that a Sufi genealogy has been built – if in an unknown period – as is the case with Udero Lal, since a *tazkira* refers to him as a disciple of the same Bahauddin Zakariyya already mentioned. The complexity of the figures is an indication of the intensity of circulation and the borrowing of cultural and religious patterns between groups whose main identification was neither Islam nor Hinduism. It can also be seen that the use of the term 'Sufism' is reductive because it does not allow for the restoration of the fact that Sufism was itself open to other cults, and could therefore incorporate some parts of them.

Regarding the circulation of the Sindhis between different cults, we saw that the Hindus participated in the cults of the *pir*, and the Muslims could also worship Hindu deities. In rural Sindh, they worshipped the smallpox goddess Sitala when epidemics struck the village (Thakur 1959: 120). In fact, the main religious element the Sindhis were sharing was the devotional practice of the cults. While this approach to religion was characteristic of regional Sufism at that time, the impact of the Bhagti, the Sindhi form of the Bhakti, and thus the interaction between Sufism and Bhagti, cannot be underestimated. In the religiosity of Sindh, the devotional relationship of a follower with a spiritual Master was prevalent, rather than the focus being on affiliation to an institutionalized religion. Nonetheless, while it was common to have several spiritual masters belonging to different religions, the Sindhis of the late nineteenth century were more and more inclined to identify themselves with a religion as it would be acknowledged by the colonial power.

As Richard Burton noted as early as 1851, it is indeed the worship of the intercessors that constitutes the common religious idiom of Hindus and Muslims (Burton 1851: 325). More than a century later, Motilal Jotwani would call the Sindhi Sufis 'the Great Integrators' (Jotwani 1996: 150–8). Nonetheless, this religious culture based on devotion and emotion needed a place to be embodied, a territory where the Sufi songs could be sung, and the rituals performed. Thus, the shrine plays a leading role in their devotional agency, and this culture has been called a 'shrine culture' by some scholars, or more precisely, the '*dargah* culture', – this being a place where specific worship belonging to the saints' cults was performed. In the context of South Asia, such places have been introduced as the very places where a shared religious culture was forming.

The morphology of the *darbar* culture of Sindh can be partially complemented by the study of the *episteme* as it appears in the *pothis*. The *pothi* is a kind of codex which functions as a vade mecum – bringing together writings of various types, such as prayers, mystical poetry in Sindhi, excerpts from sacred texts, folkloric narratives and treatises on divination. These different categories allow us to bring to light a first characteristic of the *episteme* of Sindh before on the eve of British colonization. If the *pothi* indicates the existence of a shared culture, how can one restore its importance in the Sindh of the nineteenth century? The shared culture can be circumscribed by looking at the language used and the people who transmitted it, especially in scrutinizing the religious literature produced in Sindhi by various communities. These corpuses of religious literature in Sindhi are composed of oral traditions, or sometimes handwritten traditions, which are generally classified as folkloric.

However, they have in common that they refer to a devotional conception of Islam rather than to the orthodox normative conception, as seen in the manuscripts and early works printed in the nineteenth century. For Michel Foucault, the episteme refers to 'the set of relations that can unite discursive practices at a given epistemological time, which give rise to epistemological figures, to sciences, and possibly to formalized systems' (Foucault 1969: 251). In the context of South Asian Islam, a few specialists have worked on these materials, but no major study has really attempted to restore the importance of these corpuses. However, the religious corpus used by the majority of the Sindhis was composed in a Sindhi dialect. Other vernacular languages were also used less prominently, especially Punjabi, Siraiki, Hindi or Gujarati.

These languages had in common that they were not cosmopolitan languages, such as Arabic, Sanskrit or Persian. From the seventeenth and eighteenth centuries onwards, though, there was an exuberance of poetic composition in the vernacular languages, and Sufi literature represents the majority of this production. The concerned traditions were characterized by the use of vernacular languages, the devotional accentuation of sacred literatures and musical performances with the use of instruments. Devotional literature in Sindhi thus formed the basis of a culture that transcended social, religious and ethnic divisions. This culture would be called Sindhian culture, which refers to a set of social, religious and cultural traits that existed in the Sindhi area at the time when it encompassed the southern present Punjab, and also the territories of Rajasthan and Gujarat. Muslim religious elites, like the Naqshbandis, certainly did not accept all of them. This shared religious culture was not transmitted by the Ulemas or the pandits. It was mainly conveyed by poetry and music performed in the *darbar*. While some segments of Sindhi society had their own transmitters, this culture was primarily passed on to the villages by the caste musicians (*manghanar* or *mirasi*).

Furthermore, in Sindh as well as in other parts of colonial India, the word *darbar* was used by different religious persuasions – for example, the Sikhs. Beyond the use of the word by different religious groups, the recomposition of a religious scene is attested to by the creation and the development of several important Nanakpanthi *darbar*s throughout Sindh, the attempt to centralize the Daryapanth and the making of Hindu Sufi paths. The issue of the foundation of Nanakpanthi *darbar*s in colonial Sindh still deserves to be addressed, but this process should be seen as reflecting the transformation of the Sikh community when, in the second half of the nineteenth century, the first attempt to rationalize and uniformize the Sikh tradition was implemented. This process of normalizing the Sikh tradition was centred on Punjab, and it did not concern the Sindhi Nanakpanthis who were heterodox Sikhs and as such, they did not follow the requirements of the Khalsa.

They were organized in separate communities, and they did not follow the tenets of the Khalsa order as instituted by the last Sikh Guru, Guru Gobind Singh (1666–1708). It included a code of conduct, and only the official institution embodied by the guru was able to provide salvation through one's following the code (Oberoi 1994: 62 *passim*). Rituals framed the whole Khalsa Sikh identity, along with other compulsory duties such as, for the men, wearing the five attributes (long hair, beard, iron bangle, wooden comb and dagger). In Sindh, many Nanakpanthis belonged to a subgroup known as the Udasis, who followed the tradition of Shri Chand, the eldest son of Guru Nanak who was not recognized as *guru* by the mainstream Sikh community.[10]

Interestingly, although some *darbars* had been created in the late eighteenth century, there was a renaissance of the Nanakpanthi *darbars* in the second half of the nineteenth century. For example, the Halani *darbar* was reconstructed and a dome was added to the main shrine at this time.

Another aspect of the religious recomposition in colonial Sindh was the attempt made to create a centralized path devoted to Jhulelal, then known as Amar Lal or Udero Lal, in the late nineteenth and early twentieth centuries. Jhulelal was probably a modern figure of the Vedic god Varun, the god of the Indus River. He is briefly mentioned in historical sources, but in the second half of the nineteenth century, there was obviously an attempt (rooted in an alliance between Sindhi literati and wealthy merchants, an emerging middle class in sum) to create a community based in his worship, probably inspired by the Sikhs. There was at this time a growing similarity between the iconography of Guru Nanak and Jhulelal, as well as an attempt to impose a specific script, the Khudawadi, as the Sikhs had their own script, the Gurmukhi.

The attempt to create a community of Jhulelal's followers can be observed throughout two main events which occurred in the last decade of the nineteenth century. A new *darbar* was built on the bank of the Indus River in Sukkur, this coming to be known as Jinda Pir. It was engendered by a will of the Hindus to develop a distinct Hindu cult of Khwaja Khizr, also known as Zinda Pir, after they had been expelled from the main sanctuary located on an island in the Indus River. The other event was a meeting organized by several Hindu *panchayat*s of Sindh at Udero Lal, in the main *darbar* devoted to Jhulelal, which was located about 50 kilometres north of Hyderabad. This recomposition pervading the religious borders also reflected the construction of a middle class that was ongoing throughout the showdown between different social groups that were emerging, as well as new trends across the whole Indian subcontinent.

The birth of a middle class and the emergence of Hindu Sufi paths

The last process involved in the recomposition of the religious scene in Sindh was the making of the Hindu Sufi paths. As we saw, Narsain closely related the spread of Hindu Sufism to the influence of the Amils, a process which is confirmed by Jethmal Parsram. But the three characters who would start a Hindu Sufi path only partly corroborated her assertion. As a matter of fact, Mulchand Faqir (1883–1962) was born in a zamindar family, while Nimano Faqir (1888–1963) belonged to a business family. Finally, Rai Rochaldas (1879–1957) was the son of a civil servant working in colonial administration. Thus, it is difficult to claim they were Amils, but in fact, the core point is that they had been educated in British schools and, furthermore, they became the Sufi masters of the rising middle class.

Another distinction cannot be overshadowed. Despite their different backgrounds, the three individuals started their Sufi quests through being the followers of Muslim Sufi masters, and it is because of partition that they would eventually found an 'autonomous' Hindu Sufi path. Nevertheless, throughout their lives, each founder always claimed to be the follower of a Muslim Master who was settled in Pakistan. This does not mean that no Hindu Sufi path had already existed in Sindh, as Dalpat Sufi attests.[11] But partition created a new and unexpected situation that would compel the Hindu Sufis to create new *darbar*s in order for their Sufi persuasion to be maintained. Before partition, none of the three figures had created a distinct path, let alone a *darbar*, in Sindh.

The creation of the Hindu Sufi *darbar*s was the result of both the historical and the political circumstances – namely the migration to India and the personality of each founder. The social milieu and the religious training of each of the three Hindu Sufis are now to be examined in order for us to understand how their *darbar*s would be framed and shaped in India after partition. First, we will examine, the life of Rochaldas Mansharamani, which is well documented. He was born in 1879 in Rohri, in the north of Sindh, to a family that his hagiographers call modest.[12] His family included seven children, and he himself was the youngest of the four sons. His father was a cleric in the department of engineering and he died when Rochaldas was very young. His office was transferred to his eldest son, who was then sixteen years of age, and his zeal enabled him to climb the ranks rapidly until he became chief officer of the municipality of Rohri. Another of his brothers became an entrepreneur and made his fortune very quickly.

The family frequented the ashram of Vasan Shah and, by the age of eight, Rochaldas spent entire nights participating in devotional singing sessions.[13]

Vasan Shah had already taken a vow of poverty and Rochaldas also adopted this way of life. Additionally, he was moved to tears by the melodies sung by the *sharnai*s during the processions of *tazia*s for Moharram.[14] In 1901, aged 22, Rochaldas married and settled in Hyderabad to enrol as a student at the medical college of the city. He lived with a cousin who spent his time with his spiritual Master, a certain Sayyid Qutub Ali Shah. Rochaldas asked to meet him and he was quickly initiated. Qutub Ali Shah then had an enormous influence on Rochaldas, and he was considered the pole (*qutub*) of his time.[15] In the Sufi technical lexicon, a *qutub* is a Sufi who has reached the highest degree on the path, that of *insal kamil*, or 'perfect man'.

Qutub Ali Shah was a descendant in direct line from the great Sohrawardi Sufi Jalal al-Din Bukhari Makhdum-i Jahaniyyan Jahangasht (1308–84), who was one of the masters of the second Sohrawardiyya period, then based in Utch near Bahawalpur in Punjab. He was named *shaykh al-islam* by the sultan of Delhi Muhammad bin Tughluq. On the maternal side, Qutub Ali Shah was a descendant from Sayyid Ali Sarmast, the successor of Lal Shahbaz Qalandar. The fame of Qutub Ali Shah was such that many Sufis of Sindh came to pay him homage. This was the case, for example, with Sayyid Rakhiyyal Shah (1846–1940), a Qadiri who was a writer of very popular *kalam*s in Sindhi, Balochi and Persian. As we shall see, he was Mulchand's Sufi Master.

One hagiographer specifies that, as soon as he was initiated, Rochaldas embarked on the path of divine realization. During the nine years he was taught by Qutub Ali Shah, Rochaldas followed three key precepts: deep devotion to his Master, total obedience and absolute submission. Soon after attaining his medical doctorate in 1904, Rochaldas was sent to Aden, where he stayed there for two years. His blind devotion to the poor was such that, one day, an Arab woman asked him: 'Dada, are you a kafir or a momin?' 'I am a kafir', replied Rochaldas. 'No, no!' retorted the woman, 'you must be a kafir [non-Muslim] just from your carnal envelope, but in your heart you are a momin [a Muslim])!' Back in Sindh in 1905, he held various positions, and once his five-year contract with the government expired, his brother advised him to become a private practitioner. But when Qutub Ali Shah learned of it, he wrote him a letter: 'If I had wished him to make money, I would not have asked him to terminate his contract with the government.' Rochaldas decided to set up dispensaries for the poor – first in Rohri, Karachi and then in Hyderabad. He specialized in eye surgery, and studied Ayurveda and homeopathy; surgical operations were also performed for free.

Rochaldas had a special devotion to Krishna and, for him, the two additional attributes that Krishna possessed were love (*prem/ishq*) and a bad reputation (*ninda/malamat*). For his disciples, Rochaldas had attained perfection in love and virtuous conduct. He was also a Master in *pranayama* yoga, to which I shall return. He explained that the first time he had tried to expel his breath from his body, he had found himself wandering high in the sky above the port on the Indus at Rohri. Hadi Bakhsh, the son and successor of Qutub, presented him as an example of a person who had attained perfection on the spiritual and worldly level. Perhaps it is for this reason that Rochaldas was the *mehndibardar*, the one who bore the sacred henna,[16] during the *urs* of Qutub Ali Shah.

On several occasions, the tradition affirms that Rochaldas refused to show off his powers and the spiritual degree that he had reached: he simply refused to show them in public. He hardly spoke, and did not reveal the spiritual degree he had attained. It is said that Rochaldas possessed immense occult powers, but he never used them: he considered them to be obstacles on the spiritual path. One day, when he visited disciples in Lucknow, Vasan Shah appeared to him and said, 'A divine purpose is hidden behind everything, every language, every sound and every letter. Each letter of each language contains the knowledge of uniqueness, non-duality. If the *jiva* discovers the latent divine meaning, he will obtain salvation. It is primordial language or childish language.' By the grace of Vasan Shah, Rochaldas began to speak a new language. Rochaldas used the acrostics to suggest a spiritual or divine term coming from a letter or a sound.

When partition occurred in 1947, Rochaldas was living in Karachi and decided to stay in Pakistan. But in January of 1948, his son Hari was threatened with death and his house was plundered by an uncontrollable crowd; thus, he decided to emigrate to India with his family. They stayed in Surat, Bhuj and finally in Kalyan. Meanwhile, the Indian government had decided to host the Sindhi refugees in a suburb of Kalyan, located around 60 kilometres from Bombay. In the past, the British had built camps for the army, but the barracks had been emptied after the end of the Second World War. In August of 1949, a new township was created with the name of Ulhasnagar and, near the main road,[17] Rochaldas decided to build a *darbar* in a neighbourhood he named

Figure 1.1 Three Hindu Sufis with their Muslim *murshids*. (a) Qutub Ali Shah, (b) Rochaldas, (c) Rakhiyyal Shah, (d) Mulchand Faqir, (e) Sakhi Qabul Muhammad II and (f) Nimano Faqir.

Shantinargar – or, 'the place of happiness'. In November of 1957, Rochaldas contracted jaundice and decided not to take care of himself. He died on 10 December. His son Hari succeeded him on the *gaddi*.

Mulchand Navani, later known as Mulchand Faqir, was born to Parumal Navani, who was a deputy collector in the revenue department. The Navani family in Sehwan Sharif was one of the two Hindu families with the Kanungos who used to perform *mehndi* since centuries during the *urs* of Lal Shahbaz Qalandar since centuries. They performed the *mehndi* on the second day of the *urs*, the nineteenth day of Shaban. According to local tradition, Meru and Nao were two brothers who used to take care of Lal Shahbaz Qalandar by providing food for him. Very grateful to them, Lal Shahbaz decided they would lead the *mehndi* ritual after his death, when his own *urs* would be celebrated.

Mulchand studied up to class 6 at the Hiranand Academy in Hyderabad. It is said that he was able to speak good English. However, his childhood is similar to that of nearly all saints. He did not play with his friends, but was strongly attracted to meditation. Once, Rakhiyyal Shah (1846–1940), a high-level Sufi of the Qadiriyya, came to pay homage to Lal Shahbaz Qalandar. Rakhiyyal Shah al-Qadiri had been born in the village Halim Shah of Tehsil Mirpur, Balochistan. His father, Miyyan Nur Maḥmad Shah, shifted to the *dargah* of Fatehpur in Tehsil Khandwa, where Rakhiyyal Shah was brought up. It was at about the age of forty that Rakhiyyal Shah adopted the Sufi path and went to the *dargah* of Jhok Sharif, where he stayed under the guidance of his Master. He sang *kalam*s in Sindhi, Baluchi and Persian. When he met Mulchand, Rakhiyyal Shah was a Sayyid from Fathepur, a village in the Kachhi plain about 100 kilometres from Jacobabad, but located in the Sindhi-speaking part of Baluchistan. He was a devout follower of the *sajadah nashin* of Jhok Sharif. His Sufi poetry in Sindhi is voluminous and his verses (*kafis*) are still a part of the main poetry, which is sung in the *urs* of Jhok Sharif (Boivin 2012b).

Rakhiyyal Shah quickly noticed that Mulchand was not playing with other children. He might have said that the boy would become a *pohtal*, a local term for those who have reached 'the colour of God' (*Allah rang*), as it is explained by Nabi Bakhsh Baloch (Baloch 1985: vol. II 100).

Mulchand became Rakhiyyal Shah's disciple, his *taleb*, and he was initiated by him. In Sindhi, it is said that he took the name 'nam wanhan' from him, because during initiation, the Master gives his disciple a word on which he will perform meditation. It is interesting to observe that Mulchand was not initiated by a local Sufi Master. He was thus independent from the local Sufis, and his only connection with Sufism in Sehwan was directly through Lal Shahbaz Qalandar. Later on, Mulchand married a woman named Suratbhai, but despite his marriage, he wanted to remain secluded. He would take *bhang*, a narcotic beverage, every day, and he also played *ektara*, a one-string guitar. He hardly spoke and accepted plans to meet very few people. Despite his reclusion, though, Mulchand nevertheless performed the *mehndi* ceremony of Lal Shahbaz Qalandar in Sehwan until his death. It is said that he also regularly attended the *dhamal*,[18] often in company with another Hindu Sufi, Faqir Sobhraj (1901–81), who is the author of a *kalam*.

Ruqi Bhai was born into a rich Hindu family of Shikarpur. She was a Hindu female Sufi who was a follower of the Faruqi *silsilo* in Daraza, in Northern Sindh. She was married in a Sufi-devoted Hindu family and visited Daraza with her husband. After his death, she decided to visit the holy places of Hinduism, but in Haridwar,[19] she dreamt of a saint who was calling her. He told her he was the Master of the Darazi order and that he wanted her to come. She was initiated by Sakhi Qabul Muhammad II (1842–1925), who changed her name from Ruqi Bhai to Nimano Faqir. She then spent her days reading holy scriptures or in meditation. In 1947, with the new Master's permission, she migrated to India to open in Baroda the Sakhi Kutiyya place of worship and human welfare. In 1955, she had edited the Sindhi *kalam* of Sachal Sarmast, and was herself the author of a Sindhi *kalam* with the title of *Haqq mawjud*. Her verses are still sung in different places of India and abroad. After her death in 1963, her ashes were buried in Daraza close to Sachal Sarmast.

Despite an obvious diversity, the Hindu Sufis belonged to two main social groups: the merchants and the civil servants. Additionally, two of them originated from Northern Sindh, coming from cities such as Shikarpur and Rohri. This could be a clue suggesting that the devotional centres of Sindh had shifted north sometime after the British conquest, despite the role played by the Hyderabadi Amils in the spread of the Sufi culture. Furthermore, only Nimano Faqir was the scion of a merchant family, and she was also the sole woman in the group.

In terms of Sufi affiliation, the Hindu Sufis were affiliated to three main Sufi traditions of Sindh: Lal Shahbaz Qalandar in Sehwan Sharif, Daraza and Tando Jahaniyya in Hyderabad. Furthermore, it is interesting to observe that the Sufi centre of Jhok Sharif plays a pivotal role since most of the Hindu Sufis were in touch with Jhok, directly or indirectly, often through their own Sufi Master. Finally, it looks as if the two main Sufi traditions that were very popular among the Hindus were Daraza and Jhok. Jhok, contrary to Daraza, is located in Southern Sindh and, in this respect, one can observe that while Shah Abd al-Latif's poetry was highly praised, his *darbar* at Bhit Shah is not mentioned as a reference point, and no link has been mentioned between the local *sajjada nashin* and the *faqirs*.

Partition in Sindh

Regarding partition and migration, it is a common trope to claim that Sindh did not suffer the violence experienced by Punjab. In a special issue of *South Asia: Journal of South Asian Studies*, Kumar and Kothari claim that the main trauma for the Sindhis did not come from the Muslims in Sindh, but from the behaviour of the Indian administration and local Hindus who did not welcome them, and who often openly discriminated against the Hindu Sindhis who were accused of not being 'true' Hindus (Kumar and Kothari 2016: 776). In 1941, the Hindus made up about 21 per cent of the total population of Sindh, including 6 per cent of the scheduled castes; therefore, they would have numbered at less than 1 million – exactly 0.9 million. And since the scheduled castes mostly stayed in Pakistan, and a number of other Hindus did not migrate, the migrant Hindus would have been closer to 0.8 million, if not less. Nonetheless, there is a kind of consensus that they numbered around 1 million.

Why did the Sindhis migrate to India? This resulted from an array of factors. Despite the so-called lack of violence, rumours could have played a leading role – especially since dramatic reports about Punjab were reaching the province, leading many people to feel 'uncertain of the future' (Zamindar 2007: 66). Additionally, there was a precedent of communal violence in Sindh, this being the 'Sukkur riots', which had been related to the Manzilgah Affair. The Muslims of Sukkur had claimed a building supposed to be a mosque, built by the Mughal emperor Akbar, should be reopened as such. But the local Hindus opposed this rehabilitation since it was located in the harbour on the Indus River, from which the pilgrims reached the sacred site of Sadh Belo. Over the course of three months, between December of 1939 and February of 1940, about 120 people were killed in the resulting riots, most of them Hindu (105).[20] The first victim was the famous Bhagat Kanwar Ram. Furthermore, the 'Sukkur riots' occurred beyond the city, in other cities such as Rohri, and also in other parts of Sindh, such as in Lakki, and this spread of the riots fuelled later unrest.

Thus, even if it never reached the level of violence in Punjab, it is irrelevant to claim there was no communal violence in Sindh. The role played by politicians, both from the Muslim League and then from Pakistan, the Sindh Congress, and later on the Indian government, is not always easy to disentangle from behind the official discourse which was a genuine attempt at trying to convince the Hindus to stay. Also, after independence, a dramatic event precipitated the migration of Hindus into India. On 1 September 1947, sabotage derailed a train near Nawab Shah, and an armed crowd threw themselves on Sikhs, killing fifteen and wounding seventeen (Khuhro, 1998: 320). By early November of 1947, 246,000 Hindus had already left Sindh by sea, air or rail. As of 1 January 1948, it was estimated that nearly 500,000 people had sought refuge in India. Hindus from interior Sindh enjoyed special trains chartered by the Sindh government.

On 6 January 1948, the riots triggered by the Muslim refugees, the Mohajirs,[21] who flocked to the capital of the young state, forced Hindus to accelerate their exodus. Two hundred Sikhs from the inner Sindh, who were to have been evacuated by boat, were installed in a temple in the city centre. During the night, a crowd of 8,000 Mohajir surrounded the temple compound and set fire to it, forcing the Sikhs out. The Mohajir threw themselves on the Sikhs and began to stab them. Hamida Khuhro suggests that the police were more or less complacent, and that his father, Sindh's chief minister Muhammad Ayyub Khuhro, had to come and fire upon the assailants themselves in order to calm them down (Khuhro 1998: 326). It was only when the army intervened in the early afternoon of the next day that the order was restored. The death toll ended up being between what was reported by the daily, *Dawn*, at forty-two Sikhs killed and eighty-two wounded (8 January 1948), and the figures reported elsewhere as numbering fifteen killed and many looted, according to Sindh chief minister Muhammad Ayyub Khuhro (Khuhro 1998: 327).

In spite of Khuhro's efforts, which were criticized by then Pakistani prime minister Liaqat Ali Khan, 600 Hindu families demanded evacuation within two days, and in a week's time, 11,000 Hindus left Karachi (*Dawn*, 13 January 1948). The chief minister of Sindh, Muhammad Ayyub Khuhro, arrested 500 Mohajirs. He had to enact a government directive in order to prohibit owners from selling their property. He hoped to stop the panic that had taken hold of the Hindus, who were afraid of being dispossessed, and to deter the Mohajirs from threatening the Hindus in hopes that they would sell their goods at low prices. The Indian government had chartered ships from Bombay and, in December, with the addition of a train, 140,000 Hindus crossed the border. Additionally, the congressional office in Karachi was attacked. The immediate consequence was that, on 14 January, the government of India appointed a director general of evacuation to formally assist non-Muslims who wanted to migrate from Sindh to India.

Conclusion

In this chapter, the aim has been to introduce the three main Hindu Sufi figures who created paths to be spread throughout independent India. A first step towards this goal, before exploring these individuals, was to draw the social and religious scene in colonial Sindh, in which all the three were born and grew up. They all lived during a very hectic time, from the apex of British colonization on to the nationalist fight and finally partition. They were all initiated to the Sufi path through Muslim *murshid*s, while in some cases they might also have been initiated in parallel on a Hindu path. In sociological terms, these figures belonged to the well-known middle classes Max Weber studied. Drawing on Narsain's thesis written in the 1930s, it becomes obvious that the Sufi path fitted these individual's middle-class way of life, but nevertheless, the point alone does not answer the question of why they finally chose a Sufi path rather than a Hindu one, since they were all three Hindu, and they remained Hindu throughout their lifetimes. No relevant answer can be provided without a survey of the socio-religious situation prevailing in colonial Sindh, when the three Hindu Sufis were born in the late nineteenth century.

In Sindh, the main social structure was a quasi-feudal system, with a civil servant class and the groups involved in trade, but the policy implemented by the British commissioners, especially Sir Bartle Frere, gave birth to the Sindhi intelligentsia. For historical reasons, the Hindus were at the vanguard of the objectification of Sufism, which started after Ernst Trump's printing of the *Shah jo Risalo*. The Sufi terminology made up the main lexicon used for expressing ideas of mystical love and tolerance, also forming the core of the Hindu traditions related to the *sants* and the Nanakpanth. In a context where Sufi ideology was the main channel for expressing devotion, the Hindu intelligentsia became more and more involved in Sufism. The reshaping of Sindhi spirituality occurred when the Theosophical Society was created. The society provided a universal stage for spreading the ideology of the Sufism of Sindh, along with more humanist values.

The impact of British colonization in Sindh was twofold. First, it contributed to the objectification of Sufism, enthroning it as the fundamental of Sindhi culture at large. The second consequence was a renewal of religiosity in relation to the spread of a composite middle class. It was marked by the emergence of the *darbars*, spreading a *darbar* culture. From the 1920s onwards, there was an increase of the riots between Hindus and Muslims, a growing tension that culminated with partition. However, the situation created by partition was totally new, with, as a most chaotic background, the horrible massacres occurring across the two countries between Hindus, Muslims and Sikhs.

Partition was one of the primary traumatic events that occurred in the course of twentieth-century world history. Hundreds of thousands people had to leave their ancestral place to migrate to an unknown country, sometimes with a very different culture and environment. Even if the Hindu Sindhis were not targeted by mass massacres, as happened in Punjab, they had to face the trauma of leaving all of their belongings and their ancestral home in a very short time, and in a context where they were fearing for their lives in the new state. Furthermore, the Sindhis had no new territory where they could settle, despite their attempts to build such a space in Kutch, as was the case to the Punjabis and Bengalis whose provinces were divided between India and Pakistan. Therefore, the Sindhis had to settle in a new environment where, on many occasions, they were not welcomed.

The three Sufis discussed in this chapter found different ways to deal with the issue of partition, but none migrated as soon as the independence of both the countries was proclaimed on the 14th and the 15th of August in 1947. Mulchand never migrated, despite the constant requests made by his then Indian followers. Rochaldas and Nimano migrated in 1948, and according to Nimano's official narrative, she was asked by her *murshid* to go to Baroda to spread the Darazi message of peace and tolerance. In the case of Rochaldas, his migration came due to the threat he had faced with his family in Karachi.

In the different migration processes we have examined, a number of continuities can be deciphered. The process of legitimizing authority was quite similar in the three *darbar*s noted here. It was established as a progression of what had been previously accepted: the founder of the *darbar* in India was already the follower of a *murshid*, now based in the country of Pakistan. It was made clear that, in different circumstances as related to Rochaldas and Nimano, the Pakistani *murshid* did visit the Indian *darbar*s as a final way of legitimizing them. Mulchand's case was different since, being from Pakistan, he had already been given the full power to initiate disciples to his heir, Gehimal Motwani, while he himself decided to stay in Sehwan Sharif. In this respect, partition did not alter the dynamics of authority, without which no Sufi path can develop.

The new settlement and the making of the *darbar*s

Partition's consequences are still a subject of academic dispute, despite the numerous works which have already been devoted to the issue. Hindu Sindhi elders are still currently publishing their vision of the partition and migration.[1] There are also important academic works and essays collecting different narratives of the dramatic event. In this respect, it is worth mentioning the last publications by Saaz Aggarwal, Nandita Bhavnani and Rita Kothari (see Bibliography). The aim of this chapter is far from addressing the issue of partition at large, or even that of the migration of the Hindu Sindhis who started leaving Sindh especially after the Karachi riots in January 1948.

However, the issue of partition needs to be addressed in a very specific way, for the simple reason that some Hindu Sufis decided to migrate to India while others decided to stay in Pakistan. This said, among the three main Hindu Sufi figures under study, only Mulchand decided to stay in Sehwan, his birthplace. Consequently, it is relevant to wonder if there could be a relation between the decision regarding migration and the Sufi affiliation or belonging of the three figures. Furthermore, is there enough relevance to ask the question? Were the Hindu Sufis' decisions resulting from the same argument as other Hindu Sindhis, or were there specific issues? Last, is it possible to link the fact that Mulchand decided not to migrate to his own Sufi belonging and conception, and to the place where he was living?

As we saw before, Sindh had drawn – for centuries – a kind of specific religiosity based on devotion, and which largely considered faith as being located beyond any formal belonging to an institutionalized religion. This did not mean people should not belong to any religion, for the daily rituals and other rites of passage such as births, betrothals, weddings and deaths. It meant instead that the finality of all the built religions went beyond this; it was located in the belief of the Oneness of God, whatever the name given to him. This devotional religiosity was embodied in persons, saints known as a *pir* or *guru*. These sacralized persons were seen as being the mediators between the believers and God. The role they played in the life of the Sindhis, whatever their social condition might be, was central. This condition means that, for the Sindhis who had decided to leave Sindh and to migrate to India, it was impossible not to migrate with their religious legacy.

It was not possible to shift the physical structure of the *darbar*, however. In many cases, the original *darbar* was left in Sindh and a new one was built in India. Many *darbar*s were transferred from Sindh to India from 1947 onwards. Of course, this means that the followers never thought they would come back to the land of their ancestors. More research needs to be undertaken on this neglected issue of transference, knowing that the Hindu Sindhis were not the only migrants to be concerned. Nonetheless, two of the Hindu Sufis did not really transfer a *darbar* from Sindh. For the first, his *darbar* was to be a creation – Rai Rochaldas had not had any *darbar* in Sindh – and as for the other, Nimano Faqir, she was asked by her Sufi Master in Sindh to go to India for the purpose of creating a 'branch' of the *dargah* of Daraza, which was the headquarters of the Daraza *silsila*.[2] The reasons for selecting a place and space were varied, but they always involved a process of sacralization which was crucial in the settlement of the Hindu Sindhis in India. Furthermore, the sacralization of a territory could not work without a process of legitimization. How was the Hindu Sufis' authority legitimized? The process was always rooted in Sindh proper since the Hindu Sufis kept up relations with the Muslim masters who were in Sindh.

Building the *darbar*s in India

The Sufi Hindus under study were facing partition just like other Hindu Sindhis. If one wishes to take into account some variation among them, it must depend on the location of the respective Hindu Sufis. Obviously, there was a difference between those living in small cities, such as Sehwan Sharif, and others who had been established in big cities, especially Karachi, as was the case for Rai Rochaldas. In the context of migration of Sindhi religious figures to India, the transference of a Sindhi *darbar* usually follows the migration of its *gaddi nashin*.[3] Hence, a number of important *darbars* of Sindh were recreated in India by the *gaddi nashins* who had migrated. The *darbars* in Sindh were most of the time preserved with different arrangements regarding their management. But, often, the now Indian *gaddi nashins* or their followers would provide money to some keepers who were in charge of maintaining the initial *darbar*. Furthermore, despite the fluctuant diplomatic relations between Pakistan and India, it was always possible to travel across the border.

For example, there are Sadh Belo – which was transferred from Sukkur to Mumbai (Maharashtra) – and the Kathwaro Darbar, which was transferred from Shikarpur to Nagpur (Madhya Pradesh). Another important *darbar* was located in Halani, between Nausharo Firuz and Khairpur. It is a historical place about 40 kilometres south of Daraza, in Sindh, where the Talpurs had defeated the Kalhoras in 1783. Baba Sukhdev Sahib created the *darbar* four years afterward in 1787. His spiritual level impressed a lot the Talpur mirs who regularly granted the *darbar* with lands. In 1947, the *gaddi nashin* decided to migrate to India and he settled in Ajmer, in Rajasthan. Once, when he had to go to Mumbai for a surgery, he bought a flat which became another spiritual centre. Finally, it is important to note that the Halani path has three different *darbars*, two in India and one in Pakistan, and they are managed by the eighth *gaddi nashin*, Baba Sadhuram.

In Ulhasnagar, there is the *darbar* of Sain Vasan Shah, whose original sanctuary is in Rohri. Wasan Shah (1848–1928) was a disciple of Paru Shah. Sain Vasan Shah became famous for reciting the *banis* of Shri Guru Nanak and the *kalams* of the Sufis. The *bhajans* which are attributed to him display an interesting interwoven vocabulary, showing indiscriminate use of *didar* and *darshan* (Jotwani 1968: 117). The booklet published by his *darbar* in Ulhasnagar clearly indicates he was an 'integrator', since his spiritual genealogy goes back to the Sufis of Sindh, including Shah Latif, Bedil, Rohal Shah and others (Jotwani 1968: 208). He was one of the spiritual masters of Ram Panjwani.

The transferred *darbars* in India operated in different manners, but a number of similarities can be drawn. The *gaddi nashin* was usually the direct heir of the tradition, and other forms of legitimation were implemented through official narratives, which themselves are usually published in books written both in

Devanagari and in Arabic Sindhi scripts, and of course in the Sindhi language. The legitimation also works through the genealogical charts exhibited in the main entrance of the *darbars*. Additionally, the iconography provides a sense of continuity, contrary to architecture. In the Mumbai Sadh Belo, for example, it is difficult to see any architectural continuity with the Sadh Belo settled in the island in the Indus River, in Sukkur.

Sometimes, the Indian *darbar* is seen as a branch of the initial one located in Sindh. The relationship between them can be good, or sometimes non-existent.

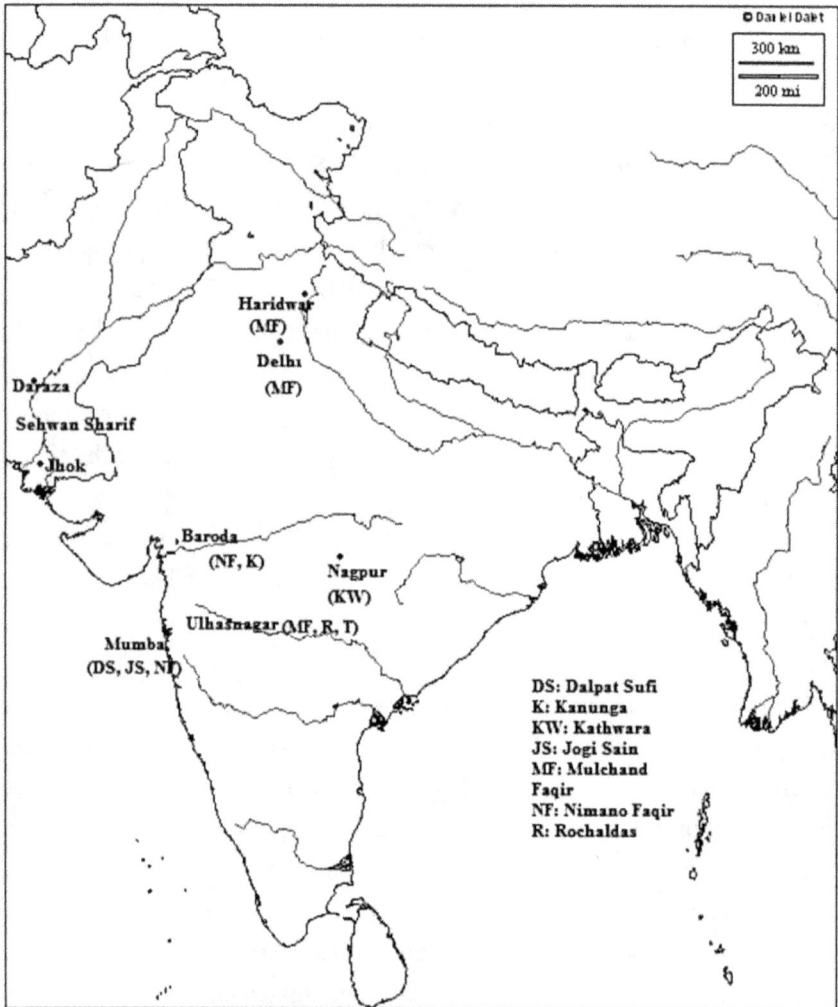

Figure 2.1 Sufi seats from Sindh in India.

But despite this situation, the sanctuaries claim to belong to the same tradition. In the case of Sain Vasan Shah's tradition, the Indian *darbar* openly claims his Sufi affiliation, with this connection of course being among other religious references, including the *isht devta* of the Hindu Sindhis of India, Jhulelal. The permanence of the Sufi reference can be observed through the Sindhi vernacular vocabulary that is used on the posters. Some words, such as *shahanshah* and *darvish*, are very common, and there is also the *faqeeri dhamal*. The *gaddi nashin* is the fourth descendant of Vasan Shah and his official title is 'Hazra Hazoor Darvish Sai Parmanand Sahab'. Except for his name of Parmanand, all of the other terms are borrowed from the Sufi lexicon in Sindhi.

However, the case of the Hindu Sufi *darbar* could have been framed through a different scenario. As a matter of fact, none of the three Sufi figures focused upon here did run a *darbar*, or even an *astano*, in Sindh. They were themselves the followers of a Sufi Master, who was always Muslim. Consequently, it is obviously the migration to India that played a role in the foundation of a *darbar*. Thus, we can reasonably claim that the creation of a Sufi *darbar* was an answer given in the context of a traumatic event, that of partition followed by migration. Nevertheless, one can claim this scenario was restricted to the Hindu Sufis: the transference of the above-mentioned *darbar*s answered the same issue. Thus, let us turn now to the issue of the creation of a Sufi *darbar* in India, having explored the reasons for migration as well as those for non-migration.

In fact, all three figures focused upon here belong to three different scenarios: Rochaldas migrated due to the violence of 6 January 1948; Nimano Faqir apparently migrated due to her Sufi Master's request; and Mulchand Faqir did not migrate, while his main disciple Gehimal Motwani did. While they belonged to well-to-do Hindu families of Sindh as part of the emerging middle classes, migration does not seem to have been a crucial issue. Even regarding Rochaldas, his biographer clearly states that he had not planned to leave Sindh before the January riots. In the first months after partition, Rochaldas was working as a medical doctor in the sanatorium he had created in Karachi. But during the dramatic events of 6 January, his son Hari was threatened with death and his house was looted.

Although it is not openly stated, the narrative clearly alludes to the fact that the spread of violence throughout Sindh was not perpetrated by the Muslim

Sindhis, but by the Mohajirs who clearly wanted to take over the houses of the Hindus, at least in Karachi. Even before the riots, a number of cases are known where Mohajirs took a house by force while its owners had left for work (Zamindar 2007: 67). Rochaldas could have decided to migrate mainly in order to protect his family. As a matter of fact, a number of Hindus had sent their wives and children to India already, while they were staying in Sindh. Obviously, they were still hoping that their families could come back, but unfortunately, they were themselves compelled to migrate to India.

In a small town such as Sehwan Sharif, Mulchand could have not felt any threat, and therefore, there was no reason for him to leave the place where his ancestors had been settled since centuries. Contrary to other cities in Northern Sindh – for instance, Sukkur, following the Manzilgah riots – no communal violence had ever been registered. Maybe this is due to the spirit of toleration which prevailed in Sehwan, at a point when a Sehwani literati Fateh Muhammad Sehwani (1882–1942), himself a Muslim who was involved in the Manzilgah Affair, advocated the Hindus' claim. Furthermore, Mulchand's family was perfectly integrated in the dominant groups of the town through the main ritual role they were playing in the *mehndi* procession during the annual festival devoted to Lal Shahbaz Qalandar. The Nawanis, his family, had also counted among them a number of literati who had been at the vanguard of the literary renaissance of nineteenth-century Sindh. Notwithstanding, the large majority of the Hindu population of Sehwan migrated to India, as for example the Thakurs who were running Jhulelal's temple in the northwestern part of the town.

Until his death in 1962, Mulchand lived as a recluse, probably leaving his dwelling place only for performing the *mehndi* of Lal Shahbaz Qalandar. Interestingly, his main disciple, Gehimal Motwani (1904–71), decided to migrate. Belonging to the same milieu of middle classes employed by the British government, he was deputy collector and thus posted at different places across Sindh, including Sehwan Sharif. The divergence between Mulchand and Gehimal regarding migration provides an interesting information: in fact, the Sufi life did not spill over into professional and private life. Also, the geographical closeness between a Master and his disciple was not at all necessary.

The date of Nimano's migration to India is not really known, but it could have been in the early 1950s. Here again, it could have resulted from a threat, or any other emergency. Notwithstanding, it is not clear why she did migrate, and why she did settle in Baroda, now Vadodara, in Gujarat. In relation to the first point, there are two distinct narratives. Firstly, that she wanted to 'spread the good word' of the Sakhi – the generic name given to the Sufi masters of Daraza, but designating especially Sachal Sarmast. She would have been granted permission by the *sajjada nashin* of Daraza. Secondly, but less common, the narrative suggests that she was asked by her Sufi Master of Daraza to go to India for the same purpose. Since it is said that she asked permission of her Master, and knowing that none of them had ever asked any other followers to perform the same duty, it is reasonable to think the first narrative is the most probable. Furthermore, why Baroda? Here, the answer is consistent: because there was an important group of followers of the Daraza *silsila*, and finally, they could have asked the Sakhi to send a Sufi from the tradition to them, after they had migrated from Sindh to Baroda.

Authority, the legitimization process and succession

Every time a sacred place is created, the issue of authority is raised, often coupled with that of legitimacy. There is no space here to review all of the different modes of authority and legitimacy. Nevertheless, regarding the latter, a frequent matter of discourse is that somebody had obeyed a superior being, most often having been met in a dream. Another way of offering legitimacy is to build a shrine in commemoration of an event in relation to a superior being. Still another process can be related to the will to spread a spiritual message. In the case of Sindhi shrines, including the Hindu Sindhi Sufi *darbar*s, the situation was more specific as well as more varied. Of course, the three Sufis under study here were disciples of Sufi masters in Sindh, but their affiliations were of different natures.

In some cases, they would have created their own path, although they still claimed to be the staunch follower of such and such Sufi *murshid*s. Thus, in India, the dynamic was more that of a creation than the building of a shrine directly affiliated to an original one located in Sindh. But the fact that a shrine, and thus a path, was created did not mean the relations between the Hindu Sufi and his or her Master, usually a Muslim living in Pakistan, were weakened by partition and migration. The close relationship known in the Sufi context as *piri-muridi*, or the relation between Master and disciple, was never broken. Obviously, the legitimizing link was formed more through an individual, a Master, rather than through an institution, such as a *tariqa*, the name given to an institutionalized Sufi order.

This strong spiritual affiliation was exhibited in a number of circumstances, the most spectacular being the visit of the Pakistani *murshid* to his now Indian Hindu followers. The climax of the relation could be for the very foundation of the Indian *darbar*, or for the *dastarbandi*, or coronation, of a successor after a deceased Master in India. Otherwise, the visit could be paid by the Pakistani *murshid* for no special reason, only for him to offer a blessing, or if a neologism is relevant here, to 'baraka-ize' the new shrine. In the spiritual hierarchy, the Master of the original shrine located in Sindh would always be considered as owning more *baraka* than the head of the Indian shrine. In the case of Mulchand, who did not migrate, his main disciple Gehimal Motwani created the first shrine in Ulhasnagar with his Master's approval, although it is not clear whether it started to 'work' before or after Mulchand's demise.

In the case of Rochaldas's Sufi path, the coronation ceremony is performed when a new *gaddi nashin* is enthroned: it is named with the Sufi lexicon of *dastarbandi*, the coronation with the turban, the *dastar*, or sometimes *pag*, which is a symbol of the spiritual power. Interestingly, it is probable that the ties with the Pakistani Master were reinforced after Rochaldas's demise. As a matter of fact, Gajwani does not refer to a *dastarbandi* of Rochaldas. But he mentions that there was a *dastarbandi* for Hari and Damodar, his two successors. In both cases, the *sajjada nashin* of Jahaniyya, Nur Husayn Shah, who is still the Master of the *silsilo*, came to Ulhasnagar in 1957 to tie a turban of ochre cloth around Hari's head (Gajwani 2000: 199). Gajwani provides more details for Damodar's *dastarbandi* in 1980: 'He (Nur Husayn Shah) first applied the tilak on the forehead of Sri Damodar, tied dastar (folded sheet of ochre cloth) around his head and then blessed him. ... Thus Sri H. M. Damodar was formally consecrated to the spiritual seat after Dada Sai (Dr) R. M. Hari in the lineage of Sai Rochaldas Sahib' (Gajwani 2000: 294–5).

Interestingly, the *dastarbandi* is performed every year when R. M. Hari's *versi* is celebrated, but not by Nur Husayn Shah. It is of interest to observe that, while the ceremony is Muslim Sufi, so to say, the Hindu belonging of the *gadi nashin* is exhibited through the application of the *tilak*, the red dot on the forehead. And it was not a Hindu priest who put it on the front, but the Muslim *sajjada nashin*, Nur Husayn Shah. Furthermore, the funeral rituals performed before the *dastarband* were all Hindu, and specifically Sindhi Hindu, done on the twelfth day after the death instead of on the thirteenth day as they are performed in most Hindu communities. Nonetheless, this very Sufi ceremony is not regularly performed in the two other Hindu Sufi paths.

Nimano's spiritual authority on the Sakhi Kuthiyya was consecrated in 1956, when the new *sajjada nashin* of Daraza, Pir Khwaja Abd al-Haqq II (1915–78) visited the shrine. After Nimano's death in 1962, another woman she called her spiritual daughter was in charge of the *kutiyya*: Pushpa Tilly Jindani (Faruqi 2002: 113). Later on, the Sakhi Kutiyya was looked after by Nirmal Jani, who was apparently the son of a staunch devotee. In 1999, a new location was chosen where a new building was soon established with the name of 'Nimanal Sangam'. Another place was inaugurated in Bombay, and then in the 2000s, in Hong Kong and Malaga, Spain. Although Nimano's tradition was 'hinduized' to some extent, *kalams* written by Sindhi Sufis like Sachal Sarmast are still sung every day. It seems, nevertheless, that there are no more relations with the Daraza *silsilo*.

Nimano Faqir died on 23 March 1963 in the *kuthiyya*. Her cremation took place on the spot and her ashes were carried to Daraza, where a grave sheltered them. Nimano never claimed to have created a 'gaddi', although the one who is currently in charge of the *kuthiyya* presents himself as *gaddi nashin*. Thapan's informants maintained that it was a certain Jivat Bhai, who died in 1979, who would have succeeded Nimano (Thapan 2005: 212). During my visit to Nimanal Sangam in May of 2012, my first informant was Kamla, who is the sister-in-law of the *gaddi nashin*, Nirmal Jani. She was ten years old when Nimano died in 1963. According to the official tradition she described, Nimano would have designated Nirmal Jani to give the name (*nam*) for initiation, and from the information collected by Thapan, Nirmal Jani would be the son of a disciple of Nimano. But it does not say how he became the spiritual successor of Nimano, a status that is fully accepted by Nimano's followers.

Regardless, one of the biggest annual celebrations happens on 24 March, the day after the anniversary of his death. It is said that, in March of 1963, while sitting in the middle of a group of disciples, Nimano asked that a devotional musical session, known as *satsang*, be organized on the 24th of each month. She died on the 23rd following that day, and her funeral was organized for the 24th. This figure then became sacred, and an inscription above the entrance of the *darbar* reads: *24 ware sai ki jai*.

Mulchand's case is different since he belonged to the renunciant Sufis. Although he was initiated by Rakhiyyal Shah, his *murshid* is not especially venerated and I do not remember seeing his portrait in the places dedicated to Mulchand. Furthermore, even his relationship with Sehwan Sharif and Lal Shahbaz Qalandar is not displayed. Mulchand was a recluse, and he spent most of his time lost in meditation. Nonetheless, he himself initiated disciples, though only three, although there is no consensus about this among his followers: Daulatram Chaudhry, Gehimal Motwani, and his brother Tirthdas Motwani. His main disciple was undoubtedly Gehimal Motwani (1904–71).

Gehimal Ainani, who took the name of Motwani after migration to India, was from a family originating from Jhangara, a village located south-west of Sehwan, very close to the Manchhar Lake. He belonged to the Amil community and, since he worked for British administration, he settled in a number of towns in Sindh. He was posted twice in Sehwan as *mukhthyarkar* (revenue officer), where he therefore stayed for some years. It is nevertheless through one Daulatram Chaudhry that he came to know about Mulchand. Although Mulchand did not wish to make disciples, Gehimal was quite impressed by him during their first meeting. Gehimal finally 'took nam' (*nam vathan*) from Mulchand.

After partition, Gehimal migrated to India and he came five times to Sehwan in order to ask Mulchand to come with him to India. Because most of his followers had migrated to India, they arranged a tomb *(maqbaro)* when Mulchand was still alive in a compound located at the western side of Lal Shahbaz Qalandar's shrine (*mazar*). The place is also known as *Mulan Faqir jo asthan*. Other places devoted to him, known as *kuthiyya*, were built in Ulhasnagar, Bombay and Delhi. However, this case of a Sufi Hindu path is specific since it was founded by the main disciple of a Master.

After Gehimal's demise, it seems that two branches tried to manage Mulchand's legacy. The first one is related to what Max Weber coined 'hereditary charisma': Gehimal's family. His young brother, Tirathdas, was in charge of the community. His own son, Daulatram, is in the process of building

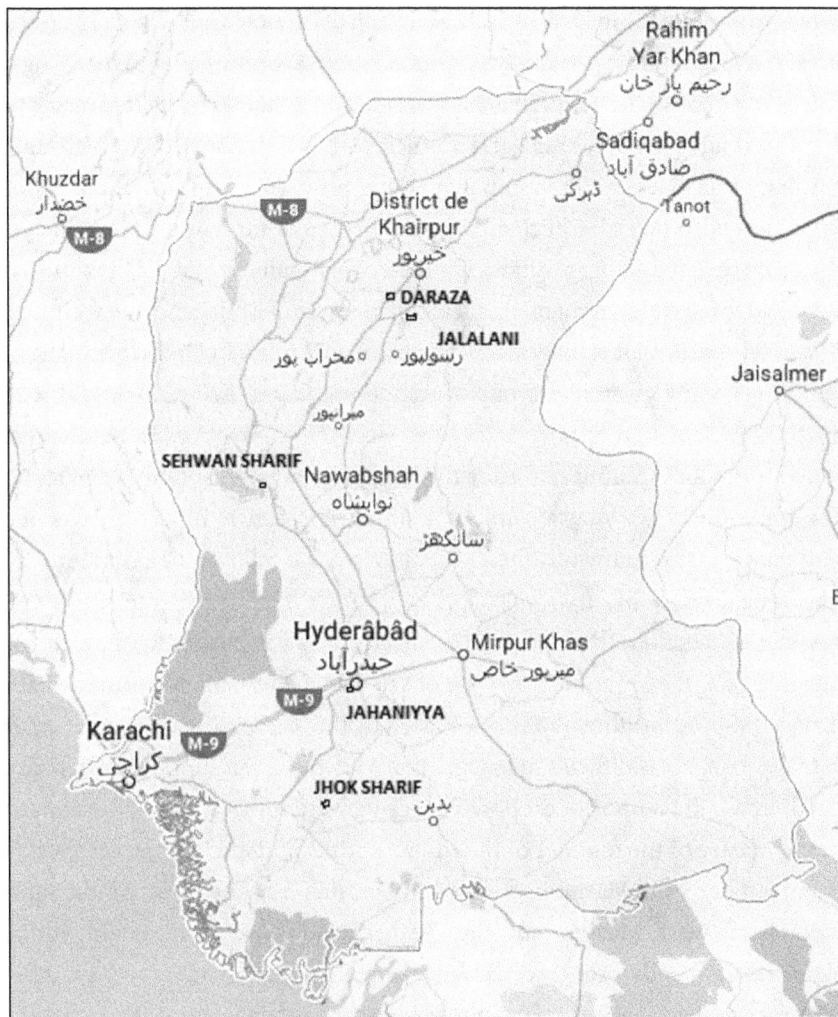

Figure 2.2 Hindu Sufi figures and their Sufi connections in Sindh.

a new Mul Kutiyya in the basement of his building. As we saw previously, the shrine was organized and ready for the *versi* for his death anniversary on 20 November 2012. But it is a modest structure, mostly arranged through the portraits put on the *samadhi*. Nonetheless, the new Mul Kutiyya could work as an alternative to the distant *darbar* in Haridwar.

The second branch is that of Basant Jethwani, the head of the followers who are not Gehimal's family members. After the closure of Mul Kutiyya in Ulhasnagar, the three main followers, who are Basant, Sonu and Devi, decided to build a new *darbar* in Haridwar. The location of the new *darbar* is explained by Basant: 'We don't have the Sindhu anymore, so we are now going to the Ganga.' The new *darbar* was inaugurated on 5 April for Mulchand's birth anniversary.

According to his will, Mulchand was neither burnt nor buried in the ground. His body was placed in the tomb in a sitting position, thanks to a small door which has been placed. Mulchand was buried in the sitting position, which is said to be the meditating position, with lots of salt-balls so that his flesh melted away and the skeleton remained. A leading follower of Mulchand and Gehimal, Basant Jethwani, claims that this tradition is called *sami*. In Sindh, the name of *sami* is generally given to a group of wandering *faqir*s. According to Dalpat's poetry, the *sami*s are clearly associated with the Verangins (or Berangins), which is the local Sindhi name for the Nathpanthis (Dalpat Sufi 1965: 54–5). The tradition of burying a saint in a sitting position is indeed that of the Nathpanthis, also known as the *jogi*s. They are the followers of Gorakhnath, who is believed to be an *avatar* of Shiva. Though it is tempting to consider a possible connection, the Nathpanthis never put salt in the tomb; they do use sugar. In fact, they renounce any use of salt after being initiated into the path (Briggs 1998: 40). Although the role played by the Nathpanthis in Sindh comes in many forms, it is difficult to assume that Mulchand was in touch with them.

All in all, the authority exercised by a migrant Sufi was always legitimized by the Master of the founder of the Indian shrine, and in all of the three cases examined here, the Master had stayed in Pakistan. For the three Hindu Sufis, the Master was a Muslim, and thus he had no reason to migrate to India. Unfortunately, only oral tradition can help us to understand and examine the process of authority and legitimacy, and no other trace of the same has remained, such as might be seen in documents or private archives related to the construction of the shrines. Now that this issue has been addressed, the next step is to take into account the space: How was the space of the shrine organized? Following which rules or patterns, if there were any?

Naming the shrine in India as a first step

Before dealing with the organization of space at Rochaldas, it is necessary to observe that all the three *darbar*s do not exhibit on the outside that they are religious, or even spiritual buildings. No such markers are displayed: no dome, no *shikara*, nor a *gurudwara* like facade. The only element to inform passer-by about the nature of the building is a plate. In these three cases, how the text is written. The words used in the inscription cannot mean anything to the people who do not belong to the community of followers, who, at least, are not Sindhi. In Rochaldas's *darbar*, the text is written in two alphabets: Arabic-Sindhi and Devanagari. In Nimano's, it is in Devanagari and Roman, while in Mulchand's *darbar* located in the sacred Hindu city of Haridwar, it is only in Devanagari.

The text of Rochaldas's *darbar* states 'Rohri dham' – the abode of Rohri, or seat of Rohri. It is a clear reference to the native city of Rochaldas, knowing he had not created a *darbar* there, but rather a dispensary, as well as in Karachi and Hyderabad. Also, there is a reference to the Hindu ideology of the *char dham*, the four sacred places a Hindu is supposed to visit. While the word *darbar* was currently used in conversations, Rai Rochaldas obviously discarded its use in favour of the official inscription whose function was to inform passer-by of the nature of the place. Furthermore, there is no allusion to him in the naming, not even via the use of a word referring to a spiritual leader. It is a geographical reference, as if Rochaldas had wished to locate his *darbar* in the sacred geography of India, in adding a fifth *dham*, the 'Rohri dham', as well as an extension of his lost native country. Consequently, we can state that naming a place is the first step in its sacralization.

The process was different with Nimano's *darbar*. Regarding the first building she would have overseen, only the name has reached us, this being the Sakhi Kuthiyya, while the new one, built after Nimano's death and in another area of Vadodara, is named Nimanal Sangam. The shifting in the name deserves some examination. The Sakhi Kuthiyya would mean something like the abode of the generous. Nonetheless, the Sindhi word *kuthiyya* comes from *kuthi*, a term for naming a modest building, a cottage or even a hut. In Sindhi, here the word *sakhi* is a *laqab* of the Masters of the Daraza *silsila*, in Sindh. It is a kind of honorific title they have been given for generations, while *sakhi* is simultaneously a very commonly used term in Sufi poetry for naming the Sufi himself. All in all, the naming of the place referred to the original *dargah* in Sindh, and furthermore to the spiritual head. After Nimano's demise, and the building of a new shrine, the name was: Nimanal Sangam, or Nimano Meeting Place, or Meeting with Nimano, the ending –al expressing endearment in

Sindhi. Consequently, there is a shifting from the Muslim Master to the Hindu follower.

In the case of Mulchand, the situation is more complicated. Because, finally, if we include Mulchand's place in Sehwan Sharif, in Pakistan, there have been three different places devoted to him: the Mulchand Kafi in Sehwan,[4] where there is a tomb or *maqbaro*, the Mul Kuthiyya in Ulhasnagar, and finally the present Dada Sain Kuthir in Haridwar. In the main entrance of the latter, the inscription is given in Devanagari: 'Om - Dada Sain *kutir*'. Interestingly, the Sindhi word *kuthiyya* has been removed in favour of *kutir*, a Hindi word, and the names of the venerated *murshid*s are not displayed. Instead, we find two honorific titles: *dada*, which is in Sindhi paternal grandfather (or *dado*), a nickname which is given to any elder, and *sain*, which is Master in Sindhi. One can wonder why Dada, who is Gehimal, precedes Sain that is Mulchand, when it is known that Mulchand was Gehimal's *murshid*. It was decided by Sonu, Basant's wife, and her explanation was that she had never met Mulchand, while Gehimal had been her *murshid*. She was given *nam* by him. The two names are preceded by *om*, the sacred Hindu syllable, which gives a final Hindu touch to the *kutīr*.

Sacralizing the new territory

In terms of architecture, it is hazardous to speak of a Sufi style. The Sufi shrines were built in innumerable architectural styles, which reflect local and historical styles from all over the Muslim world. Thus, more than an architectural style, what gives a Sufi shrine a specificity is how the space is organized. Nonetheless, if a specific feature was to be mentioned for Sufi shrines, it would be the dome (*gunbaz*), although this is not even restricted to the Sufi shrine, but can be used for any tomb. The *gunbaz* is said to represent the heaven and, in South Asia, it is an identity marker that allows somebody to immediately identify a building as Muslim, despite a few exceptions.[5]

In the case of the Sufi shrines of India, there is only one building which is the original one, built just after the Master's migration. The two others, Mulchand's one in Haridwar and Nimano's one in Vadodara, were rebuilt. Thus, I do not know how the first versions of their shrines appeared since I was not able to find any photograph. Under these conditions, I am compelled to go further in starting by focusing on Rochaldas's *darbar*. However, it not being rebuilt does not mean that the *darbar* has not changed since its first building. Of course, refurbishments were accomplished, and additional spaces were built in the compound, but they did not modify in depth the initial structure of the space. I mean to note that what the founder wanted to express through the organization of the space has not been inevitably challenged at all.

The *darbar* of Rai Rochaldas is set up on a pretty large field in Shantinagar, an area located close to the main Kalyan-Badalpur road that divides Ulhasnagar in two parts, north and south. The area is made mainly of small houses and no buildings occur except along the main road. The *darbar* of Rochaldas was built in the 1950s in a sparsely populated neighbourhood of Ulhasnagar in Shantinagar. It is surrounded by an enclosure wall about two meters high. The garden is well maintained which offers an appreciable shade in warm season. It cannot be said that the *darbar* is built in a particular architectural style: it does not belong to any religious tradition – neither Sufi, nor Hindu, nor Sikh – and includes no artefact allowing outsiders to know it is a sacred place. The *darbar* is not decorated with any tower or dome, maybe except one considered the pole of Lal Shahbaz Qalandar, which is high and thus can be seen from far away. Therefore, there is nothing relating the building to a place of worship, apart from the discreet inscription affixed near the front door.

The buildings are built of cement and covered with a sloping tiled roof. The most impressive building is the multi storey *gaddi nashin* residence, which is extended by a hall that houses the communal kitchen (*langar*). The *gaddi nashin*'s flat stands in the top floor. Crossing the entrance door, the visitor enters a huge room with, in the centre, a built-in pool. Above the pool, there are rocks with, in the middle, a small statue of Shiva in the position of the mahayogi. It is a quite modern flat with a bar, offering a saloon with comfortable armchairs. There are also paintings of mountain scenes showing the Alps, as well as a statue of young girl which looks like an eighteenth-century European sculpture. There is also a vase with colourful flowers.

Other buildings accommodate pilgrims. On the religious level, the two most significant elements are the *alam* and the *samadhi*. The *alam* is the name given to a medium-sized space near the main entrance. This term of Arabic origin is used for metonymy and signifies the whole space. It is a small square

Figure 2.3 Lal Shahbaz Qalandar's *alam* in Rochaldas's *darbar.*

courtyard, enclosed by four walls, at the top of which floats the red banner of Lal Shahbaz Qalandar. It was added to the *darbar* after Rochaldas had a dream in which Lal Shahbaz Qalandar asked him to celebrate his *urs* every year, as it was celebrated at Sehwan Sharif in Sindh. The Arabic-origin word *urs* depicts the mystical marriage realized between the Sufi and the God at the time of death. It is in fact the big annual festival (*melo*) that brings together the greatest number of pilgrims and an accompanying fair, a vogue, and many cultural events such as contests of stories and Sufi poetry.

In the *darbar*, the *sanctum sanctorum* is made up of the *samadhi*. It is a relatively large room accessed by a staircase. What is striking is the great sobriety of the place, since the *darbar* is devoid of any inscription and any decorative element. It is clear that iconography plays a special role. Indeed, the *samadhi* proper is an altar that houses several images of divinities and spiritual masters, both Hindu and Muslim. Epigraphic discourse is almost non-existent, apart from inscriptions that make iconography intelligible. This situation is not specific to the *darbar* of Rochaldas: it is found in other *darbar*s. It is similar to the Nimanal Sangam, its annex of Bombay, and the Dada Sain Kuthir of Haridwar. Before returning to the role played by iconography in these sacred spaces, one must dwell on the resemblances and differences that mark the Sangam and the Kutir.

The *darbar* of Rochaldas is the most spacious. The other two are limited to a single building, which consists mainly of two parts: the place where the *gaddi nashin* and the pilgrims stay on the one hand, and the *darbar* proper on the other. If we stop to discuss the decorum, the Nimanal Sangam is more supplied. The altar which the devotees face is composed of several elements, including a kind of throne which is intended for the *gaddi nashin*. That said, the function of the two *darbar*s is not really comparable. Nimanal Sangam receives devotees daily, while the Dada Sain Kuthir is mostly invested in by pilgrims for the anniversary of the death (*versi*) of Mulchand Faqir and Gehimal. Thus, the spatial structures of the *darbar*s do not correspond to a single matrix. This depends on the specific use of each *darbar*. In the three cases studied, the *darbar* proper consists of a large room which is relatively undecorated. In any case, the identifying element in the three *darbar*s occurs in iconography, to which I shall return (Chapter 4).

As we already know, in 1947, Gehimal decided to migrate to India, where he was employed by the Indian administration. In India, he got authorization from Mulchand, through a letter, to initiate disciples since Mulchand did not want him to bring them to Sehwan. According to a version reported by some followers, Mulchand did not want his spiritual knowledge to be transmitted and exhibited: this was the main reason why he did not migrate to India. However, his disciple and successor Gehimal initiated three ladies: Sonu Jethwani, Devi Naik and Gopi Gurbuxani. The first one was living in Delhi, and the two others in suburbs of Bombay. Gehimal was very worried that Mulchand did not want to migrate to India. In 1957, as he had understood that Mulchand would spend the last years of his life in Sehwan, he asked to take a picture of him in a local studio. It is the only picture of Mulchand Faqir. In 1953, Gehimal started the first celebration of Mulchand's *versi*, when he was still alive. All night long, he sang *kalam*s of Sufi poets of Sindh, such as Bedil, Bekas and also Lal Shahbaz Qalandar.

Gehimal also wished to build a *darbar* in the name of Mulchand. Unfortunately, his job kept him busy in Delhi and he died at the early age of 67. Gehimal had gotten land in Ulhasnagar from one Shri Vasumal. A 'Sufi faqir' had been living there, but after Shri Vasumal's death, his family sold the

(a)   (b)

Figure 2.4 External view of two Indian *darbar*s, Haridwar and Vadodara. (a) The Dada Sain Kuthir, Haridwar, 2012 and (b) The Nimanal Sangam, Vadodara, 2012.

land to Gehimal for 2,500 rupees. Gehimal started to build a wall surrounding the land, and the building's foundations for the *darbar* named Mul Kuthiyya. Unfortunately, Gehimal died as soon as 1971 and, when the first *versi* of Mulchand was celebrated in 1972 in the Kuthiyya, it was in an open air since no building had been constructed yet. The building of the *darbar* was funded by the three female followers of Gehimal – namely Sonu, Gopi and Devi – and also Tirthdas, his brother who was living in Ulhasnagar.

His own followers had the duty to build the *darbar*. The Mul Kutiyya was located in Ulhasnagar because most of the followers were there, in an area known as 'Sehwani Paro', the 'Sehwani area' where a number of Sehwani Thakurs were settled.[6] Gehimal was given a piece of land almost facing a temple of Jhulelal Lal that had recently been built by Sehwani Thakurs. A very small structure was built, and it was consequently called *kutiyya*, a Sindhi word meaning a cottage or a hut. No facilities were provided, such as toilets or electricity. A kitchen was nevertheless built since the sharing of food is a primary element of religious rituals in the Indian subcontinent. It was decided that the *versi* of Mulchand and that of Gehimal would be celebrated every year. *Satsang*s would be performed every Friday evening.

After Gehimal's death, his brother Tirthdas Motwani took care of the Mul Kutiyya, and after his death, it quickly appeared that nobody among the followers was able to manage the *darbar*. But due to family duties, and because they lived in Delhi, far away from Ulhasnagar, Sonu and Basant started to celebrate the *versi*s in their home in New Delhi. After some years, the three main followers – Sonu, Basant and Devi (Gopi had passed away in the meanwhile) – decided to sell the *darbar*.

Conclusion

The main achievement in the process of creating each of the *darbar*s in India was the building of a shrine, this having been preceded by a meaningful action: the naming of the respective places. Throughout this last process, a Sufi path was to appropriate a distinct identity, where no link with any *tariqa* or Master was displayed – not even the Sufi genealogy. In most cases, only a word identified it as a religious place, as in the case of Rohri *dham*. In the case of Mulchand and Nimano, the used word of *kuthiyya* was very local (*deshi*), since it was a Sindhi term, and for a non-Sindhi person, nothing religious was definitively attested throughout it. Only the study of the vocabulary used for the shrine is quite informative about the evolution the followers have been through regarding what they wanted the shrine to be.

Regarding the building proper, architecture was not a language to express a Sufi connection, or any religious and/or spiritual affiliation. Most of the time, no religious identity was exhibited, and the *darbar* looked like any other building, any non-religious structure, to an extent that only the plate can more or less provide a religious belonging. Of course, such a policy is questionable since, in the case of a dominant religious identity, the promoters would want the religious identity of the building to be visible through its size, but especially through the height of the tower, so that the building could be seen from as far away as possible. Already, we mentioned the bell tower for the Christians, the *minar* for the Muslims, and the *shikara* for the Hindus. One will argue this is a symbolic link with the heaven usually conceived as the abode of God. But more pragmatically, it is a way for claiming supremacy and thus domination. It is not a coincidence that, in some countries, the non-dominant religious buildings cannot be adorned with a tower.

Consequently, the *darbar* in India prioritizes a local, or better an internal, identity. This means that the identity as represented by the mass of the followers is privileged. The discourse which is expressed does not aim at reaching non-followers in the area where the *darbar* is located. The planned influence of the *darbar* is thus quite community-based. Of course, the first explanation coming to mind is that the somewhat 'ambiguous' religious identity of the *darbar* does not allow for a full exposure in the late twentieth century and early twenty-first century. As a matter of fact, though, this is the first and more obvious difference between the *darbar* in Sindh and the *darbar* in India: the lack of any religious and/or spiritual affiliation. The existence of a *darbar* is known only to those who are related to it. It is noteworthy to add that all of the religious buildings of the Indian Sindhis do not share the same feature. For example, the *gurdwara*s, in Vadodara, in Pune or in Ulhasnagari, openly exhibit a 'Sikh' identity, with a characteristic facade, towers and sculpture. The same observation can be made of the extensions of the non-Sufi *darbar*s, in India as well as overseas.

Building and sacralizing the building are two important steps in establishing a *darbar*. Yet, these are not the final steps. For the followers, the goal they want to reach is to another world, another reality, which we call a mystical realm. For them, what really matters is the agency of the internal side of the *darbar* – in other words, how the *darbar* is framed to facilitate this mystical pilgrimage towards God. Once again, it is a room where every Sufi path exhibits a specific 'Sufi' identity, as well as specific techniques and means for reaching the main goal. They can mirror the founder's conception, or the Sufi belonging of the place. Consequently, the next chapter will examine the making of the mystical space of the *darbar*, which is a virtual space built throughout the singing of Sufi poetry. It is thus after exposing this capital framing process that the daily rituals and the annual fairs will be examined.

Sufi poetry and the production of the mystical space

As is true in the case of all religious buildings, it is relevant to state that at least two types of spaces are framing the shrines being discussed here. The first type is the physical space. In the previous chapter, we saw how the organization of a space can already prepare a follower to reach the meeting with God. This is related to how the different rooms are distributed, where the aim is to gradually put the follower into a special state of mind. Another main component can be the architecture. Since this element is the most visible or even spectacular, its role should not be undervalued. In the case of the Sufi Hindu *darbars*, the new political situation imposed to build structures that looked anonymous from the outside. Only a discreet plate provides the 'identity' of the places.

The second type of space is the symbolic space which is only created and arranged to implement a mystical representation where the sole purpose is to facilitate what is the final goal of the followers: the mystical meeting with the saint, and through him with God. In Sufi terminology, it is known as the *fana fi'llah*, and the Sufis of Sindh, including the Hindu Sufis, have very often explicitly referred to it in Sindhi poetry. There are a number of ways to work on the follower's mind. In this chapter, my intention is to focus on the second type of space: the mystical space. I wish to address the issue of how a mystical space is created. The creation of a mystical space aims at putting the devotee in such a position that he is ready to meet God.

This process is implemented through three dynamics converging towards the same goal. The transfer from the physical world to the mystical world is accomplished through iconography and rituals, to which I shall return in the next chapter. But another dimension plays a fundamental role: Sufi poetry. The Sufi poetry works at different levels in the transfer. It contributes to the creation of an imaginal world of reference, as well as the ideology of the 'unity of being', *wahdat-e wujud*, the Persian version of the Arabic *wahdat al-wujud*, introduced as the encompassing paradigm which should be the basis of all human relations, and also the basis of the relationship between mankind and God. It is the combination of these three components – poetry, iconography and rituals – that allows the follower to be placed in the mystical space of the *darbar*. I agree that this process is that of all religious places. The word *darbar* could be replaced by church, mosque or *mandir*. But the cases under study here, involving the Hindu Sufis, strongly highlight that a shared religious culture, here between Islam and Hinduism, has been at work for centuries.

All of the three components express articulate discourses, but I claim that, for these discourses to meet and to merge, a necessary structure is the existence of an ideology that plays a leading role in the process. In using the concept of ideology, I differ from David Lorenzen's statement, which gives ideology a broad meaning, and a somewhat loose one, especially when he claims that ideology is a description of the structure of a society (Lorenzen 1996: 3). Maybe in a more Marxist understanding, I would consider an ideology as an intellectual framework, involving a condition of knowledge working as a prerequisite for the implementation of a number of processes, including a process of merging different religious traditions not as a syncretism, or a hybridization, but as a new agency of its own. After the Sufi corpus, I shall focus on the *wahdat-e wujud*, a principle without which the meeting of Sufism and Hinduism would not have been possible. A last part of the chapter will deal with Hindu references in the Muslim Sufi poetry.

Bhakti and Vedanta

This chapter wishes to introduce the varied corpus of Sufi poetry, mostly written in Sindhi, that is used by the Hindu Sufis in the *darbars*. For framing these corpuses, I have selected the main references quoted by the Hindu Sufis in their writings, as well as those collected in interviews with them. Different Indian Sindhi authors claim that the Sindhi Sufi corpus can be divided into two parts: the Bhakti corpus of Sufism and the Vedanta corpus of Sufism. Such a formulation implies that Sufism was influenced by one or the other Hindu movement. In a first step, I decided to follow this cleavage in my introduction to the different Sufi corpuses as used by the Hindu Sufis. In this respect, I started using this terminology of 'Bhakti' and 'Vedanta', drawing especially on Motilal Jotwani's writing (Jotwani 1996).

But, Jotwani takes these references for granted: he never explains what, in his own understanding, are Bhakti and Vedanta. This suggests that the meanings are supposed to be already known by the reader. Nevertheless, Jotwani does not refer to the Neo-Vedanta. When talking about the Vedanta, he quotes Sankara's work dated in the eighth century, where the main concept of the doctrine is the Advaita, or 'absolute non-dualism' (Jotwani 1996: 23). Furthermore, regarding the Bhakti, he clearly refers to the Nirguni Bhakti: 'The ultimate Reality is One, without guna or rupa, that is, without attributes or forms' (Jotwani 1996: 157). Unfortunately, there is no comprehensive argumentation supplying his claim that 'Shah Abdul Latif (was) a late participant in the Bhakti movement' (Jotwani 1996: 121).

Of course, these labels should have to be discussed, but after some time, it appeared to me they were used interchangeably[1] – not only by Jotwani but also by most of the Hindu Sindhi authors, as well as Muslim Sindhis and colonial literature. The main reason behind this was that, as was recently demonstrated by John Hawley, the idea of the Bhakti movement in early-twentieth-century India had been reframed by the Hindu literati in the context of the nascent nationalist movement (Hawley 2015). Since then, the Bhakti movement has been introduced as a social movement that aimed at unifying the Hindu population and instituting a kind of egalitarian society.

This said, it was quite logical that the Sindhi literati refer to the Bhakti interchangeably with Vedanta, since it is well accepted that these movements share a number of characteristics with Sufism, in terms of beliefs as well as of organization. As we shall see, the historical data gives evidence that the late-nineteenth-century Sindhi literati were in touch with the Vedanta, more exactly the Neo- or Modern Vedanta, instead of any historical Bhakti movement. Consequently, it is necessary to understand why the Sindhi literati constantly refer to the Bhakti, but before we get to this discussion, let us summarize the main features of the Bhakti movement.

Born around the sixth century, the Bhakti movement – whose initial meaning in Sanskrit is to share – was never unified, but scholars identify a number of shared features among all of the components of the movement. Mostly, the core of devotion was a Vishnuite tradition, mainly centred on his *avatar* Krishna, as well as Rama, although there is also a minor Shivaite Bhakti. First, all the Bhakti poets were critical to the institutionalized religion, here not only Brahmanical Hinduism but also Islam, and consequently they criticized with virulence the caste system. Another of the main characteristics of the Bhakti was that a number of devotees gathered around a spiritual Master, and the devotees could be renunciant or housekeepers. The spiritual Master was himself the heir of the founder, usually an ascetic who had been granted a revelation by a god, in Sanskrit or in a vernacular language. The innumerable sects resulting from this process were known as *sampradaya*, literally 'transmission' in Sanskrit.

Moreover, the condition for reaching salvation was mostly the loving relationship between the Master and his disciple, rather than the caste duties or the performance of given rituals. Thus, it is also, theoretically, an individual decision to become a member of a *sampradaya*. The Bhakti literature is replete of verses stating the pain due to the separation from God, and the joy of the union with him. Another meaningful cleavage appeared in the whole Bhakti movement at the later part of the fifteenth century: the Nirguni current, 'without attributes', and the Saguni current, 'with attributes'. The basis of the distinction is a different theological conception of God. The Saguni tradition has been dominant in the Hindu community for about a thousand years, or even more.

The Nirguni tradition was more influential in Northern India, especially in Punjab, where the Sikh tradition historically derived from the Nirguni tradition of the Bhakti. According to Lorenzen, the Nirguni Bhakti was closer to the Advaita, or non-duality, as Kabir's poetry wonderfully illustrates, with other Nirguni poets such as Guru Nanak or Dadu Dayal. Another main difference between both streams is that the Saguni poets, for example Mira Bai and Tulsidas, underscored the role played by the *avatars*, while the Nirguni poets denied or downgraded them. Nonetheless, both streams gave a prominent place to hagiography, and especially to the stories (*katha*) devoted to the founders and the great saints (*sant*) of specific sectarian traditions (Lorenzen 1996: 17).

However, as Hawley puts it in Chapter 7 of his book, the Bhakti movement had many significations, depending on the people, the regions and the caste.

Among the many disagreements, there is the issue which has been debated for centuries among the Hindu Vishnuite authors, as to whether the Sufis were a part of the Bhakti or not. Of course, this issue is far and away from the scope of the present study, as well as from the author's abilities. Notwithstanding, it is easy to find many shared characteristics between the Bhakti movement and Sufism, especially as it stood in colonial Sindh. The core of the religiosity is the expression of emotion throughout the singing of poetry.

It remains the main issue of the spread of the Bhakti movement to Sindh. Unfortunately, this issue has hardly been addressed by scholars. Ajwani devotes some pages to the issue of Bhakti, though, and according to him, the main innovation of the Bhakti was through a *sant-kavi*, Jaya Deva (twelfth century), who expressed the longing of the soul to find the union or absorption with God, Rama or Krishna. Then, he goes further in stating that in Sindh, due to its geographical isolation, the Bhakti was spread only in the sixteenth century (Ajwani 1970: 52). But while he mentions the name of Tulsidas and Surdas, he does not provide any clue for evidence of the influence of these *sants* on the spiritual life of Sindh. He quotes other names such as Dadu, before concluding the abstract in claiming that Guru Nanak was the greatest poet of the Bhakti.

Indeed, it is a seductive hypothesis that the Bhakti could have permeated Sindh through the teaching of Guru Nanak. As we already saw, Guru Nanak and Sikhism historically derived from the Bhakti, and especially Guru Nanak's teaching as preserved in the Granth Sahib. In nineteenth-century Sindh, the Nanakpanth, or 'the path of Nanak', was probably the dominant religious path among the Hindu Sindhis. However, there is evidence of the active participation of Sindhis in the new Vedanta. Therefore, I think it is more relevant to use the sole term of Vedanta. Briefly put, they were both used to refer to the meeting between Sufism and Hinduism through a similarity of concepts, rather than providing evidence that the Muslim Sufi poets had a thorough knowledge of the Bhakti or the Vedanta, and thus could have been influenced by them.

The classical Sufi corpus

The idea of Sufism as built by the intelligentsia in late nineteenth-century Sindh started from the hypothesis that there was a congruence between

Sufism and Vedanta: the Sufi concept of *wahdat-e wujud*, or the unity of being, was in Vedantic parlance *advaita*, the non-duality or Oneness of God. Their conception embraced other religious schools claiming the same statement, mostly belonging to the *sant*s, with Kabir, Mirabai[2] and Guru Nanak as the heralds. Sometimes, Sufi poetry authored by non-Sindhis also played a liturgical role during the performances. One can quote Bulhe Shah or Ghulam Farid, the latter being a Siraiki-speaking author, this being a language in which many Sindhis also composed poetry.

The core of the poetry sung during the religious performance is in Sindhi, meaning that it is in one of the Sindhi dialects. In this respect, it is relevant to identify two distinct corpuses: the classical corpus and the modern corpus. The classical corpus is simultaneously a pan-Sindhi repertoire. Through this expression, I want to highlight that some Sindhi poets are much acclaimed and that the devotees of all of the Sufis' *darbar*s, Hindu and Muslim, are fond of their poetry, to the point where it is used as the devotional reservoir for their prayers. The three most popular poets are called the 'trinity of the Sindhi poets' by Ram Panjwani (Panjwani 1987: 29): ShahAbd al-Latif, Sachal Sarmast and Sami. The three Sufis of the trinity share a legacy pertaining to the religious culture of Sindh. As coined by Motilal Jotwani in his book on the Sufis of Sindh, they were the 'Great Integrators' (Motwani 1986: 150).[3] For him, this means that they were, and here he spoke especially of Shah Latif and Sachal, 'the late participaters in the Bhakti movement which had a major impact in Sindh through the spread of Guru Nanak's teaching' (Motwani 1986: 155).

In the literary field, Sindhi scholars label them as the heralds of the Classical Sufi poetry and Classical Sindhi literature.[4] I find it relevant to refer to the category of classical poetry because the literary forms they used, as well as the motifs they dealt with, became the patterns for the following authors. Let us briefly introduce their personality, as well as the main features of their poetry, before turning to the second corpus, that of the Modern Sufi poets.

Shah Abd al-Latif Bhittai (1689–1752), or Shah Latif or Shah, was a Sindhi Sufi poet who is acclaimed by all Sindhis as the greatest poet of Sindh and the Sindhi language. He was the great-grandson of Shah Abd al-Karim, or Shah Karim. He was born in Hala in a Sayyid family. Many legends were framed about him, although it is still difficult to trace his historical character. Nonetheless, he was very fascinated by the *jogi*s, considering them the models of renunciation. He probably travelled with them on a number of Hindu pilgrimages, including Dwarka and Hinglaj. The technical vocabulary used by Shah Latif to name the *jogis* gives evidence that they were Nathpanthis, and that they were therefore an important religious community in eighteenth-century Sindh.

His verses are so popular among the Sindhis that most are familiar enough with them that they can be quoted or recognized with ease. Shah is the symbol of Sindhi culture for Muslims as well as for Hindus, in Pakistan as well as in India. Such fame is based on the fact that he incorporated the main characters of Sindhi folklore into his work, thereby making it accessible to Sindhis across the social spectrum while also appealing to a sense of unity among Sindhis. His emphasis on the *wahdat-e wujud* furthered his resonance among different populations because it indicated that distinctions, especially religious, were disposable in the face of unity. Among his influences, Jalal al-Din Rumi was so dominant that his poetry is sometimes called the *Masnawi* of Sindh.[5]

Although many studies have been devoted to Shah Latif, his work still proves fertile ground for more analysis. For example, through his treatment of musicians in his poetry, Shah gives evidence of the importance of music both to him personally and, historically, to the region. In 'Sur Sorath', a much-acclaimed chapter of the poetical work the *Shah jo Risalo*, the minstrel Bijal defies Rao Diach, the king of Junagarh. The power of his lyre (*chang*) is such that the queens start crying and the forts begin to crumble. The many terms used by the poet to describe the minstrel, as *charan, mirasi, jajik* or *manghanar*, reflect not only his own interest in music but also the role played by the musician in the regional society. Shah Latif attributes a kind of magic power to him. 'Sur Sorath' comes across as an allegory for music's all-powerful sway over human beings and nature. The figure of the 'mendicant minstrel', the *charan*, is dominant throughout Shah Latif's poetry. Regarding the instruments, although the *chang* is the most quoted, one can find reference to others – like the *kamach*, for example.

Another neglected issue addressed by Shah Latif is the tragedy of Karbala. In the *Shah jo Risalo*, there is another chapter (*sur*) of special interest: *Sur Kedaro*. The whole chapter is devoted to the martyrdom (*shahadat*) of the third Shia imam, Husayn. A thorough study should be made on the reasons for which Shah Latif introduced a Shia topic in his poetry; he was likely influenced by Persia, where the *marsiyyo* genre, the dirge devoted to the martyrdom of Husayn and his family, was booming. Shah Latif's references to the tragedy of Karbala distinguish him from his predecessors in classic Sindhi Sufi poetry.

Shah Latif is the first Sindhi poet to write a *marsiyyo*[6] in Sindhi, and after him, the genre was adopted by many other poets. His *marsiyyo* did not strictly follow the format of the Persian dirge; instead, *Sur Kedaro* is divided into four parts. The first focuses on the coming of Moharram, the month of mourning for the martyrdom of Husayn. The second part comments on the apparently helpless state of imams during the ensuing conflict. The third part is about their bravery in fighting and how their murder was a part of God's plan, and the fourth deals with their union with God after death. Shah Latif's depictions of the different episodes of the battle are made very vivid with precise details.

Sachal Sarmast (1739–1825) was another main Sufi poet of Sindh who composed several works in Sindhi, Siraiki and Persian. Named Khwaja Salah al-Din Hafiz Abd al-Wahhab by birth, he was given the *laqab* of Sachal Sarmast, meaning the 'truthful one with an intoxicated head'. He was the son of the *sajjada nashin* of Daraza, Khwaja Muhammad Hafiz, also known as Sahib Dino I, and brother of the *sajjada nashin* Khwaja Abd al-Haqq. He thus belonged to the Darazi *silsila* located close to Khairpur in Northern Sindh. Although he had never owned a piece of land, he was in charge of looking after the business affairs of the Sufi lodge, the *khanaqah*.

There is a legend according to which Shah Latif met Sachal Sarmast. When he was about seven, it is said that Shah Latif came to pay homage to the local *murshid*. After seeing Sachal, he is said to have exclaimed: 'This God-gifted child will one day uncover those divine secrets which I have still kept concealed'. Sachal Sarmast's attributes were those of a *bayragin*, a stick with two forked ends, an *asa*, a stick, a *tanbura*, a stringed instrument, and a *kishti*, a bowl. These attributes highlight what was Sachal's conception of Sufism. The *bayragin* and the *kishti* are the symbol of renunciation. Like his Sufi predecessors, he used to play music and sing, and also to perform ecstatic dances. In his poetry, he was a staunch extoller of the doctrine of *wahdat-e wujud* – as, for example, when he states: 'God is the Unique Manifestation everywhere and all have come from Him'. His religious conception attracted the wrath of some religious leaders who tried to kill him. The legend states that the swords passed through his body as if it was water.

Chainrai Bachomal Dattaramani (1743–1850), better known as Sami, was a Sindhi Hindu saint poet, who is known by many as a Hindu Sufi.[7] He was born in a well-to-do family in Shikarpur. He was himself a cloth merchant and travelled a great deal between Shikarpur and Amritsar in Punjab. After getting married when he was about 30, he got in touch with Swami Meghraj, who taught him Vedanta in original Sanskrit for about ten years. He is the most influential Sindhi author of the Bhakti, with a strong devotion for the god Krishna. He was the author of a huge Sindhi poetical work known as *Sami jo sloka*, and he wrote in the Gurmukhi script, which is one of the scripts used by the Sindhi Hindus. His poetry went through several editions, including one recently published in Karachi in 2002 (see bibliography). This edition ends with a glossary composed by Abd al-Karim Sindilo, who, interestingly, had already published a glossary of Sachal Sarmast's poetry (Sindilo 1984).

Although the Bhakti he expressed encapsulated many similarities with the *wahdat-e- wujud*, Sami frequently referred to typical Hindu concepts, such as illusion, *maya*, or the transmigration of the soul (Sami 2002: 3–12). He mentioned quite often the Veds (Vedas) as the final religious scripture. The Hindu references are nevertheless entangled with Sufism. He used the technical lexicon of Sufism, devoting a chapter of his *slok*s to *ishq*, *mohabat* or the *faqir*s. His *slok*s finally contains the famous claim first expressed by Mansur Hallaj:[8] *Ana al-haqq*, or 'I am God', that was as we saw before a real refrain in Sachal's work (Allana 1983: 146–7). Furthermore, some of Sami's verses perfectly expressed the concept of *wahdat-e wujud*, as for example:

Khalq men khaliq, khalq subh khaliq men

In the Creation is the Creator, the Creation is in the Creator
(Allana 1983: 148–9)

The classical Sufi corpus is praised by the Hindu Sufis since such poetry is made of two meaningful features: the use of Sindhi local figures and themes, and the importance given to music. But above all, they all claim the unity of God. Beyond these shared features, some distinctions should be mentioned. Shah Latif retains a unique place in Sindhi poetry and literature, and needless to say, not all of his chapters (*sur*s) are equally appreciated by the Hindu Sufis. Sachal was a Muslim Sufi who made a lot of references to the Hindu gods, an issue I shall examine in the next section. Finally, Sami was a Hindu whose poetry perfectly interweaves the Bhakti legacy and Sufi heritage. A last distinction should be made regarding language. While Shah Latif's poetry can be difficult to understand, especially in terms of the somewhat ancient vocabulary he uses, Sachal and especially Sami are far more accessible. The evidence is given by the fact that the technical lexicon of Shah's poetry was the object of a study as soon as 1913 by Mirza Qalich Beg, while, as we saw above, similar works were only recently published for Sachal and Sami.

The modern Sufi corpus

Besides the classical corpus, the modern Sufi corpus plays a capital role for framing the mystical space. The word 'modern' is principally employed in opposition to that of classical. It also refers to another period of Sufi poetry, although the chronology of the Sufis' lives can be seen to overlap. The main distinction between the classical and modern Sufi poetry is a shifting in the dominant literary forms, and above all in the themes addressed by the poets. In the strict literary field, some of them are not much praised by the specialists of Sindhi literature. Such scholars usually underscore the fact that their poetry did not reach the standard of the classical Sufi poets. For example, in his *History of Sindhi Literature*, L. H. Ajwani wrote: 'As poets, however, they cannot be placed in the front rank' (Ajwani 1970: 154). Obviously, what is of interest here is not their literary value, but the success they meet in the circle of the Hindu Sufi *darbars*.

For a number of reasons, including my lack of skill in this area, it is not my aim here to discuss this issue. I wish only to illustrate the Sufi poetry that is the most popular among the Sufi Hindu circles of India. In this respect, Qutub Ali Shah (1810–1910) deserves to be mentioned first. He was a famous Sufi from Hyderabad who had many followers among the Muslims and the Hindus of Sindh. He was a strong advocate of *wahdat-e wujud*, a *wujudi*, and his poetry is dotted with references to Hindu concepts and characters. For instance, he uses the word *darshan* for vision as much as *didar*. One of his most important followers was Rai Rochaldas. His *dargah* is located in Jahaniyya, a neighbourhood in Hyderabad.

Qutub Ali Shah was fond of Krishna. His poetry is still very famous among the Hindu Sindhis of India, and one of his poems is a kind of hymn to the Hindu Sufis: *Sakhi sabhajal*, whose Sindhi text with an English translation is given in the annex. It is a short poem with a refrain (*thal*) and four stanzas. We can say it is an archetypal *wujudi* poem because of the following features. Above all, it summarized many of the current middle-class expectations, and is simultaneously well adapted to the modern life because of its brevity – making it fit especially well the very busy traders' way of life, as they cannot spent too much time in praying. The main purpose of the reciter is expressed from the refrain itself: to obtain the blessing (*fazal*), and through it, the grace (*rahim*) of the Master. Qutub Ali Shah introduces himself as *hek nimani*, a humble devotee, but the word *nimani* is female. It is a common feature of South Asian literature to represent the Sufi as the female lover, the bride, longing to be married to her love, the bridegroom who is God.

It is to be sung in the *sur asa purbi*, *sur* being the Sindhi word for *rag*. It is an interesting association of two *surs*. The first one is named *asa*, probably borrowed from the Sikhs but seldom heard today. The *sur asa* is related to hope, inspiration and courage. The *sur purbi*, a vernacularized form of *purvi*, implies the follower to be quiet and serious, as well as mystical. This one, too, is not commonly heard today. Furthermore, the verses are mostly oriented towards two themes. First, God is named after three different words: the Master (*malik*), the Creator (*khaliq*) and the Guide (*murshid*). It means he is all powerful, but also the only one who can remove the pain (*dard*). And suppressing the *dard* is to obtain the divine vision, although it is not expressly stated in the poetry. Furthermore, God is the one who knows everything and another verse clearly refers to the *wahdat-e wujud*: *to bin byo nahe ko malik*, or 'None but You is the Master'.

Qutub Ali Shah's *Sakhi sabhajal* is probably one of the two most popular Sufi poems among the Hindu Sufis, along with another one authored by Dalpat Sufi, *Sufi so jo sachu pachhani*, or 'The Sufi is the one who knows the Truth (God)'. Before turning to it and to the English translation provided by H. M. Hari, it is relevant to observe that the poem is quoted by different Sufi figures as being the best expression of what Sufism is. It is quoted in English by H. M. Hari in his book (Hari 1982: 16–17), quoted again by S. L. Gajwani in his two books, and also by Sakhi Qabul Muhammad Faruqi, the *sajjada nashin* of Daraza. The latter quotes, word for word, Hari's translation, after giving the Sindhi text (Faruqi 2002: 35–6). Thus, we can see there is a convergence of views between different Sufi paths.[9] In comparison with Qutub Ali Shah's piece, one could claim Dalpat Sufi's one is much more 'Sufistic'. What does it mean? It means it is not devoted to the common worshipper, to the simple follower of the path, the *murid*. It was written for someone who has been initiated into the Sufi path.

Thus, the poem doesn't deal with daily problems, with smoothing the pains of life, or being granted a direct vision of God. It rather deals with the importance of taming the Ego, the absolute prerequisite for the merging with God. This issue is the most addressed issue throughout the poem. It is about 'burning the Ego' (*jani*) or to 'Transform the Ego into the Self', or to 'find the self in the Self'. Different words are used by Dalpat for naming the Ego and the Self. They mostly belong to the Sindhi root *pan*, but in different shapes, such as *ap* or *apna*. Throughout this poem, it is said that the Sufi is beyond the common human nature, in terms of seeing or happiness. Another main message is expressed: the Sufi is the one who 'knows no religion, sees One in all'. These words clearly refer to the *wahdat-e wujud*, and are the main reason why it is praised by such persons as Sakhi Qabul Muhammad Faruqi and R. M. Hari.

Another much-acclaimed Sufi among the Hindu Sufis is Bedil. Faqir Qadir Bakhsh (1814–72), also known as Bedil – literally, without a heart – was a Sufi born in Rohri, belonging to the Qadiriyya (Bedil 2012).[10] In his teens, he went to Sehwan Sharif, where he is reported to have been vouchsafed spiritual visions. He also visited Jhok Sharif and Daraza since he was a staunch follower of Sachal Sarmast. He wrote copiously on mystical topics in Persian, Sindhi, Siraiki and Urdu, and is the author of eighteen works, mainly in Persian and in Sindhi. Most of his writings are devoted to Sufism, and he described numerous Sufi concepts in prose and poetry. He also wrote a commentary on Abd al-Qadir al-Jilani's *qasidas*, the renowned Sufi from the twelfth century who was the founder of the powerful Sufi brotherhood of the Qadiriyya. According to his verses, Bedil can be regarded as a *wujudi*, as he states, for example, that a *dervish* is neither a Shia nor a Sunni. The true Sufi is a 'witness of the Truth', *shahid-e haqiqat*; he understands that union with the beloved is the only escape from plurality.

Bedil was the scion of a Qurayshi[11] family that migrated from Multan two generations back. The most remarkable part about Bedil is that he authored many *masnawi*s in Persian, and other literature in Arabic. Rochaldas seems to have been particularly fond of his Sindhi and Siraiki poetry. In his spiritual dialogues, Bedil is the second most quoted poet, after Shah Abd al-Latif, and before Sachal. He is also more quoted than the Jahaniyyan lineage, whose members were the *murshid*s of Rochaldas, such as Qutub Ali Shah and his son, Hadi Bakhsh. Rochaldas was born in Rohri, like Bedil, but seven years after his demise. Answering a disciple who asked him to recite Bedil's poetry, Rochaldas stated: 'The lyrics of Bedil Sahib are excellent, but his language is very difficult' (Hari 1995: 193). Nonetheless, he referred frequently to his poetry when he wished to explain a Sufi concept or notion.

Among the Hindu Sufi paths, some followers of the Sufi masters themselves authored Sufi poetry in Sindhi. Every path broadly uses the classical Sindhi Sufi poets, as well as the modern Sufi poets, but they also refer to a repertoire which arose inside the community. Most of the time, the poetry has been authored by the founder of the path, or his Master. Here, there is a tradition that deserves to be mentioned. Since a Master is supposed to provide inspiration to his *murids*, even if a *murid* composes Sufi poetry, it will be attributed to the Master. This untold and unwritten rule is prevalent in many religious traditions all over the world. If we want to list the community repertoire, we would have, for instance: Rochaldas, while the poetry was mainly authored by Dadi Dhan and Dadi Ganga, and Nimano Faqir. Furthermore, we can quote other paths, such as Jogi Sain or Dalpat Sufi. Interestingly, there is no *kalam* which is attributed to Mulchand Faqir, nor to Gehimal Motwani, his main follower and head of the Indian disciples. Nonetheless, some verses are attributed to both of them and are used as sung prayers during religious performances.

To use the community repertoire means that a Sufi community is autonomous, and there is no relation with any kind of centralized institutionalized paths. I am thinking here of the Sufi brotherhoods that are dominant in the landscape of Sindh, such as the Qadiriyya or the Sohrawardiyya. Belonging to a shared Sufi legacy of Sindh is implemented through the singing of pan-Sindhi *kalam*s. But the main pattern allowing a delimited group to make a community is that the members are united through the worship of a Master. The combination of the two repertoires plays a primary function in the *darbar*s.

It draws a spiritual state of mind that is an indispensable condition for reaching the goal: the merging of the follower with the Master, and from him/her to God. The singing of the Sufi poetry puts the disciple in an emotional state, which can hopefully lead to ecstasy, itself understood as being the threshold of the meeting with God.

The vernacular ideology of the *wahdat-e wujud*

Before turning to the study of the rituals as a connection between the spaces and community, we have to study the extent to which the cornerstone of all the processes, the *wahdat-e wujud*, went through a process of vernacularization. As a matter of fact, it is thanks to the process of vernacularization that this concept was able to meet that of *advaita*, and, consequently, to facilitate the meeting of Hinduism and Sufism. The expression of *wahdat-e wujud* is an extension of the central dogma of Islam, *tawhid*. It began from an attempt to provide a proper understanding as well as an explanation of the dichotomy between immanence and transcendence. Although the expression *wahdat-e wujud* is usually associated with Ibn al-Arabi,[12] he never used it himself. It probably made an appearance with his main follower, Sadr al-Din al-Qonyawi. According to William Chittick, the major problem was to understand the word *wujud*. In later Islamic history, in the debates on Ibn al-Arabi in the Indian subcontinent, the Arabic expression *wahdat al-wujud* was said to assert 'All is He' or *hama ust*, a Persian expression. In the mystical thought of the subcontinent, *wahdat-e wujud* became the equivalent of the Persian expression.

William Chittick translates *wahdat-e wujud* as 'Oneness of Being' or 'Unity of Existence' (Chittick 1997). Furthermore, he enumerates the seven different ways in which the term has been understood, without intending to be exhaustive. Instead of trying to give a definition of *wahdat-e wujud*, it is better to quote Ibn al-Arabi, who states that things borrow *wujud* (existence) from God, as the earth borrows light from the sun. Before exploring the technical lexicon of Sindhi Sufism, it is necessary to have a look at the expression *wahdat* and *wujud* in nineteenth-century colloquial Sindhi. In a Sindhi-English dictionary published in 1879, *wahadata* means unity, oneness, but there is no word equivalent to existence or *wujud* built from the Arabic root, WJD

(Shirt 1879: 865). To investigate more thoroughly, it is necessary to have a look at the early publications devoted to the technical lexicon used by Shah Abd al-Latif, who authored the paradigmatic vernacular Sufi poetry known as *Shah jo Risalo*.[13]

In the last quarter of the nineteenth century, and more than two decades after the first publication of *Shah jo Risalo* in 1866, Sindhi literati thought it necessary to publish Shah's works so that his poetry could be more accessible to the people. The first glossary was published in 1890 by Lilaram Watanmal Lalwani in a book he wrote in English, with the title *The Life, Religion, and Poetry of Shah Latif*. It includes a glossary of 'all the difficult words and expressions occurring in *Shah jo Risalo*'. While there is no word related to *wujud*, two are related to *wahdat*: *wahadaniyyat*, and *wahdat*, both translated by Lalwani as 'unity'. Nevertheless, Lalwani quotes the sentence *tuhnjo Allah hekro*, 'Your God is One' – which first appears in Shah Karim's verses and then in Shah Abd al-Latif (Lalwani 1890, vol. I: 45). Therefore, from the late nineteenth century onwards, the *wahdat*, as a central dogma of Islam, was already vernacularized by Hindu Sindhi literati in using the term *hekro*, one.

The vernacularization of the *wahdat-e wujud* was reinforced by Mirza Qalich Beg, whose final aim was to 'democratize' the reading of *Shah jo Risalo* among Sindhis of all classes. In 1913, he published in Sindhi the first book totally devoted to Shah Abd al-Latif's technical lexicon. He translated the term *wahdat* used by Shah as *hekro*, and this was followed by the explanation: *Khoda jo Nalo*, 'the name of God'. The democratization process thus meant 'vernacularizing' the terminology by a translation into Sindhi. Mirza Qalich Beg also translated the Arabic word *wahdat* as *hekra'i* (Beg 1913: 187). The expression *wahdat-e wujud* is not included in the lexicon, of course, because it was not used by Shah Abd al-Latif.

Later on, the issue of *wahdat-e wujud* was addressed by many other scholars who were specialists of Sindhi poetry, but they have hardly been able to explain it, and this includes, for example, Motilal Jotwani in his book on Shah Abd al-Latif (Jotwani 1975 (1996)). Usually, the expression is supposed to have the simple meaning that God is unique, which implies that, beyond the formal practices of a given religion, there is only one unique God who is named differently in different religions. This concept is deduced from a Quranic quotation: 'All will perish except His face' (28:88).

The Sindhi Sufi poets often refer to the concept, although they most of the time name it only as *wahdat*. The topic of Oneness or Unity is nevertheless addressed as a central issue. For example, Nasir Faqir of Jalalani Sharif (d. 1960), the follower of Sufi Hazrat Abdul Sattar Shah of Jhok Sharif, speaks of *jam wahdat jo*, 'the cup of unity' (Nasir Faqir 1972). Qutub Ali Shah accuses the believers of having forgotten what he calls the origin of Unity: *Vatin wahdat vesariyotun*, 'You forget the origin of Unity' (Qutub Ali Shah 1985: 101).

Furthermore, they often refer to the *wahdat-e wujud* by using the Sindhi word *hek*, 'one', or its derivatives. Sachal Sarmast (1739–1829), one of the most popular Sindhi poets from Daraza, in the north of Sindh, refers to the 'One' by using the Sindhi word *hekkhe* or *hekro*. In the works of Rakhiyyal Shah (1842–1940), who was Mulchand's Sufi Master, the word *hekal*, with the ending -al which is a mark of endearment in Sindhi, is used. Nimano Faqir (1880–1963), a Hindu Sufi who was a follower of Sachal Sarmast, simply uses the world *hek*. There are, nevertheless, a few occasions when poets refer explicitly to the *wahdat-e wujud*, as for example when Rakhiyyal Shah uses the term *wahad wujud thiya wahdat*, 'With One their existence became unique' (Rakhiyyal Shah 2007: 6). Qutub Ali Shah also praises *wahdat vang vujudi pa'ye* – 'Unity is adorned with the attires of Existence' (Qtub Ali Shah 1985: 38).

It is significant to see how these Sufi poets focus on the issue of 'the Oneness of God'. Although it was not conceptualized then, their efforts to express their ideas in varied formulations, in Persian or in Sindhi, echo their feeling that all members of the Sindhi community are brothers. With Sachal Sarmast, the vernacularization process reached a new step when he used a new expression, that of *haqq mawjud*, which is in fact not new in the context of Muslim thought. Nonetheless, using a new expression means a new step has been taken for establishing an interfaith dialogue.

We have observed that, in pre-partition Sindhi authors, there are but few uses of words or expressions directly based on *wahdat-e wujud*. A leading reason is perhaps that another expression, *haqq mawjud*, was being used by the Sindhis and is very close to *wahdat-e wujud*. The main user of the expression, if not the creator, was Sachal Sarmast. On the other hand, Sachal usually used the expression *haqq mawjud* coupled with another one: *sada mawjud*, that is, *sada* (always) omnipresent. In one of his poems, for example, one finds it as a refrain. Among Sachal's followers, these formulas are used as salutations.

When they write to each other, they use the expression *ishq mawjud*, and last but not least, the inscription written on the main gate of Sachal's *dargah* is *haqq mawjud*.

Interestingly, in the expression *haqq mawjud*, the word *wahdat* is replaced by that of *haqq*, while the form *wujud* has become *mawjud*. 'Truth' or 'haqq' is one of the ninety-nine names of God, and is frequently used by the Sufis for the Creator. Furthermore, it is an implicit allusion to the sentence *ana al-haqq*. The story of Mansur Hallaj (857–922), who was hung in Baghdad after he shouted *ana al-haqq*, or 'I am God', is very well known in the Islamic world. It became a key expression in the mystical poetry of Iran, Turkey, Muslim South Asia and Indonesia wherever the theories of the *wahdat-e wujud* were employed. The expression was condemned by some Sufis, but others tried to defend Hallaj's utterance. For example, Rumi explained that *ana al-haqq* was the expression of perfect selflessness when the mystic had completely forgotten himself in God. Muhammad Iqbal (1877–1938)[14] was formerly a critic of Hallaj, but finally thought that *ana al-haqq* meant the 'Infinite entering into the loving embrace of the Finite' (Schimmel 1989: 1002).

In Sindh, Hallaj is a very popular figure, and many Sufi poets mention his name in their verses.[15] Sachal Sarmast, nicknamed Mansur sani, 'the Second Mansur', was a staunch admirer and devout follower of Hallaj. In his Sindhi poetry, there are many references to him. What is the implication of replacing the word *wujud* with *mawjud*? The word *mawjud* reinforces the immanence of God since, in Arabic, *mawjud* means the very presence of God. The expression *hu mawjud* has a similar meaning: 'He is here'. The expression has already been used by Arab Muslim philosophers, for example al-Kindi (801–73) and al-Farabi (872–950). It is a clear statement of the omnipresence of God.

From the end of nineteenth century on, the Sindhi literati associated the *wahdat-e wujud* with the monism expressed by the Hindu school of *advaita vedanta*. The Sindhi understanding of *advaita vedanta* followed Vivekananda's interpretation (1863–1903) in the framework of his neo-Hinduism, which he introduced as a universal religion. It is thus more appropriate to name it Neo-Vedanta (Sooklal 1993) or Modern Vedanta (Bartley 2009). The main innovation of Neo-Vedanta introduced by Ramakhrishna was to lay stress upon social service, or *seva*. Furthermore, Ramakrishna (1836–86), Vivekananda's Master, taught that the ultimate reality behind the phenomenal world was one.

According to Vivekananda, Ramakrishna was the one who was able to put theory into practice. The Neo-Vedanta greatly attracted young Hindu Sindhis.

Sadhu Hiranand Advani (1863–93) was strongly attracted by the 'New Dispensation' and his life is quite exemplary in this regard. Hiranand Advani was born in Hyderabad in a family of Khudabadi Amils. The Khudabadi Amils were at the top of the social structure of Hyderabad. The Amils belonged to a high caste and were well-educated and well-versed in Persian. Most of them were in government service and a number of them had been *diwan*s (prime ministers) of the Talpur *mir*s. Hiranand was himself educated as a Nanakpanthi – that is, a follower of Guru Nanak, or of his son Shri Chand – but was not in the brotherhood of the Khalsa (Gidumal 1932: 40). His elder brother, Naval Rai, was the first to become a follower of Keshub Chandra Sen (1838–84), himself a follower of Ramakhrishna, and he travelled to Calcutta where he joined the Brahmo Samaj. Following Ramakrishna's egalitarian philosophy, Naval Rai and his brothers refused to bow to the Brahmans or to the *bawa*s, the Nanakpanthi priests.

Some young Hindu Sindhis from Hyderabad met Ramakrishna in his ashram on the banks of the Hugli, located in a suburb of Calcutta. In 1883, Hiranand used to spend several consecutive days and nights in the ashram. According to Hiranand's biographer, he was 'the one whom he (Ramakrishna) loved most deeply' (Gidumal 1932: 150). When he heard that Ramakrishna was seriously ill, Hiranand hastily left his work in Karachi and went to Calcutta to see the dying saint. Ramakrishna's preaching encompassed all great religions, since 'the Muhammadan Allah, the Christian God, the Nirakara Brahma were all realized in him' (Gidumal 1932 : 152). Furthermore, a central concept of Ramakrishna's Neo-Vedanta which the Sindhi literati understood as being close to *wahdat-e wujud* was the concept of *akhanda satchidananda*, 'the Indivisible and Eternal Being'.

The concept of *satchidananda* is made of three Sanskrit words. The first part, *sat*, stresses the divine as the Truth, as it is in *haqq mawjud*. Thus, *sat* corresponds to *haqq*. The second part, *chit*, roughly means consciousness, while *ananda* means bliss and happiness. *Akhanda* means non-divisible – that is, unity, *wahdat*. The expression finally emphasizes 'the glimpse of ultimate reality', and in the words of Hiranand's biographer, the 'eternal and formless Being, Who is unchangeable in his blessedness and unity'. Many Sindhi literati were convinced that Neo-Vedanta was the key to the modernization of India. A number of charitable institutions were created, for example, by Hiranand and his brothers, or by his 'disciples'. Among these were the leper asylum in Mangho Pir and an orphanage in Sukkur. Many educational institutions were also established.

Rochaldas did refer to *satchidananda* in his spiritual dialogues with his disciples. He mentioned Ramakrishna had attained *fanai* (absorption) in the goddess Kali, as well as in other incarnations such as Hanuman, Sita and Krishna, as well as Muhammad and Jesus (Hari 1995: 316). According to Rochaldas, the three words making *satchidananda* mean existence (*sat*), knowledge (*chit*) and bliss (*ananda*). Furthermore, they are the exact equivalents of *haqq* (truth), *ishq* (love) and *husn* (beauty) (Hari 1995: 195).

It is not easy to trace Neo-Vedanta in Sufi poetry. Nonetheless, Nimano Faqir used the negation of duality for emphasizing the Oneness of God, for in Sindhi, the word *akhanda*, non-divisible, does not exist. For example, Nimano employed other expressions, such as: *Allah (...) ne ahe biyyo*, 'Allah is not dual'. In this case, it is more appropriate to speak of non-duality instead of Oneness or unity, *wahdat*. Although it is not known by which Hindu *panth* Nimano was educated, one can surmise that Sami's *sloka*s were widespread among the Hindus of Northern Sindh.

Hindu references in the Sufi poetry

At this point, and before turning to the ritual, a last step is to focus on the main element explaining how Hindu Sufism is possible and at work among the Hindus. It is related to the Sufi poetry performed in the *satsang*s and other devotional events, and in this respect, the main aim here is to find out if a typology of these Sufi poets can be drawn. In his chapter on the Siraiki mystical poetry of Sindh, mostly based on Sachal and Bedil, Christopher Shackle identifies three styles: Islamic, Persian and local. Regarding the use of 'Hindu ideas and practices', he claims they are paradoxically a variation within the Islamic style, arguing that 'the paradox was, after all, admirably designed to fulfil the poets' attempts to express the insights of a pure monotheism' (Shackle 1981: 255–6).

In this section, I shall not venture to comment on such methods but rather focus on deciphering whether a special category of Sindhi Sufis is praised by the Hindu Sindhis or not. For this answer, we have to look at the authors as well as at their poetry. We will try to scrutinize how they deal with Hindu figures and/or Hindu concepts and notions. But first, for the aim of contextualization, let us summarize who are the main Muslim Sufis of Sindh whom the Hindu Sufis of India are referring to.

At different levels, there are five main Sufi Muslim poets for whom we find quotations: Shah Abd al-Latif, Sachal Sarmast and the successors Qutub Ali Shah, Dalpat Sufi and Bedil. Three categories of references can be found in Sindhi Sufi poetry authored by these poets: figures, gods and notions/concepts. In fact, references to the figure of the *jogi* date back to Shah Inat, a Sindhi Sufi poet of the seventeenth century (Ajwani 1970: 60–1). Also, we can find it in Shah Karim's poetry, but it is fully expressed in Shah Abd al-Latif's verses. The main purposes of the poets, when referring to Hindu elements, are to show there is no difference between Muslims and Hindus, and even to provide evidence that there are equivalencies. Such Muslim practice is equivalent to such Hindu practice. Nonetheless, the paradigm of Sufism is renunciation, and the *jogi* is the pattern of the renunciant.

Among the classical Sufi poets, Sachal is probably the one whose work quotes the most numerous Hindu references. For example, regarding scriptures, he mentions the Vedas, named *Bed* in his verses. Furthermore, like most of the other Muslim Sufi poets, he refers to the *pothis* (pl. *pothiyyun*) as a broad term for encompassing all of the Hindu scriptures. Frequently, he puts side by side the scriptures of the different involved religions – namely Islam, Hinduism and Christianity. His purpose is to show that reading the scriptures does not suffice for reaching God/s. The mention of the scriptures goes hand in hand with the denunciation of the different categories of priests who can spend hours on reciting the scriptures, without trying to understand the deep, or even the hidden, meanings. Talking about the different forms God can have, he writes:

Somewhere he reads *pothiyyun*
Somewhere the Quran!
Somewhere he is a Christian, somewhere Ahmed,[16]
And elsewhere he is Hanuman!

(Sachal Sarmast 1997: 75)

In his poetry, Sachal mentions different Hindu gods, such as Ram, Hanuman (as we saw above), Sita and especially Krishna. Sita was the wife of Ram and she was supposed to be a symbol of a devoted loyal wife in the *Ramayana*, an important Hindu scripture. Hanuman, another Hindu god in the *Ramayana*, was also a symbol of devotion to his Master, Ram.

Other characters of Hindu mythology are quoted – for example, Ravan and Goga. There are also a number of sacred Hindu places, such as Hinglaj, Kasi, or Kashi (Banaras), Sri Lanka and the Ganga. As was the case with Shah Abd al-Latif, Sachal uses different words to name the Hindu renunciants. We find, for instance, *gosain, jogi, nango* and *udesi*, but not varied as is the case in Shah Abd al-Latif's poetry. However, Sachal is well aware of the Hindu rituals since he talks about *mandir*, the Hindu temple, the *darsan*, the ritual of visualization of the God, the *jap sahib*, the repetition of the name of the *guru* among the Sikhs, and the *janeo*, the sacred thread symbolizing the religious initiation of the young Hindu boy.

Another Sufi Muslim poet who refers a great deal to Hindu gods is Qutub Ali Shah. In his poetry, he goes so far as asking his followers to read the Hindu scriptures he also calls *pothiyun*:

> In Lanka, in the waters of the Ganges is God, accept this without doubt.
> Ram beside Krishna (Kaniyya) does stay, know this truth.
> Sita with Laxman observes Diwali,[17] search and realize this.
> Qutub, Ram and Rahim are both within, see now, this moment.
>
> (Qutub Ali Shah 1985: 14–15)

In his verses, Qutub introduces new characters: Laxman, who is the younger brother of Ram. He also mentions Diwali, a main Hindu festival commemorating Ram's victory over Ravan, and his coming back to Ayodhya with Sita.[18] Sachal also refers to this episode of the *Ramayana*. Furthermore, it is interesting to observe that, while Krishna is a main Hindu character for Sachal Sarmast and Qutub Ali Shah, they do not mention him with the same name,[19] while, in Sachal's poetry, he is named Krishna or Shyam, maybe the most used names for the God, Qutub Ali Shah calls him Kaniyya, the Hindi equivalent being Kanhaiya, a name for Krishna when he was a teenager. Shyam would mean dark, as is the meaning of Krishna, and also as a reference to his dark complexion, which can even be dark blue.

These quotations, as is the case with many others, suffice to show that the Muslim Sufis of Sindh were mostly attracted by the Vishnuite school of Hinduism. The most quoted gods are Ram and Krishna, two *avatars* of Vishnu. While the Hindu and Sikh scriptures are broadly referred to as *pothiyun*, other Hindu deities clearly allude to the *Ramayana*, one of the gospels of Vishnuite Hinduism. Sachal mentions Hanuman while Qutub Ali Shah gives the names of Laxman and Sita, Ram and Krishna. This shows a deep influence of the Bhakti and, through it, more bridges being built between the *wujudi* Sufism and Hinduism. In terms of concept, some Hindu terms are mentioned, such as *maya* or, above all, *darsan*, the Sindhi form for *darshan*. Here, again, we can observe variations in the poetry. For example, Sachal puts *darsan* while Qutub Ali Shah puts *darshan*.

In relation to the Hindu references, a special mention should be made of what I shall name the Kandri school of Sufism. Kandri is a small town located in Rohri taluqa, in the Khaipur district. The founder of the school was Rohal Faqir (1734–1804), who was a contemporary of Sachal Sarmast. He started working in the Kalhora administration as Minister of Finances, but resigned upon becoming a renunciant in Kandra. He was a disciple of Shah Inayat from Jhok Sharif. As a staunch *wujudi*, he authored poetry in Sindhi, Siraiki and Hindi (Bhatti 2012: 86–7). In his *History of Sindhi Literature*, L. H. Ajwani states that the main feature of the period between the eighteenth century and the first half of the nineteenth century 'was the impulse given by Hindi and Vedantist literature to Sindhi poetry. Sami was the Master who could claim to have rendered the "speech of the Vedas" in the vernacular of the Sindhis, but there were several others, like Rohal and Dalpat' (Ajwani 1970: 110).

All the other Sufi poets who belonged to the Kandri school were related to Rohal Faqir, and they were all Shias. Murad Faqir (1743–96) was Rohal Faqir's brother-in-law, and his cousin, and also a staunch *wujudi*.[20] He composed poetry in Sindhi, Siraiki and Hindi (Bhatti 2012: 91–2). Murad was the father of Darya Khan and Ghulam Ali. In Jotwani's *Dictionary of Sindhi Literature*, Rohal, Murad and Darya Khan belong to the 'jnan-marg school of poetry' (Jotwani 1996: 125–6). Darya Khan (1775–1850) authored Sufi poetry in Sindhi and Siraiki. According to Ajwani, Darya Khan surpassed Ghulam Ali, as well as his other brother named Shahu Faqir. Ajwani further emphasizes that Darya Khan excelled in his verses on Krishna 'as if he were another devotee like Mirabai' (Ajwani 1970: 116).[21]

Regarding Rohal and Murad, they seem to represent Rama as the god to be reached in the mystical quest. Murad stated that the *jogis* are fascinated by Rama (Paniker 2000: 437). Already, Rohal had explicitly mentioned him as the goal to reach:

> They merged themselves in Rama, the hermits realized Him for ever,
> Everything they gave, in giving they hesitated never,
> They drove away from their minds evil thought for ever,
> Says Rohal, day and night, absorbed in Him they were,
> Happy were all Nagas at the sight of their Friend
>
> Paniker 2000: 462

It is not known the extent to which these Muslim Sufis knew Hinduism and Sikhism. Nonetheless, it is obvious that the Sufis to whom the Hindus refer possess a number of similar characteristics. First, they mostly belong to Upper Sindh, with Siraiki as a language used for Sufi poetry besides Sindhi. Second, they all belong to the *wujudi* school of the Sufism of Sindh, and thus the Naqshbandis are excluded. But even among the *wujudi* school of local Sufism, they form a group whose aim is to find out equivalencies between Islam, Hinduism and Sikhism. These selected Sufis from Sindh are probably those that refer most to the Hindu figures and concepts.

Conclusion

In this chapter, we saw how the mystical space of the *darbar* is framed. All of the material elements pertaining to the making of the mystical space are sustained by non-material elements. In these ranks stands the poetry. In order to provide the frame in which the mystical space is constructed, two corpuses of Sufi poetry have been distinguished: the classical corpus and the modern corpus. Each of them works at a different level but, above all, the different Hindu Sufi paths give them different functions in different circumstances. All in all, it is amazing to observe that, while the poetry of the greatest Sufi poet, Shah Abd al-Latif, is sung during *satsangs*, there is no ritual use during the different ceremonies. Furthermore, his poetry, which is praised by everyone as being the quintessence of Sindhi poetry and literature, does not provide data for any prayer.

The main argument pertaining to the poetry is a concept which irradiates through all of the verses: the Oneness of God, or *wahdat al-wujud*, in classical Arabic Sufi terminology. This concept was appropriated by the Sindhi Sufi poets, both Muslim and Hindu. The more remarkable point is how they succeeded in remoulding it through a process of vernacularization. The vernacularization followed two layers. On one side, it was re-coined with a different linguistic expression, compulsorily making a shift, even if a slight one, in the meaning. For example, it was the *haqq mawjud*, a core principle in Sachal's poetry, which was mostly continued by Nimano. On the other side, the main vernacularization at work was the merging of the *haqq mawjud* with the vedantic *advaita* principle, as nurtured by the neo-vedantism of Vivekananda. Thus, the Oneness of God did meet the non-duality of God, and once again, the best exponent of this working congruence was Nimano Faqir.

Once this construction is completed, the final touch for reaching God is provided by the singing of the Sufi Sindhi poetry. The study of the Sufi corpus highlighted by the singing provides a number of clues. Two kinds of repertoires are intermingled, working together. The first category is made up of Sindhi Sufis without any relation with the involved path. The exemplary example in this context is Sachal. It is noteworthy that the language he used is very accessible – more so, for instance, than Shah Abd al-Latif's. He is certainly the core of Nimano's path, but his poetry is sung in all the Sufi *darbar*s of India, and we saw that there are even special Sufi sessions organized under the name of 'Darazi *satsangs*' (See last section of chapter 5). Another category of repertoire is made up of Sufi poetry sung only in the involved Sufi path. For example, Rochaldas's poetry, usually composed by Dadi Dhan or Dadi Ganga, is hardly performed in Mulchand or Nimano's paths, although it could be – but not as a rule, as it is in his *darbar*.

We have finally observed that the corpus used by the Hindus, Sufis and non-Sufis has been built following a number of criteria. But the most significant is that the quoted Sufi poets are those who refer the most to Hinduism, not only in mentioning the figure of the *jogi* as was done by classical Sufi poets such as Shah Abd al-Latif, but going further so as to refer directly to Hindu gods, and to the episodes of the sacred Hindu scriptures. Interestingly, this trend in the *wujudi* Sufism of Sindh seems to have developed in the nineteenth century, during colonial domination.

We saw that the Sufi poetical corpus of the Hindu Sufis draws a mystical space, but both the spaces, physical and mystical, need to be connected to the followers. The link between them is operated through not only rituals but also iconography. This makes for a junction between all of the components: the masters, the followers, the physical space and the mystical space. The material support allowing for the transition from one step to another is made through ritual. The ritual itself is mostly made up of symbolic gestures in relation with, in most of the cases, sacred images of the saints pertaining to the *darbar*. Visualizing the Master is the best way to reach the merging with God, the *fana fi'llah*. Sometimes, but rarely, relics are also exhibited, not for being worshipped as a kind of idolatry, but because they are believed to strengthen the concentration of the disciple. Nonetheless, one can observe a number of distinctions between the rituals as performed in the Hindu Sufi *darbar*s in India. It is not always known how the rituals came to exist. Rarely, the origin of a ritual is explicit. Most of the time, it is said to be 'tradition', which could mean it has been performed for centuries.

Alternative Sufi structures as networking India and beyond

While the Sufi *darbar*s are diverse in terms of architecture and agency, they nonetheless share a number of characteristics. A Sufi saint who is worshipped is supposed to have made miracles, and to have delivered a spiritual teaching. Also, while the main rituals are Sufi, the social rituals performed for births, weddings and deaths are Hindu. Amazingly, the Pakistani *sajjada nashin* of Tando Jahaniyyan performed a Hindu ritual for the coronation of the new *gaddi nashin* of Rochaldas's *darbar*. The *darbar* also works as a place of pilgrimage where followers come to get rest and attain a peaceful feeling. It is thus necessary to plan accommodations where they may stay since some have engaged in long travel to visit.

While they are obviously the core of the Sufi worship, the followers are constantly in need of guidance on the Sufi path. Most *darbar*s are the centres of a spiritual network crossing over India, and sometimes abroad. A network is built following the migration and displacement of followers. Often, such followers have claimed that they have themselves been granted a spiritual place where they can perform the Sufi rituals devoted to their Master. Places such as these are like subsidiaries of the *darbar*, which would be their 'parent company'. Often, the subsidiaries are run by family members of the *darbar*'s *gaddi nashin*. The *gaddi nashin* himself regularly visits the places, grants them of his blessings and also collects the gifts made by the followers. The subsidiaries are not made of separate buildings, as the *darbar* would be, but they are organized inside a house or a flat depending on how many followers are living nearby.

Other *samadhi*s are independent Sufi structures, although their owners are required to be the follower of a Sufi Master who runs a *darbar*. Sometimes, as is the case with Jogi Sain's *samadhi* in Mumbai, one is directly linked to the spiritual authority of a Muslim *sajjada nashin* who stays in Sindh, in Pakistan. But, most of the time, the main authority of the *samadhi* is its founder. An interesting case is Molchand Kripalani's *samadhi*. It is given a specific name, the Sufi *mandir*, which offers an interesting association of a Sufi adjective with a Hindu term, *mandir*, the most common word to mean a temple. However, the most unexpected element is that Molchand Kripalani's *samadhi* is managing a Sufi pilgrimage at the *dargah* of a forgotten Sindhi Sufi located in Bijapur, Karnataka.

Among the three Hindu Sufis under study, Mulchand Faqir is an exception since he did not migrate to India. He spent his whole life in his native town of Sehwan Sharif, a very reputed centre of Sufi pilgrimage. Known as a *kafi*, a local term used for the Sufi lodge, it is a very unique Hindu Sufi place where Molchand's tomb (*maqbaro*) stands. In the Islamic Republic of Pakistan, no ritual is performed there, although the Mulchand *kafi* is private property. Unfortunately, his followers can hardly perform the pilgrimage to the *kafi* because of the difficulties involved in them getting a Pakistani visa. Consequently, the main pilgrimage place remains the *darbar* located in Haridwar, where Mulchand is venerated, as is his main follower and successor in India, Gehimal Motwani.

The *darbar* and its extensions

Beyond the specific case of Mulchand, each Sufi path has different extensions that are related to the 'centre'. The 'centre' is here considered the main *darbar*, which is usually the main residence of the *gaddi nashin* as well as the seat of the path. Regarding the relationship between the centre and the peripheral structures, one can observe differences between Rochaldas's path, Nimano's one and Mulchand's. Let us start with the latter. The purpose is to observe how Mulchand's path is managed by his followers, beyond the existence of Mulchand's *maqbaro* in Pakistan. Mulchand's case has another specific feature: the seat of the path has been shifted quite often. Before partition, it was settled in Sehwan Sharif in Pakistan after 1947. In a second period, it was shifted to Ulhasnagar after the followers had migrated to India. A transitional step can be seen as occurring in Delhi then, and finally a new shrine was built at Haridwar. Beyond this, one cannot really speak of extensions, except if the private *puja* rooms are to be taken into account. A *puja* room is usually a small room, or even a part of a room, which looks like an altar or a chapel inside a flat or a house. It is mainly made of a kind of table on which different ritual objects are placed – incense, candles, oil lamps and especially representations of the gods and the saints, whether images or statues.

I have visited two such *puja* rooms devoted to Mulchand. The first one was at Daulatram Motwani's place in Ulhasnagar, and the second at Basant Jethwani's in Delhi. The *puja* room was originally a private space for devotion. It is 'used' by an extended family, where individual devotion can be performed, as can be that of the extended family. Sometimes, nonetheless, the *puja* room can be used as a transitional *darbar*, especially when there is for any reason a lack of a *darbar*. For example, when the Mul Kuthiyya stopped its activities in Ulhasnagar, Basant's *puja* room in Delhi played the role of *darbar* for a while. This means that the main functions, including the *versi*, were arranged in the flat, with the *puja* room acting as *sanctum sanctorum*.

Recently, Daulatram Motwani has arranged a *samadhi* devoted to Mulchand in the basement of his building. The principle is not different from the one he had previously in his flat. There is only a difference in terms of size since the new space is bigger. The gallery of portraits is made up of Mulchand's picture in the heart of the pictorial agency, and one can also find the Khatwara Sahib and Gehimal Motwani, Daulatram's father. Different *versi*s are celebrated and, when I visited the *samadhi*, it was the *versi* of Daulatram's wife. All the *versi*s start with the *havan* performed by a Brahman. This is followed by a very simple ceremony, during which Sufi poetry is sung by a Sindhi bhraman, who also plays the harmonium and is accompanied by a tabla player. Some cakes are given to the visitors as *prasad*, and mostly women composed the choir who sang with the main singer.

Regarding Nimano's path, I was told there are three extensions: in Hong Kong and in Malaga, Spain and another one in Mumbai. The overseas extensions were made for the diaspora followers. In Mumbai, the extension of the Nimanal Sangam is looked after by Shobha, the *gaddi nashin*'s sister, when he is in Vadodara or abroad. It is a large room, but with almost no decoration save a huge portrait of Nimano behind a small altar. As is the case in the *sangam*, she is represented in her middle age with detached hair and with a small portrait of her Master from Daraza, this being located at the very centre of her breast. It is a painting dominated with dark colours, except her coat which is a kind of mixed rose and ochre. Nimano's eyes are brown, and she is smiling; her smile is both strong and benevolent.

Finally, Rochaldas's *darbar* has had a kind of extension through Dadi Dhan's flat in Mahim, Mumbai. Dadi Dhan Samtani (1922–2014) was born in Sukkur, Sindh, and her father was a famous lawyer. She obtained a M.A. in Philosophy from Karachi, which was then under the University of Bombay. Dadi Dhan came across to the newly bordered India in 1948 with her Master, Rochaldas. Dadi then settled with her mother and other siblings in Mahim, Bombay. She taught philosophy at the National College in Bandra. Dadi's maternal side was very close to Rochaldas, and he often visited their house in Karachi. In Mumbai, she lived in a small flat where a number of followers took care of her since she spent her last years bedridden. Despite her difficulties, she used to talk with them and to sing *kalam*s devoted to Rochaldas. There were also *versi*s organized by them in the flat, and I shall turn back to these in the portion of the chapter devoted to the *versi*s.

The network built by around *darbar* is not always easy to understand. For example, the Sufi Dar located in Chennai was built to worship Dada Ratanchand Sahib (1926–2013). It is said he was a follower of Shahanshah Baba Nebhraj Sahib, a Sindhi guru who had no close interest into Sufism. But the official narrative states he was born thanks to a miracle performed by Qutub Ali Shah. He was initiated to the Sufi path by Hari, Rochaldas's son. There are two main daily rituals. The first one is a *dua* (invocation or prayer) devoted to Abd al-Qadir Jilani, and the second is the *arti* performed to Mata. The Sufi Dar claimed to have itself two subsidiaries, the Darvesh Asthan in Delhi and the Dukh Bhanjan Darbar in Kolkatta. I mention this case to the variety of relationships that were built between a centre and other Sufi structures. A thorough study of the Sufi Dar would be needed in order to give more details.[1]

A common duty shared by the *darbar*s is related to charity. Since the origins of Sufism, charity towards the poor has been considered the practice of a main Quranic pillar, that of *zakat* or alms. But beyond the will to help the poor, starting with feeding them, the Sufi *darbar*s in India developed more specialized practices, mostly referring to the medical field. Nonetheless, it has

Figure 4.1 Shoba, the *gaddi nashin*'s sister, unveiling Nimano's picture, Mumbai.

to be said that this evolution was not restricted to the Sufi realm, and other *darbars* have followed the same trajectory. For example, the Halani *darbar* in Sion has a clinic run as a charitable institution, and the *darbar* itself stands at another location in Mumbai. In this case, the existence of two distinct spaces goes so that it is relevant to speak of a total separation of the activities: the religious activities and the non-religious activities. One can even speak of a form of secularism in this respect. The Halani clinic is a most impressive clinic where researchers are working on very innovative medical programmes.

In other *darbars*, the two activities are more complementary. Hence, the two activities are not implemented in two distant spaces. Let us take, for example, Rochaldas's *darbar*. Here, the two spaces belong to the same cluster, although they are separated. Te medical activities were in charge of Pritam Mansharamani, one of Rochaldas's sons. However, it is not possible to speak of a clinic here since the medical activities of Pritamdas, who himself was a medical doctor, were centred on distributing medications to people, mostly destitute, who came to meet him.

Medical activity is also at work in the Sufi Mandir in Sion, Mumbai. Here, there is another specialty, dentistry, as a dentist comes for a few hours almost every day, and once again it is mostly to work for destitute people who cannot afford medical treatments in a 'regular' hospital. Also, *darbars* can restrict their charitable activities to the traditional ones, excluding any medical assignments. This is the case, for instance, when it comes to the Nimanal Sangam in Vadodara. It does not prevent the *darbar* from having a 'pharmacie' whose pills are sold at very low prices.

This is not to say that local charitable and medical activities are exclusive to the Sufi *darbars*.[2] Rather, it is to see them as a historical heritage through which the social role of religion is expressed: helping the destitute. As a matter of fact, in all of the local religions, the religious classes have taken the trouble to care for, to some extent, weaker classes of their society. Otherwise, the ideology working as the basis of their authority could have lost any legitimacy for the people. Furthermore, through this action, one can see another powerful instrument of social control.

The *samadhi* as an alternative Sufi structure

All the Hindu Sufi paths of India do not have a *darbar*, namely big built structures. One could reasonably think it is related to if the devotees are numerous or not. If they are not, there is no need to build a big structure such as a *darbar*. When the devotees are not numerous, there are two scenarios involved in creating a space, here known as *samadhi*: on the one hand, the *samadhi* is reduced to an altar made in a room of a flat, usually the spiritual head's one; on the other hand, a hall has been arranged in the basement of the building where the spiritual head is living. Let us start with the first scenario, through the case study of Dalpat Sufi's *samadhi* located in Colaba, in Mumbai.

The word *samadhi* is employed in most of the North Indian languages with a number of meanings. In Hindu theology, the *samadhi* is the union with God in the Absolute. Sometimes it can be a state of high consciousness. Last, as it is used here, it is a funerary monument devoted to a saint. Since most of the Hindu saints are burnt, there is a box containing the ashes of the saint's body. In the Sindhicate context, the *samadhi* also designates different religious places. For example, in the *darbar*, the term is used for the altar, the place where the rituals are performed. In this section, the *samadhi* is an alternative Sufi place where a Sufi saint is worshipped. The main characteristic of such a space is that this religious place is not a building of its own. A number of these *samadhi*s can be found in Mumbai, including Dalpat Sufi's *samadhi* located in the southern part of Colaba.

Dalpat Sufi (d. 1841) was born in Sehwan Sharif in the Mirani family, one of the two Hindu families whose members performed the *mehndi* ceremony during the *urs* of Lal Shahbaz Qalandar. The other Hindu family was Mulchand Faqir's one, the Navanis. Dalpat was a high-ranking officer in the Talpur administration and he was thus posted in different localities of Sindh. Once when he was touring in Bubak, a village near the Manchhar Lake and not far from Sehwan, he met a guru named Asardas and he quickly became his follower. Asardas was himself a follower of the Sufi masters of Jhok Sharif. After some time, Dalpat resigned from his job and became a renunciant. Himself a follower of Jhok Sharif, he authored many Sufi *kalam*s in different languages, such as Sindhi, Hindi, Siraiki and Persian.

He founded an *astano*, a place of residence for a renunciant, in Hyderabad, on the Sipahimalani Lane. He is said to have attracted many followers, Muslims and Hindus, and the Talpur *mirs* are said to have looked after it. Among his *kalam*s, the most popular is probably the one in Sindhi that was published in India, although he did not wish his poetical work to be published. Still today, his poetry is very popular and is sung in India among his Hindu followers, as well as in several *dargah*s located in Sindh and run by Muslim *sajjada nashin*s, as for example in Jhok Sharif. Dalpat's style is shaped by his knowledge of Persian and Sanskrit, and he is probably one of the best Sufis to explain what is the *wahdat-e wujud* in Sindhi, as we already saw earlier.

Dalpat's Sindhi *kalam* was, and still is, very popular, and can be seen as a kind of meeting point between all of the Hindu Sufi traditions. For example, it is said that Mulchand was delighted when his followers sang Dalpat's poetry. It is also sung at Jhok Sharif in Sindh and in many other Sufi centres. Last but not least, his *kalam* titled *Sufi so jo panchhani* is seen by many, Hindus and Muslims, as the best explanation of who a Sufi is (see Annex 1). Other Sufi *kalam*s were composed by his followers, but they remain unpublished. Here, there is kind of paradox between the high value given to his poetry, in India as well as in Pakistan, and the few followers his *darbar* in Colaba has.

After Dalpat's death, his *astano* in Hyderabad became a pilgrimage centre under the guidance of his successor, Keshavram Sipahimalani. The place was known as Guru Sehwani's place. After partition, and contrary to the three other

Sufis discussed here, no monumental *darbar* or temple was built in memory of Dalpat Sufi. It is probably because Dalpat Sufi, as it is the case for other Sufis, for example Mulchand Faqir, did not claim to create a Sufi path. In fact, he was himself opposed to the creation of a Sufi path in his name, which would have been embodied in a *darbar*. Thus, it is his successor, Keshavram Sipahimalani, who did create a new Sufi path. The Sipahimalanis were a well-known Amil family of Hyderabad.

Nonetheless, there is a *samadhi* for Dalpat located in Colaba, in Mumbai, and kept by Dalpat's main follower's descendant, named Dhuru Sipahimalani, or better Dhuru Sain. He is the fourth successor of Keshavram, and the fifth after Dalpat. He is unmarried and lives alone with his sister. He claims that, as it was already the case with his father named Lachmandas, he is not *gaddi nashin*: he only takes care of the *samadhi* in order to give access to it to Dalpat's followers – but he does not play any spiritual function. And, as a matter of fact, he has got a knowledge bout Sufism, and je can speak and read Sindhi. Notwithstanding, his paternal aunt was a mystic, and she did compose a Sufi *kalam* in Sindhi, which is still unpublished. It is handwritten in a school notebook. The author is strongly inspired by Dalpat Sufi's *kalam*.

Dalpat's *samadhi* is in Colaba, the older part of Mumbai which is the heart of British colonization. Today, it is the largest tourist area in the megacity. The *samadhi* is made of a huge room belonging to Dhuru and his sister's flat, which is located in a luxurious building in a residential area of Mumbai. The agency of the *samadhi* follows the basic rules of any Sindhi *samadhi*, Sufi or otherwise. The core of the place is the altar, whose main components belong to two categories: pictures of gods, saints and Dhuru's predecessors, and relics. It is interesting to have a look at the size of the different pictures. The biggest are those of four predecessors of Dhuru, in black and white, and adorned with garlands of withered flowers. Two portraits of gods are in colour: Krishna with Radha, in a large size, and Guru Nanak. There is also a small statue of Shiva with the snake (*nanga*) and another one of Vishnu. The usual Sindhi Hindu pantheon is almost complete; only Jhulelal is absent.

The relics are made up of two items: the sandals (*chakriyun*) and the canes, known as *bayragins*. There are five pairs of *chakriyuns*, including those of Dalpat. In fact, these are the only remains from the Sufi saint. The *chakriyuns* are wooden sandals that are the symbol of renunciation in the Indic world among the Hindus, Muslims and other religious persuasions. The ones which are attributed to Dalpat are the most worn. The other relics are the *bayragins*. In Sindh, once again irrespective of religious belonging, they are the mark of renunciation. Thus, the *samadhi* highlights that Dalpat was a renunciant. It thus refers to the second part of his life, when he gave up his post in the Talpur administration in order to become a Sufi renunciant.

In Dalpat's *samadhi*, the devotional performances are limited. Contrary to other *samadhis*, there are no regular *satsangs*. The main performance is for Dalpat's *versi*, which is celebrated during the month of Badho, a solar month spreading from the middle of August to the middle of September, soon after the festival of Dasserah.[3] It is mostly made up of the singing of Sufi songs in Sindhi, but I do not know how many people attend the performance. In fact, it is difficult to know how many people have paid visits to Dalpat's *samadhi*. Other versis are arranged for Dalpat's successors, including Dhuru's father. If one follows the criteria applied to other *samadhis*, it is not relevant to take Dalpat's *samadhi* as representative. A thorough study, involving an enquiry into the private life of Dhuru, would be necessary before doing so.

In Mumbai, there is also Jogi Sain's *samadhi* in the district of Powai, in the northern part of the city, while Colaba is located at the extreme south. Parsuram Keswani, better known as Jogi Sain (1898–1998), was a Hindu follower of Nasir Muhammad Faqir al-Qadiri (1835–1960). Interestingly, his name of Jogi Sain refers to the important figure of renunciation in Sindh. The *jogi*, a vernacular form of yogi, is usually the model of renunciation in Sindhi Sufi poetry, especially in Shah Abd al-Latif's work. The *jogi* in a Sindhicate context was a Shivaite renunciant belonging to the Nathpanthi, an ascetic order founded by Gorakhnath, in which meditation was tied to breath control.

Nasir Muhammad was born in Jalalani and, from his early childhood on, he had visions involving Abd al-Qadir al-Jilani. In one of them, the founder of the Qadiriyya told him it was time for him to reach Jhok Sharif, to take *nam* from the Sufi Master (Jogi Sain 1996: 4). Nasir Muhammad spent many years in Jhok Sharif, and he was initiated to the Qadiri *tariqa* by the *sajjada nashin*, Sufi Abd al-Sattar Shah. He started by cleaning the stable of his Master's mare, and went through all of the different fasts usually practised by the Sufis. When he had reached the highest spiritual degree, that of salvation, Abd al-Sattar allowed him to give *nam*. Nasir Muhammad was buried in a small *dargah* located in the village where he was born, Jalalani Sharif.

Jogi Sain was Nasir Faqir's principal disciple, and he migrated to India in the wake of partition. After his demise, his son Daulat carried on the Sufi legacy, first by publishing his father's *kalam* (Jogi Sain 1996). Regarding the mystical Sufi poetry, Jogi Sain was fond of Bedil's work. As we saw in the previous chapter, Bedil was a primary poet of the modern Sufi corpus. His work was composed in many different languages, and he was one of the Sindhi Sufi who did produce a *kalam* in Persian, with the name of *Dil kusha*, or 'Awaken your heart'. Jogi Sain had it translated into Sindhi by Professor D. K. Mansharamani and published in Mumbai in 1996. It was distributed for Jogi Sain's birthday, on 15 August 1996. Later on, in 2013, at the occasion of Sadiq Muhammad's *urs*, Daulat Keswani distributed an English translation from the Sindhi version, which is available online (http://www.mysufi.in).

Dil Kusha is totally devoted to the issue of *zikr*, the Sufi mediation. It is made of 283 sentences related to *zikr*. In the introduction, probably written by Daulat Kesvani, there are interesting parallels drawn with Sultan Bahu's poetry, he being an important seventeenth-century Sufi from Punjab, Abd al-Qadir al-Jilani, and, not surprisingly, the Guru Granth Sahib, from which copious abstracts are given. The *Dil Kusha* reflects a very classical conception of Sufism in pointing out the importance of associating the repetition of the *nam*, the one given by the Master during the initiation, with breath, for reaching the vision of God. Bedil, himself a Qadiri Sufi, advocates the silent and personal *zikr*, or *zikr khafi*. The *zikr* allows one to annihilate the Ego, which is a prerequisite for being merged with God.

The most interesting point in Jogi Sain selecting the *Dil Kusha* as a breviary is that it is full of Quranic references. Bedil clearly claims that the *zikr* is mentioned both in the Quran and by the Prophet Muhammad. Furthermore, there are several sentences (especially from n°67 to n°70) stating the superiority of Muhammad over the other prophets and all saints. Another main Islamic reference is devoted to the Shia figures: Ali, Hasan, Husain and the Imam Mahdi (from n°109 to n°113). Last, Bedil mentions a number of Sufi saints: Bayazid Bistami, Junaid, Mansur Hallaj, Shams Tabrizi, Lal Shahbaz Qalandar, Attar, Rumi and even Bu Ali Qalandar.[4] Briefly put, the *Dil Kusha* is full of Islamic references. It can sound unexpected to make such a comment regarding a Sufi work, but this one displays an unusual representation of Sufism in late-nineteenth-century Sindh. Another clue comes from the array of the mentioned Sufis who belong to the early phase of Arabic Sufism, such as Junaid.

The importance given to Islam in Jogi Sain's path, as well as to the personal aspects of both Jogi Sain and Daulat, shows that they are the most 'Islamicized' Hindu Sufis. Jogi Sain used to wear a Muslim turban, as well as the beard. Jogi Sain and his son Daulat Keswani were followers of the Jalalani *tariqa*, whose *dargah* is located in Northern Sindh close to Khairpur. As a matter of fact, the Pakistani *sajjada nashin*, Sain Oshaq Ali Faqir, still has many followers in India and, in 2012, he toured different cities of the country to meet them, starting with Mumbai and utilizing Daulat Keswani as a guide. Although he used to live for part of the year in London, Daulat Kesvani also runs a *samadhi* devoted to his father in Powai, Mumbai. The *samadhi* is organized in the main room of a flat, and as is the case in most of them, the iconographical setup expresses the relations they have with different saintly figures and Sufi paths.

The iconography exhibited in the *samadhi* gives the unique and authentic spiritual identity of the place, and of the mystical inclinations of Jogi Sain's path. The most unexpected figure is that of Ali, the first Shia imam, who is also looked upon by a majority of the Sufi *tariqa*s as being the first in the chain of transmission of the tradition. Interestingly, while the Shias have produced an important iconography of their imams, especially in Iran, this representation of Ali does not fit with the usual Shia canon.[5] Unfortunately, the origin of Ali's representation cannot be traced, but he is represented as a warrior wearing a leather cuirass and a helmet, while in the 'orthodox' Shia representation, he is wearing 'civil' clothes, a kind of long dress called *abaya* which is worn in the Middle East and a turban. However, a very similar portrait of Ali is exhibited in the Doda Mard Haqani Kafi, a Sufi lodge devoted to an alleged disciple of Lal Shahbaz Qalandar in Sehwan Sharif, in Sindh.

In Jogi Sain's *samadhi*, religious performance is based on two basic practices: the *satsang* and the *versi*. During the *satsang*, Sufi songs in Sindhi are performed, starting with Jogi Sain's *kalam*. Four *versi*s are celebrated throughout the year: Dada Dastgit Badhsha (in other words, Abd al-Qadir al-Jilani), Jogi Sain, Shah Inayat (from Jhok Sharif) and Nasir Faqir. In fact, the dates of all of these death anniversaries are taken as sacred: the 11, the 15, the 17 and the 27. The credo of Jogi Sain's path follows that of the other Hindu Sufi paths. The Master gives the *nam* to his disciple with a specific technique for meditation that can be revealed only through initiation. Daulat himself received the *nam* in 1958 when he was twenty years old from Nasir Faqir, himself. The goal is to reach ecstasy, named *kafiyyat* by Daulat Kesvaram.

The Sufi *mandir* and the pilgrimage to Bijapur

In the heart of the Sindhi colony of Sion, in Mumbai, there is a very discrete building on a narrow lane. Above the main door, it is written in Latin and Arabic Sindhi scripts: Sufi *mandir*. As a sort of oxymoron, it echoes the 'Hindu *dargah*' of Tando Ahmad Khan in Sindh, examined in Chapter 7, since it brings together the two terms which are usually not put together. But in the case of the Sufi *mandir*, this is the building that is designated by a Hindu name, while in Sindh the building refers to Sufism.[6] The Sufi *mandir* hosts the *samadhi* of Molchand[7] Kripalani (1887–1980), a Hindu Sufi who migrated from Sindh to India during partition. On the ground, there is a room with a number of photos of the Sufi masters, as well as a quotation from Ali. Molchand Kripalani was born in Hyderabad in 1887 in a Krishnaite family (Kripalani 1986: 3). He studied at the Wilson College in Bombay and was the follower of a number of Sufis in Sindh, and especially of Mohsin Shah, the *gaddi nashin* of Tando Saindad near Tando Muhammad Khan (Kripalani 1986: 38), a Sufi who was affiliated to the Qalandariyya.

Additionally, he was a staunch follower of Pir Data Dastgir, the South Asian name given to Abd al-Qadir al-Jilani (d. 1192), the Sufi Master from Baghdad. Al-Jilani was the founder of the Qadiriyya and his popularity was such that numerous Muslims and Hindus use to celebrate his death anniversary, the 11th (or Yarhen) of Rabi al-Sani. For Molchand, the number 11 was consequently sacred. Still, Yarhen is a great festival celebrated at the Sufi *mandir*. In the *mandir*, the portrait of Pir Data Dastgir overlooks all of the saints' images. Molchand visited many Sufi places in India and he used to attend every year, with his followers, the *urs* of Muinuddin Chishti (1142–1236) at Ajmer Sharif. Another Islamic reference in the *mandir* is related to Ali, but contrary to Jogi Sain's *samadhi*, it is not a picture but a long quotation from him, exhibited in the main corridor leading to the altar.

Molchand was also very active in terms of publications. He could have played a leading role in the translation of the *Diwan Dastgir*, the poetry of Abd al-Qadir Jilani, that was officially translated from Persian into Sindhi by Kalyan Advani and published in 1979. Among his remarkable literary production, he published a translation into Sindhi of Farid al-Din Attar's famous *Tazkira al-awliyya*. Furthermore, Kripalani translated Ghazzali's *Ilhya ulum al-din*, 'The Revival of Religious Sciences'. Both books were translated from an English translation (Gajwani 1997: 40–1). It is thus a rare example of when a Hindu Sufi was not only interested by Sufism as an Islamic production but also by some other works, such as Ghazzali's treatise. Abu Hamid Muhammad al-Ghazzali (1058–1111) was one of the most important Muslim thinkers, as a *mujaddid* or renovator, and through this book he was able to reconcile Sufism and Islamic theology.

After partition, Molchand was worried that it was difficult for Hindu Sindhi Sufis to pay a visit to the Sufi places in Sindh, now in Pakistan. Since he knew that a Sufi Master from Jhok Sharif, Sayyid Shah Mehmud Shah al-Qadiri,[8] had been buried in Bijapur,[9] in Karnataka, he decided to look for his grave. Sayyid Shah Mehmud Shah al-Qadiri was the Master of Shah Inayat of Jhok Sharif. In 1965, he was able to discover the *dargah* and he started to celebrate the *melo* every year from the 17th to the 19th of Moharram, as it is celebrated in Jhok Sharif. Furthermore, since the *dargah* was found in a dilapidated state, he succeeded in finding funding to rebuild it, including a dome, in 1972. Later on, in 1978, Molchand started to build a place for pilgrims to stay close to the *dargah*. Known as the Sufi Asthan, it was completed after his death in 1981.

Interestingly, although I do not know what the relations were between Molchand and the *sajjada nashin* of Jhok, the official website devoted to Jhok Sharif claims to have a *dargah* in Bijapur which is affiliated with Jhok (http://www.sufisattari.com). Under the heading 'affiliated dargahs', the 'Hazrat Soofi Abdul Malik' is mentioned. Some years back, there was also a beautiful anthropomorphic calligraphy that was attributed to a follower from Bijapur. It has been removed from the website.

Mulchand Kafi

Mulchand is the only Hindu Sufi among the three figures who did not migrate to India. He is also the only Hindu Sufi figure to be granted two *darbar*s: one located in India, the other in Pakistan. This situation reflects a unique feature resulting from partition: the Master disagreed with his main disciple and future successor, Gehimal Motwani. How do we explain the fact that Mulchand did not migrate to India? The most convincing explanation is the local milieu. As we saw before, through his family, Mulchand was extremely well integrated into the mystical network of Sehwan Sharif. During his lifetime, he had thought of the place where he wanted to stay after his death. His *samadhi* was thus built, but it is said that the structure under which it rested felt down, so that his followers had to build a new one.

In Mulchand's biography, published by Gehimal Motwani in 1965, there is discussion of a funerary built structure called a *samadhi* which the followers had planned to build for Mulchand. It looks like a huge square slab, under a kind of *chattri*, a dome-shaped pavilion that is a frequently used architectural structure in South Asia, except that in this case the dome has been replaced by a pointed roof with four sides. The final building as it eventually came to exist is different, mainly because it is not an open space but a closed space. The square slab is there, but it is inside a kind of small house, as if it has been built around the slab, with a narrow space to circulate all around it. The house is amid a pretty huge space, a *kafi*, and other built structures can be found here. One of them is used to store different artefacts that are paraded during Lal Shahbaz's *mehndi* procession.

No other ceremony or ritual is performed here except for the *mehndi* of Lal Shahbaz Qalandar. Mulchand's birthday is not celebrated. The tomb of Mulchand is located inside a small house. It is a pretty large square made with bricks, and its size is much bigger than that of other tombs. No picture or inscription can be found. Mulchand's first successor was Chandmal Chandrani, a local Hindu from Sehwan. But, in 1971, he decided to migrate to India, and his son Kanya Lal, who had a vegetable shop in the Shahi Bazar in Sehwan, refused to take care of the Mulchand Kafi. Mohan Lal, who was Mulchand's nephew, finally took care of it. Also, he took on the duty of performing the *mehndi* during the *urs* of Lal Shahbaz Qalandar.

Mohan Lal passed away in 1981 and his son Ramchand began to perform the *mehndi*; he is still in charge. Ramchand is an Amil, but his mother was a Thakur.[10] He lives in a huge *haveli* from the eighteenth century with his joint

Figure 4.2 Mulchand's tomb in Sehwan Sharif.

family, including his wife, brother and sister. Ramchand was a pharmacist and he retired some years ago. His sister Champra takes care of the space where Mulchand's tomb stands, locally known as a *kafi*. She used to come and look after it, and she also put a new *chador* on Mulchand's tomb. Interestingly, the *chador*s which are available in Sehwan come with Quranic inscriptions.

It can hardly be asserted that Mulchand is venerated in Sehwan. According to Ramchand, nothing is arranged in his name. The main event occurring in Mulchand Kafi is the procession of the *mehndi* for the *urs* of Lal Shahbaz Qalandar, which starts from the *kafi*. Before the procession, two main events are arranged. First is the *dastarbandi* of Ramchand. As we saw before, this is the coronation, when the ceremonial turban (*pag*) is put on his head. It is followed by a musical session with musicians and dancers from Punjab. The apex of the listening to spiritual music is the singing of the famous song devoted to Lal Shahbaz Qalandar, *Dam dama mast qalandar*. The third is the preparation of the *mehndi* under a canopy.

Finally, Mulchand Faqir is known in Sehwan as a *mehndibardar*. His *kafi* does not work like the other *kafi*s in the town. Usually, the *sajjada nashin* stays for welcoming the *murid*s, and provides them advice and amulets (*tawiz*). Ramchand did not play such a role. And no *faqir* stays in Mulchand Kafi. Only

Ramchand's family used to come, but the *kafi* is closed most of the time. The only time in a year when it plays a social and religious role is the time of the *mehndi* procession, on the 19th Shaban. Such a situation is quite contradictory to the spread of Mulchand's cult in India. It is nevertheless not easy to understand why such a cult did not grow in Sehwan, Mulchand's birthplace and the town where he spent all of his life.

The most striking point here is that cults of Sufi saints are displayed in all of the other *kafis* of Sehwan. The ancestors' tombs are always the most sacred place in the *kafi*, and the death birthday of most of them is celebrated every year: it is a main tool to keep the community united. Among them, there is another Hindu Sufi lodge, that of Lal Das, and the *gaddi nashin*'s spiritual duty is similar to any other *sajjada nashin*s in Sehwan, as a spiritual Master who initiates followers to the Sufi path. It is therefore relevant to wonder why not a single celebration related to Mulchand is arranged in his *kafi*. Unfortunately, Ramchand is not very talkative. A possible explanation is that the Hindu population of Pakistan, including Sindh, is more and more under the threat of the radical Muslims of the country. Such a threat creates a deleterious environment.[11]

Conclusion

Among the Hindu Sufis of India, the *darbar* is the dominant built structure. In relation to the three figures under study, there is diversity regarding their agency and size. Nonetheless, the *sanctum sanctorum* is always made of an altar, where the most displayed elements are pictures of the Sufi saints, and of the gods or Guru Granth Sahib. The Sindhis of India who are involved in Sufism are scattered all over the country. Consequently, there was a need to build alternative structures for keeping the followers in touch with the Sufi Master and his path. The first alternative structure is a structure affiliated to one of the three studied *darbars*. The alternative structure can also reflect the diaspora followers, where subsidiaries could have been created. In another configuration, an alternative structure can be born from the radiation of a follower, as was the case with Dadi Dhan in Mulund, in Mumbai. She was a devotee of Rai Rochaldas, but since she had herself reached a very high spiritual level, her small flat became a de facto *samadhi*. Lastly, a *samadhi* as an extension of a *darbar* can be created from the will of a follower. There is the case of Daulatram Motwani, Gehimal Motwani's nephew, who recently created a *samadhi* in the basement of his building in Ulhasnagar.

Other *samadhi*s are reduced to a room in a flat. This suggests that the followers are not so numerous. It also implies that the Sufi rituals are restricted to *satsang*s, because no procession is possible in such a space. In this type of *samadhi*, since no architectural item can be exhibited, the identification of the Sufi path is focused on the altar. The two most meaningful elements in the process of distinction are the pictures of the Sufi masters, and, in the case of Dalpat Sufi, some relics. The main feature is, however, the limited performance of Sufi rituals. The Sufi *mandir* of Molchand Kripalani is singular, not only because of its name, which can be understood as a slogan showing that there is no contradiction to being a Hindu Sufi. The distinction does not come from the setup because the core is the altar, which is similar to any other Sufi Hindu *samadhi*.

The singularity of the Sufi *mandir* is due to the attempt made by its founder to invent a Sufi pilgrimage in India. The process leading to this is still very intermingled because, in the narrative found in Molchand's biography, there is no mention that Abd al-Malik's *dargah* in Bijapur is affiliated to Jhok Sharif, while the official website of Sufi Ataullah Sattari, the *sajjada nashin* of Jhok, claims it is. However, this attempt at creating a Muslim Sufi pilgrimage from Sindh in India is unique, but, unfortunately, it does not look to be very successful. A last alternatively built structure was another unique case: the Mulchand Kafi. Located in Sehwan Sharif, where Mulchand decided to stay, it was planned at a time when his followers, who had migrated to India, still thought it would be possible for them to easily cross the border. In the 1950s, Gehimal visited Sehwan twice during Mulchand's lifetime. Now, it is almost impossible for Mulchand's followers to obtain a Pakistani visa.

In the alternative Sufi structure, due to the limited space, it is tempting to give huge importance to the discourse displayed through exhibiting portraits. But what would be the relevance, following this approach, to speaking of a more Islamicized or a more hinduized Sufi *samadhi*? As a matter of fact, it is really amazing, and thus meaningful, that a Sufi, whatever his religious belonging may be, refers to Ali, who is acclaimed by most of the Sufi *tariqas* as being the first Sufi, or to Abd al-Qadir al-Jilani, who is the most venerated Sufi all over South Asia. Rather, this study is to focus on the processes and dynamics that were built for, more than seventy years after partition, keeping a Sufi tradition alive among the Sindhis. In addressing this issue, we already shift to the issue of the transmission of the Sufi legacy among the Hindu Sindhis of India.

Rituals as connecting spaces and community

While the physical spaces the Sufis built refer to different repertoires among each group of followers, we can also observe that they were not significant in terms of architecture. Only a plate shows off these spaces as a religiously built complex. A basic structure shared by the different Hindu Sufi paths is nonetheless the *samadhi*, a kind of altar hosting the portraits of the masters, those from Sindh who are usually Muslim and the deceased Indian masters. The *samadhi* is a nexus around which a number of processes operate, not only in relying on the physical and the mystical spaces. It also operates the connection between the spaces and the body of followers, which I shall call the community.

The connecting process between spaces and community works at different levels. The two main dynamics are produced by the iconography and the rituals. The iconography is of special importance in the context of Hinduism. It is due to the cardinal role played by the *darshan* or visualization of God in the general economy of Hindu worship. Furthermore, it meets the process of *didar*, the visualization of the Sufi Master. It will be necessary to carefully examine how the Hindu Sufis converted, to some extent, the Sufi *didar* into the Hindu *darshan*, knowing that some Sufi masters such as Qutub Ali Shah had already paved the way – for example, in using them interchangeably. The iconography was much used in all of the cultures and civilizations, and when it was canonically forbidden, the followers did find ways to circumvent the prohibition or they developed other mental supports such as calligraphy.

This chapter consequently aims at analysing the interaction between the two complementary spaces, the physical and the mystical, and the community. It will address issues such as how the physical space impacts community worship, and how the disposition of the built elements are supposed to facilitate the followers' travel on the mystical path for reaching the merging in God as well as the transformation resulting in becoming God.

The study of the rituals as connecting spaces and community once again displays a huge range of different practices. Beyond this variety, one can decipher some structural similarities. In all of the Hindu Sufi paths, there is an initiation to the path given by the Master. Furthermore, meditation is one of the most significant practices, but the Hindu Sufi masters have different conceptions related to it. Nevertheless, most of the practices emphasize breath control, a common practice in the Sufism of South Asia. The Sufi poets constantly refer to breath, or *dam*. But the Sufi paths can also keep specific rituals, such as the *dhamal* at Rochaldas's *darbar*, while other such practices labelled as 'Islamic' in the Hindu 'radical' milieu[1] had to be removed.

Finally, the articulation between spaces and community will be approached through the study of the rituals proper. They will be put into two categories: the daily rituals and the annual fairs. Since the *darbar*s were created about seventy years back, the evolution of the rituals has followed the evolution of the Hindu society and culture of India. The ability of the paths to be flexible was a main condition for them surviving in Hindu-dominated India, and also the process of rigidification of Hinduism. The study of the rituals in these two contexts, daily and annual, will provide an opportunity for illustrating the different strategies implemented by the Hindu Sufis to face such challenges.

Iconography as an idiom of transference

The decisive role of iconography is due to the fact that the Sindhi *darbar*s of India are not centred on tombs, unlike those of Sindh: none of them contain any tomb or cenotaph. This is the point of major divergence from the paradigm of the *dargah*. In India, it is actually the *samadhi* that replaces the tomb. But, if the sanctuaries of the three Hindu Sufis discussed here have a *samadhi*, two of them also have a grave in Pakistan. Mulchand's remains were buried in a tomb in Sehwan Sharif. Nimano Faqir was cremated, but his ashes were deposited in a tomb in the *dargah* compound in Daraza, Pakistan, near that of Sachal Sarmast. No tomb is therefore located in India, which explains why the photographic portrait polarizes the sacredness of the space in place of the tomb, as is the case in the *dargah*s of Sindh. It materializes a presence, and almost all of the rituals are realized in front of it.

Additionally, the iconography traces the genealogy, often pluri-confessional, in which the founder of the *darbar* is inscribed, and thus locates the *darbar* at the crossroads of multiple religious heritages. Beyond this function, it is also the iconography that informs us about the relations of power within the community of disciples, for example, the position of the *gaddi nashin* vis-a-vis the founder. But, once again, the situations are varied. The most widely used iconography is that of the *darbar* of Rochaldas, while that of the Dada Sain Kuthir has three elements and that of the Nimanal Sangam only two. The representations are usually photographs that are sometimes re-coloured. The most widespread representation is a large portrait of Nimano Faqir, who is in bust and with his hair unfurled, in which is inlaid a portrait of his Master (*murshid*), Sakhi Qabul Muhammad II (1842–1925).

Therefore, Nimano Faqir and Sakhi Qabul Muhammad constitute the two Sufi referents in the Nimanal Sangam. One can wonder about the absence of a representation of Sachal Sarmast, who was at the origin of the creation of the Sakhi Kuthiyya founded by Nimano Faqir in Baroda, and later on Vadodara. Moreover, in the same *darbar*, another absence is to be noted in the iconographic decorum: that of Krishna. Krishna plays a decisive role in the Dada Sain Kuthur and the *darbar* of Rochaldas, in that it overlooks iconographic compositions. This place of choice offered to Krishna comes mainly from the fact that, with Radha, he symbolizes divine love and is also a symbol of devotion, known as Bhakti, or in Sindhi Bhagti.

The iconography set-up displays a multiplicity of Sufi networks and family affiliations, and sometimes includes unexpected figures. For example, in Jogi Sain's *samadhi*, there is a portrait of the first Shia imam, Ali, the son-in-law of Prophet Muhammad.[2] This picture is not the one that is familiar among the Shias. It is, however, not really amazing since Ali is considered to be the first Sufi Master by a large majority of the Sufi brotherhood. In Molchand Kripalani's *samadhi*, also located in Mumbai, all of the iconography set-up is dominated by a single picture – that of Abd al-Qadir al-Jilani, the founder of the Qadiriyya. Here, it reflects the peculiar inclination professed by the Hindu for this important Sufi figure.

The most elaborate iconography is to be observed in the *darbar* of Rochaldas. There are three levels. The first level is that of Rochaldas and his son Hari, with a portrait on the left of Guru Nanak, below which stands the *Guru Granth Sahib*. The portraits of Rochaldas and Hari are the only ones to be sheltered under a kind of miniature kiosk (*chhatri*). The transition from the first level to the second level is carried out by a representation of the *darbar* of Lal Shahbaz Qalandar. The second level is that of Qutub Ali Shah and two of his successors: Hadi Bakhsh, who is the author of a poem (*kalam*) which is highly prized in rituals, as we shall see below, and Nur Husayn Shah, the current *sajjada nashin*. The third level consists of a representation of Krishna accompanied by Radha.

Moreover, the four walls of the *samadhi* are decorated with fairly numerous representations as well as calligraphy. Among the representations is Abd al-Qadir al-Jilani, as well as Jesus. An ecumenical orientation is therefore displayed, but it is not confirmed by the incantations given during the ritual. The other two *darbars* do not display such an array of figures and only the founder and his Master, even a Muslim, are represented.

The reduction of the decorum to a relatively uncluttered iconography is also explained by the personality of the founders: it is in fact a reflection of their lives. Nimano Faqir and Mulchand Faqir were renouncers, but although Rochaldas was not, he had placed poverty and destitution at the heart of his spiritual quest, like Vasan Shah. His *darbar*, however, is the only one where the charge of *gaddi nashin* is hereditary. Another explanation for this sobriety close to the refined is the importance accorded to the singing of mystical poetry. The visualization of the holy personages constitutes a mental condition, but access to the mystical state is realized through devotional songs in Sindhi, especially those of the Master of Rochaldas, Qutub Ali Shah. The simplicity of the device also corresponds to the simplicity of the rituals for which, once again, devotional song is the very substance of religious practice. It is therefore the enunciation of Sufi poetry that transforms the physical space of the *darbar* into a mystical space. The decoration planted by iconography is a prerequisite. This set-up contributes to put in condition to reach what will be fully realized by the song of poetry: the communion between Rochaldas and his disciples, and, through him, God.

In *Some Moments with the Master*, the narrator explains that, in the beginning, there was no picture in the *darbar* of Rochaldas. Then, one day, he visited the place, and he saw pictures of Guru Nanak, Qutub Ali Shah, Sai Baba, Ramachandra and Krishna. Rochaldas saw the narrator was astonished. The follower asked him why there were now so many pictures. Rochaldas answered that a devotee had come one day with the pictures and fixed them on the wall. At the moment, Rochaldas interestingly did not relate the pictures to any ritual, such as *darshan*. He related them to silence. The pictures do not talk, so that they can facilitate meditation for the follower (Hari 1995: 125–6).

The *darbar* of Haridwar was built thanks to the financial support of Basant and Sonu Jethwani, as well as that of Devi. Since the building was registered as a worship place, it was not possible to provide many rooms for the pilgrims. Everything had been recorded under Sonu's name. There are thus only two small rooms, but the broad roof can nevertheless work as a sleeping place. The *darbar* proper is a large room with very sober decoration. The altar itself is made of flowers and a lamp, and the pictures of the two *murshids* – Sain, who is Mulchand, and Dada, who is Gehimal – which are the focus of the worship.

Above the pictures of the *murshids*, there is also a painting of Krishna and Radha. Such a scene can also be seen in other Sindhi *darbar*s of India,

(a)   (b)

Figure 5.1 Iconographical agency in the Mulchand and Rochaldas's *samadhi*s. (a) *Mulchand's altar, Dada Sain Kuthir, Haridwar, 2012 and* (b) *Rochaldas's darbar, Ulhasnagar, 2012.*

as for example in Rai Rochaldas's *darbar* in Ulhasnagar.[3] In the re-composed Sufism produced by the Sindhi Hindu Sufis, this representation is more and more common, so that the place given to Krishna and Radha at the altar is another issue to be investigated. Krishna's worship had already developed in late-nineteenth-century Sindh among the Amils. Narsain states that, in the nineteenth century, the Vallabhachari sect[4] was accepted by some members of the Amil community (Narsain 1932: 1939). Centring their devotion on Krishna, the Vallabhacharis laid great emphasis on *pushti* (grace) and *bhakti* (devotion).

One can also understand the painting of Krishna as an identity marker of Hinduism. Many Sindhi Sufi cults managed by Hindus in India put Krishna's representation above the other pictures, as if Krishna is supposed to both protect and encompass the *murshid*s and their disciples placed underneath him. A last explanation provided by Basant Jethwani is that the love between Krishna and Radha symbolizes the 'Sufi' love (*ishq*) between God (Krishna) and his passionate devotee (Radha)[5]. According to him, Gehimal called Krishna *ashiq baghwan*, the Lord of Love. The couple of Hindu mythology is a kind of an equivalent of Majnun and Layla,[6] two characters who are frequently quoted by the Hindu Sufis. So, Mulchand was the *bhagwan* and Gehimal was his Radha. Interestingly, this implies a feminization of the disciple that follows a main literary rule of Sindhi Sufi poetry where the *murid* is often depicted as the *virahini*, the woman/soul longing for her love, namely God (Asani 1994).

In Nimano's place, the *darbar* is designed in a very stripped style. No decorative element appears, which contrasts with the Hindu temples and other sanctuaries. Compared to the other Sindhis *darbar*s of India, we must note here a very sober iconographic agency. There are two images: Nimano and Sakhi Darazi, which is a nickname given to the *sajjada nashin* of Daraza who initiated Nimano, Sakhi Qabul Muhammad II. Interestingly Nimano is represented from when she was young. Her brown hair is down. But the main element is the *gaddi*, and I suppose the *gaddi nashin* sits there when he attends the performance. There is also on the right side the Guru Granth Sahib. In Mumbai, the altar devoted to Nimano is not adorned with any picture or other element, save a huge portrait of Nimano, with her Sufi Master pictured near her heart.

Initiation and meditation

Already, we have noted that the main goal of the Sufis is to be merged in God, a formulation that designates reaching the divine state, or becoming God. For many Sufis, like for Sachal among others, it is the final stage of *ana al-haqq*, or 'I am God', the famous phrase uttered by the Sufi from Iraq, Mansur Hallaj. A number of methods can be used to have access to God, but it is indispensable to have been through the initiation. A very crucial element is the *nam*, the name. This is the main part of the Sufi initiation – to be given a name. The *nam* in Sindhi is nonetheless much more than a name. In fact, it is a word for God, or through a metonymic process, it is a simple name for God that is used as a basis for meditation, or *zikr*. The *nam*, sometimes called a *mantra*, can be a name of God, such as *om*, *hari om* or *Radhye Shyam*, another naming of Krishna and Radha, or, more rarely, some Sufi verses. The *nam* or *mantra*, also *shabd* in Rochaldas's spiritual dialogues, is given once in one's life. Beforehand, the *murshid* has a question and answer session with the disciple to see if he is ready.

The proper ritual of initiation starts with the *havan* ritual, which is performed by a Sindhi Brahman. It is said that this is a Vedic ritual when a Brahman lights a fire as a process of purification. The next step of the initiation ritual shows the importance of Krishna among the Sindhi Sufis, including Muslim Sufis such as Sachal and Qutub Ali Shah. Most of the Sufi Hindu publications start with praise for Krishna. In this step, a *puja* is performed in the name of Krishna. The *puja*, or *pudiya* in Sindhi, is the basic ritual for all of the Hindus, despite some variations. In Christopher Fuller's words, the *puja* is 'primarily a ritual to remove impurity from the deities' (Fuller 1992: 76). According to him, it is made of sixteen offerings and services that can be grouped into four main parts: invocation, offering, taking care of the statue or image and taking leave. But the core of the *puja* is the third part, when the devotee performs bathing, dressing, putting on of the sacred thread, sprinkling with perfume, adorning with flowers, burning incense, waving an oil lamp and finally offering food. Nevertheless, even this part is often reduced to three or four last elements (Fuller 1992: 67).

A meaningful way for reaching God is visualization, or *nazar nihal*, literally the vision bringing happiness, or the visualization of bliss. The expression is used by different Hindu Sufi paths, such as Mulchand's. R. M. Hari, Rochaldas's son and successor, also uses it under the form of *nazar nihal ka diya*, or the 'illumination of the visualization of bliss' (Hari 1995: 159). The word *nazar* is a word of Arabic origin and it was used by the nineteenth-century Sufi poets of Sindh. It can be translated as vision, or glance, but in any case, it emphasizes the centrality of the visualization, be it physical or spiritual. The *nazar nihal* also refers to the mystical practice when the *nam* is given by the Master to the disciple.

In fact, being given the *nam* can be a first experience of meeting God through the Master. In this scenario, the Master and the disciple are facing each other, they look in each other's eyes, and see each other as if they were one, and this one is God. The Sufi poets do not always give details about how to be granted the divine vision, usually named *didar* or *darsan*. Nonetheless, Rakhiyyal Shah claims it is a wonder (Rakhiyyal Shah 1923: 39). Qutub Ali Shah precisely says that the *darsan* can be obtained with the heart (*dil*), while for Dalpat, the *darsan* is the way to be ecstatic (*diwani*). While chanting the *nam* is the most common way to be granted the divine vision, another technique to which the Sufi poets allude is related to breath discipline. Most of the time, chanting the *nam* and breath (*dam*) is relied upon. As, for instance, when Dalpat Sufi wrote:

> Without the name of the Master
> They breathe not one breath
>
> (Dalpat Sufi 73)

Qutub Ali Shah often associates remembrance (*yad*) with breath (mainly *dam*), another spiritual technique relied to yoga, to which I shall return. In the following verses, he provides an indication that respiration is performed with the chanting of the name, *nam*. As in classical *zikr*, it is the basis on which meditation is to be performed:

> Waking up at midnight, those that chant the name (*ganhan nam*),
> They remain forever in bliss, untouched by wrong,
> Every moment within the name (*nam*) they utter,
> Those disciples stay, who are every breath (*dam*) with the name (*nam*)!
>
> (Qutub Ali Shah 1985: 54)

Qutub Ali Shah provides a number of clues related to breathing. It should be controlled from different parts of the body, but the navel plays a tremendously important role associated with the *nabh kanwal*, the 'lotus of the navel'. The symbol of the lotus is a point of convergence between Islam and Hinduism. In the Baghavad Gita, Brahma was born from a lotus spread out from Vishnu's navel (8.21.2-3). It can also refer to the *sidra al-muntaha*, the lotus (sometimes translated as jujube) of the limit, which is the name given in the Quran for the last stage reached by Prophet Muhammad before God (*surat al-najm*, 53/14):

> Waking up at midnight, those that chant the name (*ganhan nam*),
> They remain forever in bliss, untouched by wrong,
> Every moment within the name (*nam*) they utter,
> Those disciples stay, who are every breath (*dam*) with the name (*nam*)!
>
> Qutub Ali Shah 1985: 54

The role played by breath is also attested to in other Sufis of modern Sindh, such as the Qadiriyya. Rakhiyyal Shah weaves an inextricable relationship between breathing and remembrance, as in the following Sindhi verses:

> Mercy of Beloved is near me not!
> Breath by breath (*dam dam*) remembers (*yad kare*) Love my heart!
>
> Rakhiyyal Shah 2007: 23

For Rakhiyyal Shah, the breath only allows for one to do meditation that leads to the Oneness of God (Rakhiyyal Shah 2005: 39). Qutub Ali Shah is the more explicit in relation to the importance of breath in meditation. The control of breath is the best way to be closer to the Friend (*dost*), God. But, the exercising of breathing should be performed in a state of total consciousness. Thus, the separation between God and the Sufi will gradually disappear until the final union. Another goal of such breathing is to delete the self in order to finally reach the Self, another shape of God that lies inside the Sufi. Qutub Ali Shah puts it as follows:

> Every breath your Friend is
> Go within yourself and see
>
> Qutub Ali Shah 1985: 54

The issue of Sufi meditation raises a very difficult concern: the relationship between Sufi breath exercises and that of yoga, especially the breathing practice known as *pranayama*. Of course, it is beyond the scope of this study, but the Indian influence is nonetheless accepted by the specialists of Sufism, especially through the Naqshbandiyya.[7] The Hindu Naqshbandis studied by

Dahnhardt nonetheless do not give a crucial role to *pranayama*, although they sometimes refer to it (Dahnhardt 2002: 352, 358). However, Rochaldas was said to be an expert in *pranayama*, and his son Hari devoted a large part of his books to it. As we already know, his Master, Qutub Ali Shah, belonged to the Sohrawardiyya. The Sufis of Sindh we have been dealing with were mostly in touch with the Sohrawardiyya and the Qadiriyya, but the issue of breathing is addressed by all of them as a crucial matter for meditation.

The *pranayama* is a term used for the study and practice of breathing techniques. It is a stage for the different schools of yoga and for them; beyond the balance between inhalation, exhalation and retention, the final goal is the total suspension of breath. When this is achieved, life may be prolonged indefinitely, or in other words, immortality can be reached (Walker 1983: I - 174). Rochaldas's conception of *pranayama* is that expressed in the Sri Yoga Vasishtha, the book his son Hari had translated into Sindhi under the form of a dialogue between Sri Vashishtha and Sri Ramchandra (Hari 1992). Furthermore, Rochaldas refers directly to *pranayama* in the dialogues Hari edited (Hari 1995). Answering the questions of a devotee, Rochaldas argues *pranayama* is but a practice among others that leads to the annihilation of Ego. For example, there are love and devotion, and contemplation. He adds that, although *pranayama* is the most difficult, it is also the most beneficial. Some saints do no recommend it, but rather remembrance (*samaran*) and concentration (*dhyan*): 'but one can not fly with these practices' he adds (Hari 1995: 78).

Another issue addressed by Rochaldas is the role played by the word of initiation in breath exercises, which he calls *shabd* instead of *nam* in his lexicon. Rochaldas states that there are two kinds of *pranayama*: one with *shabd* and another without *shabd*. But the results they can provide are different. The *pranayama* without *shabd* can only bring physical force. Furthermore, Rochaldas describes *pranayama* as inhaling, exhaling and above all holding the breath. The state of holding the breath brings a lot of benefits. But he also says that *pranayama* is a 'primary practice and it has to be undertaken only at the earlier stages' (Hari 1995: 145). Interestingly, *pranayama* needs to be practised as long as the Ego is not under control, but once love (*ishq*) has arisen, there is no more need to perform *pranayama*.

Since the initiation has a secret side, one will not find a detailed description of the practice of meditation, although there is an obvious relationship to yoga.

While the final aim of the Sufis is to reach the divine state, other methods can be followed by the disciples to obtain spiritual benefits.

Daily rituals and informal Sufi practices

Apart from the initiation and the meditation, there are two different kinds of religious activities for the Hindu Sufi *darbars*: the daily rituals and the annual fairs. In the *darbar* of Rochaldas, the most significant daily Sufi ritual is the *dhamal*. This ritual is directly related to Lal Shahbaz Qalandar because tradition says that, under this name, he practised an ecstatic giratory dance in which he saw the supreme form of meditation (*zikr*), a position that brought him closer to Jalal al-Din Rumi (d. 1275), the celebrated founder of the brotherhood of the whirling dervishes. Through the *dhamal*, Lal Shahbaz Qalandar reached the final stage of absorption into God (*fana fi Allah*). In Sehwan Sharif, where his shrine stands, the *dhamal* is performed every day at sunset. It is performed by professional drummers in the main courtyard and hundreds of devotees start to dance to reach ecstasy. Also, a number of women participate, but in a different manner. The renunciants (*faqirs*) of Bodlo Bahar, the main follower of Lal Shahbaz who has a shrine nearby, come once a month, and they perform a beautiful whirling dance in their red skirts.

In the *darbar* of Rochaldas, the *dhamal* was adapted: it is a simple beating of drums practised in front of the *samadhi*, which plays the rhythm of the devotional song *Mast qalandar* devoted to Lal Shahbaz. The ritual is very flexible – for example, with regard to the percussionist. It so happens that it is a girl of about fifteen years. For devotees, *dhamal* means the victory of the *faqir* over his self. When he masters it, the *dhamal* is played as a celebration. The teacher asks some of the disciples to move their feet in harmony with the *dhamal* while singing *nam*, the word given by the Master who serves as a medium for meditation. *Dhamal* is therefore a medium for meditation.

The *dhamal* lasts about fifteen minutes and is divided into three parts of about five minutes each. The first part plays *Mast qalandar*, the second is a rhythm of rejoicing (*shadmano*) and the third plays again *Mast qalandar*. The worship begins early in the morning between 4.00 and 4.30. The *dhamal* is again performed from 4.30 to 4.45 in the afternoon and again from 6.45 to

7.00 in the evening. It is closed with the song of *Allah Ishwar Krishna karim*, a succession of terms drawn from Islam and Hinduism aimed at showing the convergence of the mystical quest. The ritual has gone on unchanged since 1952. The purpose of the ritual is clearly to make the *darbar* of Rochaldas a territory that extends from an original sacred territory which is located in Sindh, the holy city of Sehwan Sharif.

Another element of the daily ritual is the recitation of the *kathas*. The *kathas* are stories about the lives of the saints in whose name the *puja* is conducted. They come mainly from the life of Rochaldas as well as from sacred writings of Hinduism such as Bhagavad Gita in the interpretation given by his son Hari. Others are borrowed from the life of Sufi Sindhis, such as Nasir Muhammad Faqir (d. 1960), a Qadiri who was the disciple of the Master (*murshid*) of Jhok Sharif, a great Sufi centre located in the extreme South of Sindh. Nasir Muhammad Faqir has many followers among the Hindu Sindhis of India and is also the author of a *kalam* that was recently published in India. Again, the invocation of Jhok Sharif contributes to the construction of a network of sacred territories which are all located in Sindh.

The *arti*, the first part of the *puja*, begins at 6.00 pm. It begins with the singing of prayers devoted to Rochaldas before a devotee removes the tissue that protects the *Guru Granth Sahib*, and then it is the Sufi poem of Qutub Ali Shah titled *Sakhi sabajhal* that is sung. The *puja* ends with the *jai* (praise) formula devoted to the gods, including Guru Nanak, Jhulelal as well as *Mast qalandar*, that is, Lal Shahbaz Qalandar. Let us return to the prayer that opens the *arti*. It is composed of a short refrain that opens it with seven verses. The refrain of the *arti* is explicit:

> *Om jai Rochal Shah avtar*
> *Swami jai Rochal Shah avtar*
> *Sant sacha sain ayo puran*

> Om! Praise to the Incarnation of God, Rochal Shah
> Praise to our Master Rochal, the Incarnation of God
> O authentic saint, you are the Absolute!

In the couplets, Rochaldas is deified. After a couplet devoted to his praises, he is the benefactor of the world (*duniya ja datar*) and the Master of truth (*satguru*), who can bring the illumination of knowledge (*giyan ji jot*) and disperse the darkness. He is the personified grace, the Master (*malik*) and the lord (*sardar*). The many devotees who crowd around can see their wishes realized through the visualization of their idol (*murti jo didar*). He alone can make them cross the ocean on his nave (*bera*). This prayer makes it possible to observe that the technical lexicon of Sufism constitutes the framework of prayer.

The daily rituals are different in the Nimanal Sangam in Vadodara. It was in 1999 that the Sakhi Kuthiyya became the Nimanal Sangam, thirty-six years after the death of Nimano Faqir. This change is celebrated on 5 December of each year under the name Puj Nimano Sain Pak Astan. It is not known how the devotional practice was organized during Nimano's lifetime. Now, the *satsang* takes place every day and lasts one hour, except for on Sunday and Friday when it lasts two hours, from 5.00 to 700 pm. In the ordinary *satsang*s, the chants are not accompanied by musicians, but for those on Friday and especially Sunday, they are. The instruments are made up of an electronic keyboard and a dholak, and both are electronically amplified. The choice of the songs is made by the devotees, and no rule prevails except that they try to find themes that can be linked together.

The songs are led by Kamla, who is assisted by a choir of eight women. The rhythm is also given by a few tambourines struck by the singers and through the clapping of hands. The repertoire consists mainly of works by Sachal and Nimano. The *Sachal jo kalam* is open closeby Kamla. Women, who are separated from men, are the most numerous and active. Their heads are covered with a veil. The songs follow each other before being followed by prayers, and then by an offering of flowers. The ritual ends with a song from the *Guru Granth Sahib*.

The rituals performed in a *darbar* are also dependent on the size of the space, which is itself mostly a reflection of the present followers' number. For example, only a weekly ritual event is organized in the Maqbul Manzil, in Ulhasnagar. In this space devoted to Sachal Sarmast, a Darazi *satsang* is organized every Thursday under the supervision of Soni Kataria. The *satsang* starts at 7.00 pm and lasts until 9.00. The first part is the *arti*, when light is moved around the portraits of the altar. Every devotee is supposed to perform the *arti*, and usually, each one finishes by joining both hands and bowing to the altar. But I also observed that one woman, obviously Hindu, ends the *arti* like the Muslim's prayer, holding the open hands, then spend them on the face.

It is interesting to observe that the *satsang* is organized on Thursdays. It is well known that Thursday evening is for Muslims the beginning of Friday, which is itself the most sacred day of the week. In the Sufi *dargahs* of South Asia, the most important religious events are arranged on Thursday evenings, as for example the musical session of the qawwali. On the other hand, in a Hindu context, the *arti* performed on Thursday is also a special occasion. The *arti* is devoted to Vishnu, although it is called Bhraspativar *arti*, or the *arti* of Jupiter. It is said that this is the most beneficial sign of the planets, and that offering prayers on this day promotes greater learning and prosperity.

After the *arti*, the devotees sing Sachal's *kalam*. Two devotees are musicians: one plays harmonium and the other the tablas. Soni is the leading singer, and she knows the verses by heart. Other devotees, who are mostly women, have written in a notebook all the *kalam*s. I could see one is written in Devanagari, and another in Arabic Sindhi scripts. About twenty people attend the *satsangs*. Usually, Soni starts to sing and the others follow her. Sometimes, other forms can take the leading singer with a choir repeating each verse of Sachal's poetry. Always, as in all Hindu and Sufi rituals, the session will be achieved through the distribution of *prasad*. Throughout the year, one of the most significant events is the *urs* of Sachal Sarmast. Since it is in the Islamic calendar, the 14th of Ramazan, the date changes every year, be it in the Christian calendar or in the Hindu one named Vikram Samvat (or Sambat). Thus, Soni has to call, or is called by phone by the *sajjada nashin* of Daraza, for him to inform her of the timing.

In the context of Haridwar, a pilgrimage centre which is a stronghold of Hinduism, Basant confessed that he was compelled to withdraw some features of Mulchand's cult, which could be interpreted as Muslim. For example, it was not possible to make a pole with Mulchand's *alam* in navy blue. Neither was it possible to play the *dhamal* for the functions. In the strong Hindu neighbourhood, it was not possible to display such rituals which would be seen as Muslim. When the Sindhis migrated to India in 1947, they were often tagged as Muslims, or at least not authentic Hindus, because of the Sufi cults (Kothari 2007).

After the closure of the Mul Kutiyya, and finally its destruction, Mulchand's cult was celebrated in private spaces. His main followers had arranged in their home a 'puja room'. A *puja* room is a room, usually small, where an altar has been arranged, adorned with the pictures of gods and gurus. In the private space of a home, it is where the *puja* is performed. Such *puja* rooms were in Ulhasnagar, at Daulatram Motwani's home in Bombay, and in Delhi. In Delhi, for example, functions were performed for the birth (6 April) and death (20 November) anniversaries of the Sufi *sant*. Three main sketches are implemented: 1. singing of *bhajans*, 2. singing of Mulchand's *kalam* and 3. *bhandaro* – that is, food for all the assembly (*sangat*).

As we saw before, Popati Hiranandani claimed that Ram Panjwani introduced the Sufi *chownkis*. In her words, a *chownki* is a 'chorus singing Sufi kalams composed by Sindhi poets with the rhythmic beat of the gharo' (Hiranandani 1984: 55). The term *chowki*, or *chownki*, was maybe borrowed from the Sikh tradition, since in a dictionary published in the late nineteenth century, it is said that *chownki* is 'the reading of the scriptures of Nanak Shah' without any reference to Sufi songs (Shirt 1879: 353). However, it is used today among the Hindu Sindhis for the singing of Sufi *kalams*. It is not easy to distinguish between *chownki* and *satsang*. Beside the *chownkis*, another informal Sufi practice was another session, named *ruha ruhani*, or 'Spiritual conversations'. The topic was mostly related to God, and such conversation was often interceded with the singing of Sufi *kalams*.

In the Sindhi *darbars* of South Asia, the annual fair is meant to commemorate the death of the Sufi saint. The death is transmutated into the wedding of the Sufi with God, as a kind of metaphor through which the wedding, *urs* in Arabic, symbolizes the merging with God, namely his/her supreme union of the Sufi with God. A number of rituals are performed during the *urs*, among which the *mehndi* is at the apex of all of the *urs*. The *mehndi*, or henna, is the very symbol of the wedding (*shadi*) in South Asia. The bride is supposed to put henna on her hand. In the Sufi context, the *mehndi* is brought to the tomb, inside the *dargah*, where it is deposited at the foot of the tomb.

Annual fairs: From *urs* to *versi*

One of the main features of the modern spiritual paths is the commemoration of the events related to the founder. The first one can be his birth, and also different important events that have provided evidence that he was a superhuman creature. Another main event is his death. In the case of saints, death is understood as being the merging of the saint with God: finally, the saint is able to realize what he has been fighting for years, the meeting with God. Consequently, sadness is not the dominant mood, but rather rejoicing and happiness. In the Sufi context of South Asia, the commemoration of the union of the Sufi with God is the most important event of the liturgical year and many distinct events are organized in association with it.

As with the 'ordinary' rituals, 'extraordinary' rituals such as *dhamal*, *mehndi* or *jhando* (raising of the standard) are adapted according to the direct environment in which the *darbar* is located. The *versi*, the name given to the *urs*, commemorates the day when the Hindu Sufi left the physical world. For Rochaldas, the *versi* is celebrated according to the Hindu lunar-solar calendar of Vikram Samvat, on the third day of the dark face of the moon in the month of Margashirsa. This month, also known as Agrahayana, starts on 16 December and ends on 16 January. The celebrations last three days and are marked by the chanting of many Sufi *kalam*s, and by the *mehndi* ceremony.

As we can see in the chart of the daily programme of Rochaldas's *versi* in 2012, the daily programme lasting three days is mostly similar every day. It starts with the *dhamal*, the ritual related to Lal Shahbaz Qalandar. Nonetheless, the *dhamal* performed in Ulhasnagar is different. It is reduced to the drumming, while in Sehwan, the drumming is played for the ecstatic dance of the devotees. However, the *dhamal* obviously plays a capital role in Rochaldas's *versi*. Furthermore, *dhamal* is performed several times a day, especially on the first day when it is performed three times. The *dhamal* is played in different places inside the *darbar*. Most of the time, *dhamal* is only performed with drums and only on one occasion, the drumming is accompanied with the *shahnai*s, the flutes in the shrill sound that are very common in any religious ritual performed in Sindh.

Another important ritual is the *dastarbandi*, or the enthronement of the *gaddi nashin*. It reproduces the enthronement of the *gaddi nashin*, when the ritual was performed by Nur al-Din, the *sajjada nashin* of Tando Jahaniyyan in Pakistan. The re-enactment of his authority opens a kind of new spiritual year. For the occasion, the disciple reaffirmed his loyalty and surrendered towards the Master, as symbolized by the kissing of the *dastar*. Also (and interestingly, it is not stated in the programme), the *versi* of Rochaldas is simultaneously the

Table 5.1 Daily programme of Rochaldas's *versi* in 2012

	First day	Second day	Third day
4.00–4.30	*dhamal*	idem	idem
4.30–8.30	*kirtan*	idem	idem
9.00	breakfast	9.45: dhamal, shehnai and mehndi sahib	9.30 idem
10.00	Pooja and flag sahib dhamal		
10.30–1.00 pm	Kalam and satsang in hall	idem	10.30 idem
1.00–2.30	Bandharo sahib	idem	idem
3.30	Tea	idem	3.00 3.30
4.00	Shehnai and dhamal near flag sahib	Shehnai, mehndi sahib and ceremony dastar bandi in darbar sahib	4.00–4.45 satsang in darbar
4.30–6.45	Kalam and satsang in hall	4.15: dhamal near flag sahib 4.30 custom of embracing dastar bandi with garland in hall 5.00–5.30 kalam in darbar sahib 6.00–6.45 kalam and satsang in hall	4.45
6.45–7.00	Dhamal in darbar sahib	idem	
7.30–9.30	Bandharo sahib	idem	
10.00–4.00 am (Full night)	Kalam in hall		

urs of Lal Shahbaz Qalandar. In the late 1950s, they were celebrated separately, but now they are celebrated together. The programme clearly shows both the death anniversaries of Lal Shahbaz and Rochaldas have been harmoniously mixed.

All in all, the most intense moment of the *versi* is the procession of the *mehndi*. Shortly before his death, Rochaldas had a dream in which Lal Shahbaz Qalandar appeared. He pointed out that although the Hindu Sindhis had forgotten him, Lal Shahbaz always watched over them in India. He asked him to celebrate his *urs*, as at Sehwan. It seems that the first celebration took place in 1959, two years after the death of Rochaldas, who had left orders. For a few years, two distinct *urs* were celebrated: Lal Shahbaz's *urs* in the Islamic calendar, 18, 19 and 20 Shaban, and Rochaldas's *versi*. One year, the two anniversaries fell at the same time. From then on, it was decided to celebrate both at the same time, or, that is to say, for the *versi* of Rochaldas.

The *mehndi* procession is a significant symbolic moment of the *urs*: henna or *mehndi* symbolizes the marriage between the Sufi and God, which is to say that it represents death as their union. In Sehwan, the *mehndi* is led on the first day by the dominant group of Sayyids, the descendants of the Prophet Muhammad, and on the second and third days by Hindus who belong to two distinct families. On the third day, the *mehndi* was led by the Kanungos, but in 1962 they decided to emigrate to India and settled in Ulhasnagar, where the son of Rochaldas, Hari, asked them to lead the *mehndi* procession in the *darbar*. In Sehwan Sharif, another Hindu named Lal Das then became *mehndibardar*. Gandaram (d. 2008), the eldest of the Kanungos, inherited the charge upon his father's death in 1948, but in the 1980s he was transferred to Bangalore, far from Ulhasnagar.

At that time, the *mehndi* procession went as far as the river. There, a *puja* was performed just as it is in the shrine, ending with *Hari Om Jhulelal*. After Gandaram's demise, it would have been his brother Murlidhar who should have taken on the duty. But, he was living in Baroda, and Lachhman, the youngest brother who was himself living in Ulhaasnagar was not allowed. Thus, it was the son of Hari, Damodar, who led the *mehndi* from that point on. The *mehndi* of Lal Shahbaz makes it possible to maintain a direct link through the ritual with the lost territory of Sindh.

On the third day, the celebrations of the *versi* end with the song of the *dua*. The *dua* is the devotional supplication (*munajat*) composed by the son of Qutub Ali Shah, Roshan Ali Shah (1852–1932). The *munajat* is made of twenty-one verses composed in an Arabicized Sindhi. The Prophet Muhammad, though not named as such (but as Mustafa), is praised, and his mention is followed by *ain wasi Mustafa iana Ali Murtaza*, or 'and the heir of Mustafa, namely Ali al-Murtaza' (Roshan Ali Shah no date: 4). The last part of the verse has an amazing Shia flavour. Still more amazing is an indirect Quranic reference. It is the famous *ayat* related to the sources of authority in Islam. The Muslim believers are said to obey God, the Apostle and those vested with authority, the *ulul al-amr* (Quran 4:59). In his *munajat*, Roshan quotes exactly the same references, and also he includes Ali between the Prophet and the *ulul al-amr*: it is a kind of Muslim profession of faith, which is amazingly adopted as *dua* by Rochaldas's followers (Roshan Ali Shah no date: 5).[8]

In the *dua*, the devotees thus recite in order the names of the source of authority as put in the Quran, with the exception of Ali: God, *Khoda* in the *munajat*, Muhammad as Mustafa, Ali and the *ulul al-amr*, the Quranic expression. However, the refrain is a request addressed in simple words to the One to accept the prayers of all, Muslim as well as Hindu. The *darbar* regularly republishes the *munajat* a little before the *versi*. Each participant may have a free copy. Whereas once it was published in the Arabic Sindhi alphabet, the *darbar* began to publish it in Devanagari so that the younger generations may read it.

Two other *versis* are celebrated: that of Hari, the son and successor of Rochaldas, on 21 March, and that of Gobindram, a renunciant who was close to Rochaldas when he was in Sindh, on the first day of Holi. A last opportunity is found in the celebration of the new moon (*chand*). A hundred disciples then gather to sing *kalams*. Other *versis* are celebrated for the most outstanding followers of Rochaldas, like for example Dadi Dhan. This was not celebrated in the *darbar* of Rochaldas, but in her small apartment of Mahim, in Bombay. In this case, the physical space was reduced and the sacralization of the territory was limited to the presence of a small altar: no inscription or any specific decorum gives information on the sacred function that this place can exercise. The altar is loaded with images, most of them linked to not only the Rochaldas tradition but also other traditions such as Shri Sathya Sai Baba (1926–2011), not to be confused with Shirdi Sai Baba.[9]

Obviously, Sai Baba was a spiritual guide for Dadi Dhan since, in the daily sessions, she used to read some of his texts and to explain them with quotations from Qutub Ali Shah, Rochaldas, Bedil or Bekas. Furthermore, she had organized a trip to Puttaparthi, in Andhra Pradesh, Sai Baba's native town, where his *ashram* was built in 2012. Sai Baba claimed to be an incarnation of Shirdi Sai Baba (1838–1918).[10] His purpose was to establish the *sanatan dharma*, according to which there is only one God for all of the religions. Nobody should renounce his religion. He is said to have accomplished many miracles and his main activity was to offer *darshan* to his disciples, through which they were able to see God since he was his incarnation.

At Dadi Dhan's place, the *versi* in 2012 was marked by a succession of songs sung either by men or by women, mostly a *capella*, with one exception where a singer used an *ektaro*, a one-string instrument that serves as a drone. About 150 people were involved in the *versi*, including Pritam Mansharamani who was none other than the younger son of Rochaldas and uncle of the present *gaddi nashin.* The latter did not attend, but many disciples had travelled from Ulhasnagar. Although the majority of the songs were in Sindhi, there was also a composition of Bullhe Shah and another one of Mirabai. As far as the Sufis of Sindhis were concerned, they all belonged to the contemporary period. The most requested author was Sachal Sarmast, then Rochaldas. One of Qutub Ali Shah's *kalam*s opened the celebration and his *Sakhi sabajhal* was sung before *Dam mast qalandar*, in the version authored by Qutub Ali Shah, and the final *dua* whose author was Nasir Faqir.

In Mulchand's Sufi path, the *versi* was performed on three main occasions: 5 April (birthday of Mulchand and Gehimal), 20 November (Mulcand's death) and 29 October (Gehimal's death). The function started with the raising of Mulchand's *alam*, now known as *jhando*. Mulchand's *jhando* was navy blue. The function was carried on with the *murti*, which was made *virajman*, a ritual when the *murti* is sat on the throne. Then it was the time of invocation: a spiritual person covers his face and invites the *murshid*, and his tears start flowing in this part known as *sufiyya ji ibadat*, or the 'Sufi worship'.

After the *arti*, *prasad* was distributed among the followers and, finally, flowers were put in flowing water, usually a river. The function ended with the singing of Sufi *kalam*s, and with the performance of *dhamal*. The *dhamal* was nevertheless informal. A devotee was playing the drum and other followers were dancing on the *Mast qalandar* rhythm. At Daulatram, the *versi* started with the *havan* (fire) ceremony performed by a Sindhi Brahmin, and this goes

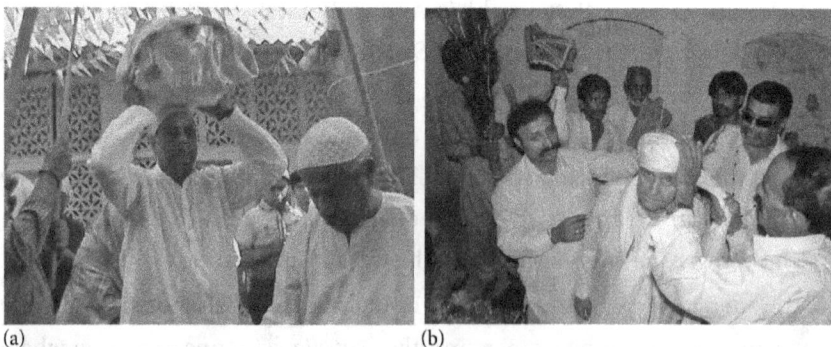

(a)   (b)

Figure 5.2 Two *mehndi*s in Ulhasnagar (India) and Sehwan Sharif (Pakistan). (a) Damodar's *mehndi* procession at Rochaldas's *darbar*, Ulhasnagar, 2012 and (b) Ramchand's *dastarbandi* before the *mehndi* procession in Sehwan Sharif, 2011.

on mainly with the chanting of Sufi songs composed by Sachal Sarmast, Shah Abd al-Latif and Qutub Ali Shah.

Many other *versis* are celebrated among the Hindu followers of the Sufis. Isarlal, who had a shrine in Rohri, was himself in touch with other local saints such as Vasan Shah and Paru Shah.[11] He was himself a disciple of the sixth *murshid* of Daraza, Sachal's *dargah*, Sakhi Qabul Muhammad II (1842–1925). In India, where his followers had migrated, his *versi* was celebrated in a flat and the main part was the singing of his poetry, with a *dholak* (cattle drum) and *ektaro* (one-string instrument). Furthermore, a kind of relic also focused the worship for the Sufi saint. It is said that he used dice in Sindh with other Sufis. The Bhatia family has kept the ivory dice, as well as the green crossed clothe on which Isar Lal played. During the *versi*, the two objects were exhibited so that the participants could touch them and then put their hands on their faces as a sort of blessing.

The 'Darazi *satsangs*'

Nonetheless, the plasticity of the Hindu Sufi cults is such that there is still a last category: the places where the 'Darazi *satsangs*' are performed. The expression 'Darazi *satsangs*' is used for naming the different musical meetings organized by the Hindu followers of Sachal Sarmast in India. Sachal Sarmast's *dargah* is located in the village of Daraza, not far from Khairpur, in Sindh. He had a large number of followers among the Hindu trade castes of Norther Sindh, and some of them transferred their love for singing Sachal's poetry to India when they migrated in the wake of partition. Beyond the accessibility of his poetry, Sachal was also a staunch *wujudi*, and he is probably the one of the Sufi poets of Sindh to use the most numerous references to Hindu gods, especially Krishna.

The 'Darazi *satsangs*' are mostly performed in Ulhasnagar and Mumbai. Usually, the followers have arranged a *samadhi* in the basement of the building where they live. From the outside, there is no inscription for identifying the place, or there are a variety of names which are given to a single place. For example, the Radha Krishin Lal *darbar* is also named Maqbul Manzil. The *darbar* was created by Faqir Radha Krishin Lal Sahib Darazi 'Krishna' (d.

1980). He was himself the author of a *kalam* (Krishin 1986) published in Ulhasnagar by Dada Hari Ram Kataria, his main follower. Radha Krishin built the *darbar* in the 1970s and, after his death, it was run by Hari Ram, who took the charge to sing Sachal's poetry. After him, it was his daughter Soni who performed the *satsang* every Thursday evening, as we saw before. Otherwise, two *versi*s are celebrated over the course of the year: Sachal's *versi* on the 14th of Ramazan, and Hari Ram's *versi* in the beginning of November. The *sajjada nashin* of Daraza has paid three visits to the *darbar*.

Another *darbar* where 'Darazi *satsang*s' are performed is the Sachal Sain *darbar*, whose official name is Rohani Rah, the 'Spiritual Path'. The entrance door is decorated by *haqq mawjud* in Arabic Sindhi script. It stood for about thirty to thirty-five years in another building, and shifted to the present one twenty years ago. It was built by Pratap Rai Rajani, who passed away in 2007. His wife Mira used to sing Sachal's poetry during the *satsang*, which is held every Sunday evening. Previously, it was organized twice a week, and it may be that the reduction to once per week could signify there is a growing lack of interest. Two *versi*s are celebrated in the *darbar*: Sachal's and Pratap's. Mira's son Jaichand daily performs the *arti* in the *darbar* at about 9.00 am.

The two *darbar*s devoted to Sachal Sarmast are located in the same area of Ulhasnagar, camp 5. The two in charge are said to have been in touch but since twenty years, they have stopped meeting for an unknown reason. Notwithstanding, still they are in touch with the *sajjada nashin* of Daraza since, in both cases, he calls on them to give the date of Sachal's *versi*. As a matter of fact, Sachal's birthday is on Ramazan in the Islamic calendar, so that the date changes every year in the Christian calendar. As in all the Sindhi *darbar*s, the walls are full of hung images. But, before deciphering the iconographical discourse, a difference is to be noted. The core of the worship in the Rohani Rah is a statue (*murti*) of Sachal Sarmast. This *murti* was obviously carved according to the 'official' picture of Sachal, which hangs on a wall at Daraza. It is said that this portrait was drawn by a Sikh follower of Sachal. Sachal is represented in majesty in a pose that could be reminiscent of Guru Nanak's iconography. In both representations, he sits on a *gaddi* with a club in his right hand, and a musical instrument, slightly different, in his left. The only difference between the two is that, in the statue, Sachal has a golden *tilak* on his forehead.

The organization of the altar is composed of Pratap's picture below Sachal's statue, and then two *sajjada nashin*s of Daraza on each side, to his right and left. Above Sachal's *murti*, there is Krishna as a flute player, without Radha, and still above this, the *darbar* of Sachal Sarmast in Daraza. In the Radha Krishin Lal *darbar*, the core of the altar is a photo of Sakhi Qabul Muhammad VI, instead of a representation of Sachal. But the whole picture set-up is dominated by an inscription in Latin alphabet: 'Sai Sachal'. In fact, most of the pictures are from the *sajjada nashin*s of Daraza, especially those of Sakhi Qabul VI and Sakhi Qabul VIII, who recently passed away. From the Hindu side in India, one can see the photos of the two *gaddi nashin*s of the Indian *darbar*, namely Radhakrishin and Hari Ram. Nonetheless, the most amazing feature is the absence of Sachal's picture, and when I asked Soni why it was Sakhi and not Sachal, she answered that Sakhi is the one who looks most like Sachal.

The Daraza school of Sufism still attracts many Hindu Sindhis of India. Already, we mentioned they organized 'Darazi *satsangs*' in Mumbai and Ulhasnagar. They gather to sing Sachal Sarmast's *kalam*. There are also other Sufi poets claiming to be 'Darazi'. This was the case for Nimano Faqir, whose Sufi poetry is very inspired by Sachal. She was also initiated to the Sufi path by Sakhi Qabul Muhammad VI. Other 'Darazi *satsangs*' are performed by Adi Ama in Ulhasnagar, Murli in Mumbai and Soni in London. I was not able to pay a visit to these places.

Conclusion

Once the virtual world of the mystic is built, the rituals can be performed. The continuity of the mystic space is made through the singing of Sufi poetry accompanying the performance of the rituals themselves. No ritual is performed without the singing of a Sufi *kalam*. Regarding the rituals, the evolution has been imposed by the political evolution in India under the rule of the BJP, as well as the growing animosity spreading between the dominant Hindus and the Muslims. Here, a number of typical Sufi rituals performed in Sindh have been suppressed, such as the *alam* or the *dhamal*. For more practical reasons, other rituals have been simplified – for instance, the *mehndi* procession at Rochaldas's *darbar*, since the *mehndibardar* left Ulhasnagar. All in all, the *darbar* mystical space shifted from a Sufi rooted framing to a more hinduized framing throughout the time of partition. Nonetheless, this evolution followed what scholars have coined the 'solidification' or 'rigidification' of religious identities in South Asia. Another factor could be the local environment.

In a large and a mostly dominant non-Sindhi India, the issue of the Sufi legacy cannot be analysed without reference to the issue of the Sindhi identity at large. The Sindhis are a very small minority in India, and since partition, they have been very active in finding efficient means to preserve and even develop the Sindhi language, which they mostly consider to be the core of a living Sindhi culture. While this topic has been studied by scholars such as Kothari and Thapan, the role given to the Sufi legacy in this process has not been given the attention it deserves. The next chapter will examine the other Sufi perspectives among the Hindu Sindhis of India. As a matter of fact, the three Sufi paths are not the only ones to deal with the Sufi legacy in independent India. The Sufi legacy of Sindh has been transmitted through other methods and means, most of them more informal than those including an initiation and the submission to a Master.

Addressing the issue of these informal ways of transmission also tackles the issue of the Sindhi identity in India, or Sindhiyyat, in relation with the Sufi legacy. Suffice it to say that the famous Sindhi cultural activist Ram Panjwani was himself convinced it was a main part of Sindhiyyat, before shifting to focus more on Jhulelal. From partition onwards, much Sufi poetry in Sindhi was published in India. Some of the most important *kalam*s are still unpublished in Pakistan – for example, Dalpat Sufi's poetry. While a few attempts were made to elaborate a kind of theological reflection on Sufism, the transmission of the Sufi legacy was represented by many as a main tool for reinforcing Sindhiyyat. Here, the target was the 'young generations', and the main question was related to the scripts to be used.

The transmission of the Sufi legacy in India

Until now, the issue of the Sufi legacy among the Hindu Sufis of India has been addressed through two primary perspectives: the physical space or *darbar*, and the mystical Sufi poetry I have depicted as framing a 'mystical space'. Between both, bridging them, are the rituals. Although the devotees performing the rituals and attending the *versis* are mostly not Sufis, in the sense that they have a job and are householders, they feel like belonging to a path, to a community whose unity is the veneration of a Sufi Master. Also, the central role played by the singing of Sufi poetry has been copiously highlighted. In this chapter, I wish to enlarge the focus of this study in scrutinizing the issue of transmission beyond the initiation between a Sufi Master and his disciple.

I intend to explore other perspectives regarding how Sindhis transmit the Sufi legacy they have imported from Sindh to India. This will show how Sufism has permeated the life of the intellectuals, such as Ram Panjwani. In dealing with such seminal figures of the Sindhi spiritual life in India, I will capture the relationship the first generation of Sindhi migrants had with Sufism, and how they merged this legacy with their own spiritual approach. Nonetheless, these spiritual souls were mostly attracted by the Sufi poetry. Another method to be investigated is the non-poetical elaboration of Sufism among the Hindu Sindhis of India. The domination of the Sufi poetry as the core of the Sufi legacy did not prevent Hindu Sufis from publishing theological works related to Sufism. Notwithstanding, these works were in a minority if compared with Sufi poetry. Furthermore, beyond the *darbar*s and the *samadhi*s, Sufi individuals have also contributed to the dissemination of Sufism among the Hindu Sindhis of India.

A last part of this chapter will be devoted to the role played by the Sindhi diaspora in the transmission of the Sufi legacy. This issue is crucial since it is directly related to another one: the transmission of the Sindhi identity, or

Sindhiyyat, to the young generations of Sindhis, and especially those who cannot read, or not even speak, Sindhi. In India, the issue is restricted, so to say, to the dilemma of two scripts: Arabic and Devanagari. But most of the young Sindhis living in other countries can only read the Latin alphabet. As we shall see, some Sindhis have already decided to publish Sufi poetry not in the Sindhi language, but in the Latin alphabet. Others are selecting the options of translating Sindhi poetry into English. Beyond this issue of script and the language to be issued for transmitting the Sufi legacy, there is the identity which the Hindu Sindhis want to express, to show off, or, in other words, the place they want to devote to the Sufi legacy in the Sindhi identity of the future generations. Mostly, these issues are closely related to each other, and they are rooted in the debates related to the scripts to be used for printing the Sindhi language.

The first Sindhi literati, such as Ram Panjwani who migrated to India in 1947, grew up in the wake of the previous generations of Sindhi intellectuals. They were those through whom, following the objectification of Sufism after the canonization of the *Shah jo Risalo* authored by Shah Abd al-Latif (d. 1752), the Sufi poetry was accepted as an epitome of Sindhi culture, and thus of Sindhi identity.

Ram Panjwani (1911–87) and the challenge of post-partition transmission

It is widely known that many contemporary Hindu gurus from India have praised the universal wisdom of the Sufis. For example, Osho published several books on Sufism.[1] Before him, in 1932, the great Rabindranath Tagore (1861–1941) had asked Gurdial Mallik (1893–1970) to deliver a series of lectures on the mystics of Sindh. Himself a Punjabi, his lectures would be published only after partition, but Mallik warmly thanks Jethmal Parsram for having introduced him to the Sufi poetry in Sindhi (Mallick 1949: vi). Also, he quotes Helena Blavatsky and he has been secretary of Annie Besant, so he was close to the Theosophical Society. His book focuses on Shah Latif and Sachal, but he also refers to other Sufi poets, such as Bekas, Bedil, Dalpat Sufi and Qutub Ali Shah.

In the Sindhi context of India, one of the first works underscoring the Sufi legacy of Sindh was published in 1955 in Ajmer. In a thick book of almost 600 pages, titled *Darvishan jo dawr*, or *The Time of the Dervishes*, Ranjit Premchand Vaswani associated poetry with biographies of the Sindhi saints, Sufi and non-Sufi. I was unable to collect any information about the author. The book starts with Guru Nanak and Jhulelal, here named Darya Shah (and Zinda Pir in the caption of the image), then going on to Paru Shah and Vasan Shah, of whom he was obviously the follower. The last part is made up of about fifty pages that are devoted to Sindhi Sufis, some Hindu but mostly Muslim. The first Muslim Sufi is, unsurprisingly, Shah Abd al-Latif, followed by Rohal, Murad, Sachal and Bedil. Dalpat Sufi's verses are not quoted within the 'Sufis' (Vaswani 1955: 514–63).

Sadhu T. L. Vaswani (1879–1966) was a prolific Sindhi *guru* who published numerous books on spirituality. In 2002, his successor J. P. Vaswani published his predecessor's writings on Sufism, but unfortunately with no date or any precision. Already, from his autobiography, it was obvious that Sufism had been an important part of his spiritual training, and he quoted many different Sufis, from Sindh and from abroad. In the texts compiled by J. P. Vaswani, one can see he is well acquainted with Sufism (Vaswani 2002). The style he uses to talk of Sufism comes through narrating a number of anecdotes. He constantly interweaves Sufi and Bhakti references and characters. For example, he writes of a 'Muslim Yogi who passed to Brahma-Nivarna, the Peace of the Eternal' (Vaswani 2002: 138).

A Sindhi played a leading role in the transmission of the Sufi legacy: Ram Panjwani. Here, my contention is to examine the place given by Ram Panjwani to the Sufi legacy of Sindh in the building of Sindhiyyat, or post-partition Indian Sindhiness. I shall briefly give a biographical sketch, especially from before partition since, usually, his life is well known after he migrated to India. In a second step, I shall focus on his conception and representation of Sufism, which occurred before the action he took which made him so popular among the Sindhis: the consecration of Jhulelal as *isht devta*, or community God, of the Hindu Sindhis of India.

Ram Panjwani was born in 1911 in Larkana in a *zamindar* family. In 1934, he graduated from the University of Bombay and started his career in education as teacher at the D. J. Sindh Government Science College in Karachi. In 1947, he was among the migrant Hindu Sindhis, and he reached Bombay where he started working as a member of the faculty of Jai Hind College, in the Sindhi department. Later on, he moved to Bombay University as the reader in the Sindhi department and headed the department from 1974 to 1976. In 1969, he had founded the Sita Sindhu Bhavan, a culture centre for the promotion of the different artistic sides of the Sindhi culture. He passed away in 1987. Twenty-five books are attributed to him, covering many different genres, and he was also a singer, a musician, an actor and a film director.

His influence was enormous on the Hindu Sindhis of India, especially since he worked hard to give them the pride to be Sindhis – and in an Indian context where the Hindu Sindhis were often despised by other Hindus. Among the Hindu Sindhis, everyone knows him, but here, I want to unveil some aspects of his life that have been darkened by his fame. The first one is the probable influence of the Theosophical Society. As it was for the majority of the Sindhi literati, be they Hindu or Muslim, the ideology of the society provided the framework for a reinterpretation of the Sufi legacy of Sindh. Already, in Sindh, Panjwani was convinced that Sufism was the core of Sindhi culture, a culture shared by all creeds and social milieus. Consequently, in 1945, thus before migrating to India, he published a book on Shah Abd al-Latif, which was republished in India in 1981 (Panjwani 1981).

The second underestimated side of Panjwani's life is the importance he gave to Sufism in the making of the Sindhi culture. This aspect is not so obvious because, as soon as the 1960s, he stopped working directly on the Sufi legacy as a main component of Sindhi culture, rather focusing on Jhulelal as the embodiment of the Sindhi culture in India. Nonetheless, Panjwani was an exemplary product of the Sufi culture of Sindh and, as was the case for most of the Sindhi intellectuals before partition, his conception of Sufism was filtered by the Theosophist ideology.

Before addressing the issue of the place he gives to Sufism in Sindhi culture, it is relevant to examine how he did conceive Sindhi Sufism through the anthologies he published in the 1950s, soon after partition. There was a brief period during which Panjwani was a migrant reaching an unknown country, after having abandoned his ancestral home that he had cherished. At the least, we can state that he was disoriented and disturbed after having experienced such a trauma. An anthology of Sufi poetry was among the first books he published in India. In 1959, he published an anthology he named *Sik ji soghat* with, as a kind of subtitle, *Sufi kalam*, which would be republished in 2000 by Thakur Chawla. About 200 poets of Sindh are mentioned, with abstracts of their poetry. No biographical sketch is provided, no date, no reference of any kind, and the most famous Sufis of Sindh appear along with lesser known poets.

Nonetheless, the three most quoted poets are Sufis, and among the most famous of Sindh. First comes Sachal Sarmast, with forty-six abstracts from his Sindhi poetry. Second is Bedil, and third is Shah Abd al-Latif, with respectively thirty-eight and thirty-six quotations. But many poets have only one abstract. Some Sufis are not Sindhi, such as the famous Punjabi poet, Bulhe Shah, but they are very few. Also, we find in the anthology many verses which are acclaimed among the Hindu Sindhis of India, such as the famous *Sakhi sabhajhal* composed by Qutub Ali Shah. In relation with the three Sufi traditions under study, we find only Nimano with two abstracts. Furthermore, the last four pages of the book are the devotional songs devoted to Jhulelal (*panjro*), along with other devotional songs (*git*), the final of which is a *pala*, a prayer sung during a ritual performed when the devotees ask for God's mercy (Panjwani 1959: 325–8). It is thus very interesting to see how Panjwani 'concludes' his Sufi anthology with literature which is related to the God community of the Hindu Sindhis, Jhulelal.

Throughout this construction, Panjwani astutely locates Jhulelal in the wake of the Sufi legacy, knowing this heritage was already the core of the cross-religious Sindhi culture. Even if this was not a totally planned formatting, one may conclude that Panjwani was already thinking of promoting a Sindhi God, Jhulelal. Jhulelal was already worshipped by some segments among the Hindus of Sindh, but as we saw before, they were in majority Nanakpanthis. The main advantage of the figure of Jhulelal was first to allow the Sindhis to be finally distinguished from the Sikhs, but also to enlarge the Sufi tradition, and finally to give evidence to the existence of a separate Hindu Sindhi identity that could be agglomerated to mainstream Hinduism as a new branch of the already innumerable sects.

For Ram Panjwani, the word Sufi was an encompassing notion reflecting a kind of state of mind rather than it being a concept working on a strictly delimited field. Under the category of 'Sufi', he could thus include poets who were not Sufis *stricto sensu* – that is to say, with no proper Sufi practice, but who were dealing with the spirit of Sufism. In this case, the main basis of Sufism was love, and love in action is tolerance. Even if Panjwani did not directly publish Sufi poetry later on, the Sufi culture was always framing his own approach to religion, and finally to life. In the complementary volume published in 1981, six years before he passed away, a contribution describes him as a Sufi. The author wrote: 'Nurtured among the Sufi traditions of Sind, he (Panjwani) has been tireless in keeping them alive in our hearts and spreading them in the younger generation' (Manghnani 1981: 15). According to the author, Panjawni had imbibed the 'spirit of Sufism' so well that he had become a worthy successor of the Sufi poets of Sindh. The author describes the spirit of Sufism as 'the divinity that dwells in man' (Manghnani 1981: 17).

As mentioned earlier, Ram Panjwani was not a philosopher, and nowhere can we find a deep and detailed explanation of what Sindhiyyat is. Nonetheless, the word is used in one of his latest books, published in 1987, the year of his death, with the title: *Sindhi ain Sindhiyaat*. We can immediately observe that he links Sindhiyyat to a language, Sindhi. And, interestingly, while the title is in Sindhi, the book of about 100 pages was published in English. In the preface, Panjwani claims that, through the book, he wishes to 'acquaint the present generation of Sindhis with their past and the glorious cultural heritage of Sind which was inhabited by their forefathers'. For him, the cultural heritage of Sindh prioritizes 'a portrayal of their (of the Sindhis) unique language and literature' (Panjwani 1987: preface).

The table of contents in the book perfectly illustrates Panjwani's conception of Sindhiyyat. The table is made of an addition of a number of cultural features. The books opens with a first chapter devoted to Jhulelal, and the second to a 'Dream realized', namely the creation of the Sita Sindhu Bhavan. The third chapter is named 'Ageless wisdom of the Sufis'. Let us start with Panjwani's depiction of a Sufi: 'He is above Time, above Space. He is above sect and above any prejudice. He sees his friend, God, in everything' (Panjwani 1987: 20). Interestingly, his statements on the Sufis, rather than on Sufism, are illustrated through quotations from non-Sindhi Sufis, such as Rumi and Hafiz.

Panjwani went further in stating that the Sufi's religion is love, and that he does not believe in formality and ceremonies: 'He does not believe that prayer in a particular kind of temple or shrine and in particular language and style as superior to other prayers' (Panjwani 1987:21). Also, Panjwani adds that suffering is an important station on the path of the Sufi who means to reach God. The control of feelings is the most important step on the Sufi path whose aims is to be closer to God. The Sufi has to go in quest of his beloved. The quest will develop into love, which will take him to the valley of oneness, *wahadaniyyat*. Thus, he will reach the knowledge, *marifat*. The next step is that of detachment, or *hirarat*. The third and last step is *fana*: he should merge himself into God through annihilating his Ego. The Ego is the main obstacle to reaching God.

The chapter on Sufism is followed by another on the 'Trinity of the Sindhi poets' – namely Shah Abd al-Latif, Sachal Sarmast and Sami.[2] Panjwani's vision of Sindh is that of 'a land of the mystic poets, who are humanists as well'. It is interesting to see how he built a link between the three of them: 'He (Shah Abd al-Latif) brings the kettle on the boil, Sachal takes the lid off from it, while Sami passes on the beverage to the rank and file of the people so that they may be brought to the intense awareness of God even when engaged in the day-to-day affairs of life' (Panjwani 1987: 29–30). Shah Abd al-Latif's poetry was of a surpassing beauty in language and thought. Panjwani quotes him in defining who is a Sufi: 'A Sufi belongs to no sect. No one can label him. He fights with his own selves and divulges nothing. He extends help even to those who are hostile to him' (Panjwani 1987: 34).

Panjwani does not escape some contradiction. On the one hand, he claims that the Sindhi language is the core of Sindhi identity, while it explains Sufism in quoting Persian-speaking poets, including Farid al-Din Attar (1145–1220). Notwithstanding, Panjwani goes so far as to mention the different stages of the Sufi quest, and in a very classical presentation based on *tariqa*, the meeting with the Sufi path, *marifa*, the knowledge after initiation and finally the *fana*, the merging with God. All in all, while he introduces the Sufism of Sindh as a milestone of Sindhi identity, he also claims that the message of the Sufis can also be found through Guru Nanak, Mirabai and Kabir, as well as in other *sants*' poetry. Consequently, and although we do not have to undermine it in the agency of Sindhi identity, Sufism is a component among others, and from the 1960s onwards, it comes after Jhulelal's worship, which can be seen as a kind of soft hinduization of the Sindhi legacy in India.

Ram Panjwani popularized 'Sufistic chownkies', to quote Popati Hiranandani (Hiranandani 1984: 55).[3] They are choral singings of Sufi *kalam*s with the rhythmic beat of the *gharo*, an earthenware pot. Finally, Ram Panjwani's understanding of Sufism is deeply reminiscent of the Theosophist representation. It is a state of mind, and it is the spirit of Sufism, more than any other belief and/or practice which give to Sindhiyyat a unique flavour. The flavour comes from the ideals of toleration and love deeply rooted in the belief of the Oneness of God, but although it was expressed in other languages, the final touch is given by the music expressed by the Sindhi language, a music that is effectively unique. When Panjwani referred to the religious culture of Sindh, he was referring to the spirit of Sufism, as if Sufism in this culture was both the ultimate referent and the provider of the technical lexicon, the way through which Sindhi identity was to be best expressed. In this respect, Ram Panjwani gave a crucial role to Sufism in the making of Sindhiyyat.

Furthermore, Panjwani was able to transmit his interest for Sindhi Sufism to some of his successors. After his death, the Sita Sindhu Bhagwan was run by a number of Sindhi 'cultural activists', but a couple among them were particularly involved: Paru (1932–2016) and Thakur Chawla (1931–2013). Paru Chala was born as Lalwani in Sehwan Sharif in 1932. Despite the strong Sufi ambiance of the city, she left at about fifteen years old and discovered the place of the Sufi legacy in Sindhi spirituality through Ram Panjwani, as she herself confessed. Like her 'master', fearing the decline of the Sindhi language, she was keen to transmit the Sindhi literary legacy to the young generations, starting with her children and grandchildren. She arranged the compilation of Sindhi literature – for example, Jhulelal's *panjra*s and *bhajan*s. Probably in 1992, according to the preface she wrote, Paru Chawla published a book titled *Chund Sindhi kalam ain dohira*, or *Anthology of Two Sindhi Literary Genres*.

The publication is very close to that of Panjwani's *Sik je soghat* since the poetry pieces are mainly from the 'trinity' – Shah Abd al-Latif, Sachal Sarmast and Sami. Nonetheless, there are other poets included, such as Bewas, Bekas and Kohji. Contemporary Indian Sindhi literati are also present, including Moti Prakash and Master Chander. She included, like Panjwani, a piece from the Pakistani Sindhi poet Shaykh Ayaz and others from a non-Sindhi author, Ghulam Farid. The book has two pieces by Ram Panjwani, a *kalam* and another one devoted to Jhulelal (Chawla 1992: 49 and 117). Two pieces are by

Rochaldas (Chawla 1992: 51 and 143), while finally a *panjra* and a *kalam* are signed by 'Paru Thakur Chawla' (Chawla 1992: 96–7).

It is interesting to see that, as late as in the 1990s, Paru Chawla published this book, as well as others, in Arabic Sindhi script, though the non-migrant Sindhis[4] in India can hardly read it. Does this choice mean she was targeting the migrant Sindhi generation only? In any case, Paru Chawla's conception of Sufism is close to Panjawni's, if not inspired by, since we know she was introduced to the Sufi legacy of Sindh through him. Obviously, she did consider Sufism as a main component of Sindhiyyat, still, when we observe that she published a Sufi anthology in the 1990s.

Non-poetic chains for the transmission of Sufism

For transmitting the Sindhi culture, and the Sufi legacy, Ram Panjwani has used many different varieties of support pertaining to different fields, such as poetry, ovels, music and singing, as well as films. On many occasions, the role played by the poetry has been highlighted, but there was another form of Sufism which was also transmitted: the non-poetic Sufism. Already, we saw that the main difference between the Sindhi Hindu Sufis and the Hindu Naqshbandis studied by Thomas Dahnhardt is the genre of their writings, and thus their approach to Sufism. Among the Naqshbandis, including the Hindu Naqshbandis, many treatises were composed to deal with theological issues.

In Sindh, save the Naqshbandis, Sufism is dominated by poetry expressing the concept of *wahdat-e wujud*. Despite the domination of poetry among the Sindhi Hindu Sufis, one can also find non-poetic writings related to Sufism, such as the Sufi school of Rai Rochaldas. His son and successor R. M. Hari (1912–80) was a prolific author, and started with the publication of the four-volume spiritual dialogues with Rochaldas, according to the notes written by his disciples. First published in Sindhi between 1959 and 1965, with the title *Ke saitun sajnan san urf Sain (Daktar) Rochaldas Sahib ji satsangi rihan*, and then reprinted, Hari prepared an English translation that was edited in 1998 by his own son and successor, H. M. Damodar, and present *gaddi nashin* of Rochaldas's *darbar*. Before scrutinizing how the book allows one to understand how Rochaldas bridges Hinduism and Sufism, as well as discovering his daily life, some comments should be made on his two other publications.[5]

As a matter of fact, in 1962, Hari published a commentary on the Shrimad Bhagavad Gita, with the subtitle *Ilm al-laduni va towhid*, or the *Divinely inspired Knowledge and the Oneness of God*. It would be translated by his son and published in English in 1982. It is Hari's commentary on the *sloka*s of the Gita, the explanations provided through the quotations of the Sufi Sindhi poets. As stated by Damodar, Hari's purpose was 'to establish there is no distinction between Vedanta and Sufism' (Hari 1982: 427). This book is a primary attempt by a Sindhi Hindu Sufi to provide a comprehensive reflection on the core topic of the encounter between Sufism and Hinduism.

In 1992, Damodar also published a translation from Sanskrit made by 'a devotee' of the *Shri Yoga Vaisishtha*, an abridged version of a spiritual dialogue between Shri Ramchandra, an incarnation of Vishnu, and Shri Vasishtha as rendered by Valmiki, the legendary author of the *Ramayana*. The text is introduced by Damodar as the main scripture of Vedanta, or the non-duality of *atma*, the God Infinite, and he claims that it was cherished by Rochaldas, who did not perform a *satsang* without reading and commenting on some verses from it. Hari put it in the shape of questions and answers, so that it would be accessible to the common reader, and even the one who is not familiar with Indian philosophy. Apparently, Hari first translated it from Sanskrit to Sindhi, but this translation was never published. Then, he started to translate it from Sindhi to English, but he could not complete this project due to his heart attack, which was followed by his death. In this book, one can hardly find any reference to Sufism, hence the technical lexicon comes from Sanskrit and Hindi.

Finally, it is worth noting that R. M. Hari did publish these books at the end of his life. It is not irrelevant to argue that they mirror a more hinduized[6] version of Sindhi Sufism, if compared with the poetry legacy. I am speaking here of Rochaldas's poetry as expressed in the verses by Dadi Dhan and Dadi Ganga. Nevertheless, a distinction is to be made between the Shrimad Bhagavad Gita and the *Shri Yoga Vaisishtha*. The latter did not aim to find bridges between Sufism and Vedanta, as can be observed throughout the technical lexicon. It is totally devoted to the philosophy of the Vedanta, and one can only very rarely find an Islamic word or expression given as the equivalent of the Sanskrit one.

In the first work, there is an obvious attempt to find parallels between both spiritual paths, but in any case, R. M. Hari starts from the Hindu text, and thus Hindu spirituality, which is followed with a comment, not always, which includes the finding of equivalents in the Sufi terminology.

The method used by R. M. Hari was comprehensive. Let us have a look at a sample: 'The stage of ecstasy and trance is absorption in the "sirgun" form of Atma. There are three ways to attain this stage. (i) Abhyas-Sumran (Recitation of mantras-zikur), (ii) Vivek- (Deep thinking-Fikur-Ghour Khouz), (iii) Dhyan (Meditation-Tasawur)' (Hari 1982: 182). Some comments are necessary here. First, Hari aimed at building equivalencies. They are first of all linguistics, lexical and then conceptual. The author never provided any contextualization regarding the Sufi technical lexicon: it is quoted only as an equivalent of a Vedantic term and concept. Second, he stays at the level of the notions, without any practical indications. Here I am speaking of the rituals that are necessary to move from one step to another. Beyond stating the similarity of the goal, the merging in God, Hari went further in claiming that the Sufi path is also similar to the Vedantic path.

In the introduction, Hari clearly argues that all of the 'perfect Masters' have mentioned the four stages which the seekers of Truth have to go through. The first one is 'Dharma=Religion=Sharyat', then 'Karma=Action=Tariqat', 'Bhakti=Devotion=Haqiqat', and 'Gyan=Perfect Knowledge of Atma=Marfat' (Hari 1982: 17–18). As expressed before, Hari's endeavour is meritorious, because it is not only, according to my knowledge, the first comprehensive attempt achieved by a Hindu Sufi with a Sindhi background to openly link Sufism with Vedanta but also a testimony to the two paradoxical trends in which the Hindu Sindhi Sufism of India was torn apart in the 1980s and the 1990s. On the one hand, it shows off a strong will to keep the Sufi legacy alive, and on the other hand, the spirituality is deeply rooted in the Hindu scriptures. In this construction, Sufism only plays the role of a non-essential repertoire and reservoir for the spirituality.

As mentioned earlier, the main written legacy published by Hari is the *Ke saitun sajnan san urf Sain (Daktar) Rochaldas Sahib ji satsangi rihan*, later on translated into English and published in 1995, and republished in 1998, with the title *Some Moments with the Master. Spiritual Dialogues with the Sufi Saint*. For Hari, a question and answer session was the best form for introducing Rochaldas's spirituality. In classical Sufism, it is a very common literary tradition known as *malfuzat*. In fact, Hari compiled the notes taken by different devotees. The pattern for each of the thirty-nine meetings is the depiction of a day as spent by Rochaldas, usually divided into two parts: singing of devotional songs and spiritual discussion, what they call *satsang*. Sometimes there is a narrator, but it is not state whether this is meant to be Hari or someone else. Sometimes Rochaldas is at home in Ulhasnagar, or he is visiting his disciples or relatives in another city of India.

Most of the issues pertaining to Sufism, and Vedanta, are addressed. A disciple asks a question of Rochaldas – most of the time after a scripture has been read, but not always. The benefit of *satsang* is itself a topic, and Rochaldas stresses the necessity to have *satsang* since reading the scripture is not sufficient. As a matter of fact, the guidance is needed through the *satguru*, to whom two sessions are devoted.

Throughout the book, we learn Rochaldas was very keen to meet other saints. One of the most interesting chapters regards his meeting with Sadhu Vaswani. On 23 May 1957, Rochaldas comes to Poona to meet him, and Sadhu Vaswani asks him to deliver a sermon. His sermon is a comment on Shah Abd al-Latif's verses, completed by quotations from the *Jap Sahib*.[7] It focuses on the importance of the *shabd* (Hari 1995: 117–23). The book also provides interesting information about the precariousness in which the Sindhi refugees lived after their migration. Rochaldas had a single room in Ulhasnagar, its function changing according to the different parts of the day and the night. At some times, it was a free dispensary, and then it would be turned into a spiritual place where *satsang*s were organized, and later on it would become a dormitory.

Turning back to the Sufi legacy as expressed in the book, we see that the main themes are the holy word (*shabd*, *jap* or *zikr*), breath control (*pranayama*), service and charity (*seva* and *dan*), annihilation of the self (*fanai*), renunciation (*vairagya*) and above all love (*ishq*), to which nine chapters are devoted. All of Rochaldas's elaborations upon these issues are rooted in literature straddling Sufi poets' quotations. Besides Sufi quotations, another method used to strengthen his argument is the narratives. The narratives can come from his own life or from the lives of saints, or even from those of other characters. For example, in an example from the last category, he refers to Majnun and Laila.

Let us take a look at a passage when Rochaldas answers a disciple's question related to the different stages of *ishq*.

Interestingly, the issue of *ishq* is addressed on the very day of Krishna's birthday, known as Janamashtmi. Many *bhajan*s are sung for the occasion and two of them, one by Mirabai and the other by Dalpat Sufi, focus on the issue of love. The first claims it has made her mad, and the second that has burnt him. Later on, Rochaldas also quotes verses from Kabir, Bedil, Sachal and Ajiz[8] (Hari 1995: 190–9). Back to the issue of the stages of *ishq*, Rochaldas starts with commenting on Hadi Bakhsh's verses. The sermon wishes to establish there are two different kinds of *ishq*: the *ishq majazi* or physical love, also understood as *saguna prem*. The other *ishq* is the *ishq haqiqi*, the mystical love or *nirguna prem*. For Rochaldas, the concentration on the form of the *guru* belongs to *ishq haqiqi*, because of his subtle nature.

Finally, while his disciples ask for more and more explanations about the difference between the two *ishq*s, Rochaldas takes two persons as symbols. Majnun is the symbol of *ishq majuzi*, while Lal Shahbaz Qalandar is the symbol of *ishq haqiqi*. Rochaldas elaborates more on the first, but later on, he will add that, at first, the beloved was a person, for example a Master, and then the beloved was God. Thus, in *ishq haqiqi*, there was no intermediary, no mediation. The reason why Rochaldas does not elaborate more on *ishq haqiqi* is because it is a matter of secrecy. One can understand that reaching the stage of *ishq haqiqi* is to reach the divine. Rochaldas gives several Sufi quotations in which the poets warn the disciple not to expose that they have gained the *ishq haqiqi*; otherwise, their destiny will be that of Mansur Hallaj. For example, Rochaldas quotes Shah Abd al-Latif's verses, where the poets express that silence is golden, and exposure is harmful, and that love is great but secrecy is greater (Hari 1995: 211).

Another author belonging to Rochaldas's school authored a non-poetic elaboration of Sufism: S. L. Gajwani, whose name was already mentioned in previous chapters. Born in 1937, he was a close follower of R. M. Hari since Hari was grateful to him for typing out the manuscript of Shrimad Bhagavad Gita and checked it many times. Beyond his small book on the Sindhi Sufi literature in independent India, his main work is titled a *Sufi Galaxy* and published in 2000, with the subtitle: *Sufi Qalandar Hazrat Sai Qutub Ali Shah, his Spiritual Successors and Select Disciples – Sufi Saints of the Present Times*.

It is amazing to observe that there is no mention of Rochaldas in the title, but only references to Qutub Ali Shah and Sufism. Gajwani nonetheless did not produce personal reflection, but rather a kind of summary of Rochaldas and Hari's thoughts.

In fact, almost half of the book is devoted to the Jahaniyyan lineage, especially to the founder Qutub Ali Shah, and two of his direct successors, Roshan Ali Shah and Hadi Bakhsh, all three having composed highly praised Sufi poetry in Sindhi. This portion is followed by a part on Bhai Gobindram (1886–1921), another disciple of Qutub Ali Shah who was very close to Rochaldas, and whose *versi* is celebrated in the *darbar* of Shantinagar. Finally, the last two parts of the work explain the life and works of both Rai Rochaldas and R. M. Hari. Gajwani underscores the fact that both had the *dastarbandi* ceremony performed by the *sajjada nashin* of Qutub Ali Shah's *dargah* from Hyderabad. The Sufi *pir* came for it from Pakistan twice, in 1957 and in 1980. All in all, Gajwani's *Sufi galaxy* questions the importance of Sufism among the Hindu Sindhis of India. As a matter of fact, though, his book only concerns Rochaldas's path – whether his enterprise reflects a main trend or is an isolated initiative.

Among the three Hindu Sufi paths under study, a last non-poetical elaboration should be mentioned: that of the Mulchand Faqir's path. Similar to Hari's work, it belongs to the *malfuzat* genre or conversations between the Master and his followers, as well as to that of the *latifas*. Mulchand's main follower and successor in India, Gehimal Motwani, published two books: *Jivan charitra Sufi Darvish Faqir Mulchand Sahib Sehwan navesi*, the *Biography of Mulchand Faqir Born in Sehwan*, and *Manzil illahi*, or the *Station of God*. The *Jiwan Charitra Sufi Darvesh Faqir Mulchand Sahab Sehwan nivasi* was published in 1965, three years after Mulchand's demise. As the title shows, the book primarily provides a spiritual biography of Mulchand, with a number of Sufi *kalam*s he authored. To some extent, the book is as much Gehimal's own story as it is Mulchand's. The seventh chapter is a description of Gehimal's meeting with Mulchand, and how he was initiated by him (*nam vathan*) (Motwani 1965: 35–45). *Manzil-e illahi*, published in 1969, is a description of the different steps for reaching the divine state.

The *Manzil illahi* exposes the main themes on which Mulchand meditated. It is interesting that Gehimal published the book some years after Mulchand's demise, and also paradoxical to some extent when one knows it is said that Mulchand did not speak, and that he did not want his tradition to be transmitted. However, the book is divided into twenty-five short chapters that are arranged according to question and answer sessions between Gehimal and Mulchand. It is significant to see how they place Rochaldas and Hari's conceptions of Hindu Sufism. Great importance is, for example, given to *pranayama*, to which the nineteenth chapter is devoted (Motwani 1969: 115–17). Not surprisingly, another chapter is devoted to the issue of 'tasawuf ain vedanta' (Sufism and Vedanta), and their similar goal of being in tune with the Infinite (Motwani 1969: 67).

The sixth chapter is about *om shabd*, namely the sacred word on which meditation is based. All of the chapters are similarly framed, in that they start with a question asked by Gehimal to Mulchand. In this case, Gehimal asks him: 'Sain, Om shabd ma'ani cha ahe?' ('Master, what is the meaning of the word Om?'). Interestingly, Mulchand references Patanjali offering his response: according to the sage (*rishi*), *om* was 'the name of god' (*ishwar jo nalo*) (Motwani 1969: 39). The very word *om* goes back to the Vedas and it is also the main provider of the divine energy, the *shakti*, but Mulchand also quotes Sachal Sarmast's poetry in his explanation (Motwani 1969: 40).

Regarding the relation between Mulchand and the Sufi poets of Sindh, one can find the same references seen in Hari and Rochaldas's work. It may be that Bedil's domination is still stronger, though. We also notice only one quotation from Shah Abd al-Latif, and two from Sachal. Otherwise, it is relevant to claim that the Sufi poetry is mainly coming from Sufi poets, such as Rohal, Murad, Darya Khan, Ghulam Ali and Kamal.[9] The choice of these poets instead of the most acclaimed, such as Shah Abd al-Latif, who was much quoted in Rochaldas's spiritual dialogues, should mean something. My hypothesis is that the selected poets signify those who were closer to the Hindu tradition, as we saw in Chapter 3. They used open and direct references to the Hindu gods.

All in all, it is difficult to evaluate the impact of the non-poetic publications among the Hindu Sufis of India and their followers. Was Hari's work read by Mulchand or Nimano's followers? In fact, what were the relations between the Hindu Sufi masters and their respective followers? Unfortunately, I was not able to collect answers for this issue. Notwithstanding this ambiguity, the role played by non-poetic literature in the transmission of Sufism is much less significant than the poetic legacy.

Other networks of transmission

The three Hindu Sufis mentioned above – namely Rochaldas, Mulchand Faqir and Nimano Faqir – were probably the three main figures of what we can call Hindu Sufism from Sindh. Nonetheless, they were not the sole figures in this trend. This can be observed through the different Sufi *kalam*s that have been published in post-partition India. In this respect, it is interesting and important to observe that a number of Sufi *kalam*s in Sindhi which have been published in India are still unpublished in Pakistan. In this respect, the small sixty-eight-page book published by Sunder Lal Gajwani in 1997 is quite useful as an introduction to the Hindu Sufis in independent India (Gajwani 1997).

Often, the other Hindu Sufis are known through their *kalam*s, although they not have been published yet. In terms of followers, one can state that they did not really give birth to a path, a *panth*. Others do not even have a place of worship, be it even a *samadhi*. In the case of Isar Lal (1835–95), there was one, but after the departure of the main followers, nobody was able to take care of it. Consequently, we could speak of individual chains of the transmission of Sufism. According to my knowledge, Bhagwan K. Ajwani (1920–2001) is not worshipped in any place in India or abroad. He nonetheless was a prolific author of Sufi poetry in Sindhi. He was born in Hingorja near Khairpur. After graduating with a B.A. in Sindh, he migrated to Delhi where he secured a job. His devotion to the Sindhi Sufis and his Sufi knowledge made the people give him the title of *Sain Raz*, or the 'Master of the Mystery'.

Isarlal or Ishwar Lal (1835–95) is one of those Hindu Sufis from Sindh who are still to be discovered. With his cousin, Lachhman Bhatia from Ahmedabad, who was a good writer of Arabic Sindhi script, Manu Bhatia took the trouble of publishing a *kalam* in two scripts: the Arabic Sindhi and the Devanagari (Isarlal 2012). Now work is ongoing on a new version in the romanized script, with an English translation. While the Sufi paths of the three figures under study here are well organized, there are other places devoted to other Hindu Sufis from Sindh. They share a main feature: their activities are not reduced to

Sufi sessions. Often, they also provide medical help and educational help to the destitute. Bhagwan Advani and Isar Lal have no *samadhi*, and their memory is embodied in the Sufi poetry they have composed.

The role of the diaspora in the transmission of the Sufi legacy

We previously saw the key role played by the Hindus of Sindh in the transmission of the Sufi legacy up through partition. The work of Jethmal Parsram is exemplary in this respect. After partition, Panjwani himself started to highlight Sufism as the core of Sindhi culture, but later on he turned to the making of Jhulelal as the community God of the Hindu Sindhis of India. But between the statement of the importance of the 'spirit of Sufism' in Sindhi culture and the Sufi practice in India among the Hindu Sindhis, what is presently the situation of Sindhi Sufism in India? Of course, the Sufi legacy is transmitted through initiation from masters to disciples, as is the norm in all of the Sufi *tariqa*s, as well as by other chains of transmission, both collective and individual.

The Sufi legacy is still apparent in the three *darbar*s examined here, although we have observed a slow but regular hinduization due to different factors, including the global hinduization of the Hindus in India, this being reinforced by the policy of the BJP which is ruling the country. Except for the *darbar*s of the three Sufi figures, and a few other places, the survival of the Sufi practice is most often private, and reduced to the singing of Sufi songs in Sindh. Here, 'private' means that it is organized by a small circle of devotees, and any event, such as the *versi* of the Master, is organized in flats. Another way through which the Sufi legacy of Sindh is transmitted is via the field of cultural events, such as *bhagat*s. The *bhagat* is a cultural artist whose repertoire straddles theatre plays, jokes, songs, prayers and folk narratives. Thus, the *bhagat*'s repertoire always includes Sufi poetry – *Shah jo Risalo* – first as well as other Sufi *kalam*s. Nonetheless, it is an oral transmission.[10]

Some non-Sindhi Sufis are also honoured through a publication, such as the most popular Sufi saint of Baghdad, Abd al-Qadir al-Jilani (Gajwani 1997: 13), whose Persian poetry was translated into Sindhi. In this category, we also find Rumi and Attar, two Sufi luminaries belonging to the Persianate world. It is noteworthy that some works were totally innovative, such as Hiro Thakur's edition of Qazi Qazan's *kalam* in 1978. Before, only seven verses (*baits*) were known, and only since they were quoted by Shah Karim in his own *kalam*. In India, a manuscript of 112 verses was discovered in a Dadupanthi monastery in Haryana, and this manuscript was edited and published by Hiro Thakur. This work is remarkable because Qazi Qazan's Sufi poetry is the oldest known Sufi poetry from Sindh – and, by the way, the oldest piece of Sindhi literature. This said, the language is difficult, and a critical edition would be most useful, as well as an English translation, although short English abstracts can be found in Panikker's anthology (Paniker 2000).

Unfortunately, Gajwani's bibliographical research stopped in the mid 1990s. Since then, only a few Sufi works have been published, so that one can surmise there is a shortage of interest. Nonetheless, the 2000s publications related to Sindhi Sufism unveil a main issue: the issue of script, coupled with that of language, with a dominant trend towards romanization although the Arabic Sindhi is still used. Gajwani decided to publish in English, and we can therefore surmise he wanted to reach the young and educated Sindhi generation of India, as well as the Diaspora Sindhis who are mostly English-speaking. At the same time, Kiku Motwani translated her father's book on Mulchand into Hindi. Once again, she wished to reach as many young Sindhis of India as possible. In both cases, the authors discarded the use of Sindhi. Another interesting publication in this regard is Sugnaram Mangadas Ladkani's book, *Siraiki kalam al-Sufiya*, published in 2000 by the Indian Institute of Sindhology.

As the title informs us, it is a 200-page anthology of Sindhi Sufi poetry in Siraiki, the Sindhi dialect mostly spoken in Northern Sindh,[11] and especially among the Baluchi population. For the majority of the specialists, it is considered the Northern dialect of Sindhi, while for others it is a distinct language from the Siraiki of South Punjab. It is a fact that many Sindhi Sufi poets, especially from Northern Sindh, composed Sufi poetry in several languages. The book opens with a short introduction on the Siraiki language and literature written by one Pritam Variyyani. The anthology is made up of *kalam*s and *dohira*s, composed by different Sufi poets from Sindh. Non-Sindhi poets are also quoted, including Bullhe Shah, Shah Bahu and Ghulam Farid (Ladkani 2000: 170–80).

In 2009, Rochaldas's *darbar* published a small booklet named *Venti ain prarthana* in romanized script. It contains *madah*s and *munajat*s, and also *arti* and *bhajan*s authored by Rochaldas, Qutub Ali Shah and Roshan Ali Shah. There is also the famous *Sakhi sabhajal* (*Venti ain prarthana* 34). In December of 2011, the Nimanal Sangam of Vadodara published a selection of Nimano Faqir's *kalam* in romanized script, titled *Nimanal Maan. Puj Nimala Sai jin ja Kalaam.* Interestingly, one cannot find Sachal's poetry, while in original Nimano's *kalam*, he was given a large part of the poetry. Guru Nanak's poetry has been kept in this new edition. The book ends with the *arti*, this preceded by a *dua jo kalam*, a text in praise of Nimano, both authored by Nirmal Jani, the present *gaddi nashin* of the Nimanal Sangam (Nimanal Maan 2011: 327–8).

Still, other recent publications in the 2010s reflect a different choice: they keep the Sindhi language, but with two different alphabets, the Arabic Sindhi and the Roman. In 2016, Manu Bhatia and his cousin Lachhman Bhatia decided to publish Isarlal's *kalam* from the manuscript they had inherited. This manuscript was written in Arabic Sindhi, and it was easier to publish it in this alphabet. Nevertheless, they quickly realized it would have been more efficient to publish it in romanized script for having a larger market: it allows to keep the use of the Sindhi language, in a script well spread among the Sindhis.

Yet, it is not a coincidence that the Diaspora Sindhis played a leading role in the 'romanization' of the Sindhi language. Following the romanized Sindhi alphabet adopted in the 18th International Sindhi Samelan in Ahmedabad in 2011, Manju Mirchandani and her husband Kamal Mirchandani definitively opted for this option, since they are based in California, in the United States. Two volumes of *Roohani Choond Sindhi kalaam* (*A Spiritual Anthology of Sindhi kalam*s) have already been published in 2008, and re-edited in 2009 and in 2012. In the first volume published before the meeting (*samelan*) in Ahmedabad, the author called the script she used 'roman', and in the second, she followed the samelan recommendations in calling it 'romanized'. The romanized script has already been used by Hindu Sufi paths that spread overseas.

The romanized Sindhi script is a kind of averaging of the official transliteration of Arabic Sindhi into Roman script used in Sindh[12] and the common 'Englishized' script the Sindhis used for writing messages, an activity that has been increased tenfold with the spread of social media. Regarding the contents of Mirchandani's *Roohani choond*, it follows the same pattern used by Panjwani and Chawla's works. Each volume offers 108 *kalam*s, with a short bibliography, while the main innovation is that every *kalam* has an English abstract composed by Manju's husband, Kamal Mirchandani. One can understand this initiative as a wish to provide some contextualization to the *kalam* as well as a will to fill in for a lack of knowledge among the young generation of overseas Sindhis.

Since then there has been something of a loss of interest in the Sufi legacy in India. Some endeavours should nevertheless be mentioned. As we already saw, Gehimal's daughter Kiku Motwani Bhalla published a Hindi translation of his biography of Mulchand Faqir (Motwani 1965: 2012). Another initiative came from a Sindhi gentleman based in Bangalore, Manu Bhatia, who wanted the *kalam* of the Sufi Master of his father and grandfather to be published.

Conclusion

Despite the many changes that Hindu Sufism in India has been through, which I shall briefly coin as hinduization, it is amazing to see how the Hindu Sufis are still active in terms of transmitting the Sufi legacy, even beyond the practices performed in the *darbar*s and the *samadhi*s. The main tool used by the Hindu Sindhis of India is publishing. As we know, they already played a leading role in this process in late nineteenth-century Sindh. In independent India, the Sindhi Hindus published books related to Sufism from the 1950s onwards. This means that, as soon as they had found a place to settle, they undertook the duty to publish Sufi-related books. Of course, Ram Panjwani will reach the highest fame, but other Hindu Sindhis were also keen to disseminate the Sufi legacy of Sindh. Sadhu T. L. Vaswani was himself partly moulded by the Sufi legacy of Sindh, as he himself expressed in his autobiography.

Nonetheless, Ram Panjwani was influential throughout his many achievements pertaining to almost all of the fields related to Sindhi culture, what he would call Sindhiyyat. He himself published Sufi anthologies as early as the 1950s. While it is impossible to know how the public Sufi cults will evolve in the future, it may be that the Sufi legacy will be more and more of a 'private affair', to quote Manu Bhatia. But the delimitation between a private cult and a public cult is not easy to find. It can be a private affair when a *versi* is organized in a private flat, but when more than 100 followers attend the event, is it still a private affair? In this case, it is at least still private if there is no institutional organization managing and organizing the event, as was the case for Isarlal's *versi* as organized by Manu Bhatia's parents.

Turning back to Ram Panjwani, we note that while he was very successful in imposing Jhulelal as the Sindhi god of India par excellence, the role of the Sufi legacy in the making of Sindhiyyat did not reach such fame. This was due to many factors, first being the need for the migrant and unwelcomed Sindhis to exhibit a Hindu identity interwoven with their Sindhi origins. Also, the personality and the charisma of Ram Panjwani were obviously instrumental in the success of the Jhulelal enterprise. It may be that the Sufi legacy lacked such a leader, but one can hardly think this was the main reason for the decline in the process of Sindhiyyat formation Sufism, generally perceived to be an Islamic expression, could hardly have been selected for being the foundation of Sindhiyyat in an independent, Hindu-dominated India.

Although it is not so developed as the poetic expression, another chain of transmission is non-poetic Sufi literature. In this field, R. M. Hari is by far the most important contributor. But, if his work is remarkable, it is difficult to know its impact on the Sindhis of India, beyond the circle of Rochaldas's followers. Among Mulchand's circle, two non-poetic works were published, but once again, it is doubtful they are widespread and well known outside of the circle of his followers. We have observed many convergences between both versions of non-poetic Sufism, both in terms of structures – or, how the books are built – and devotional references and mystical concepts.

While publishing is probably the most visible form of transmission, social networks should be added. The Hindu Sindhis have developed a powerful diaspora all over the world. Since the 2000s, the Arabic Sindhi alphabet has been mostly abandoned, with some punctual exceptions, such as Isarlal's *kalam*. The real issue the Diaspora Sindhis are facing is that of the dismissal of the Devanagari script that the young overseas Sindhis will no longer know. The main option to combat this trend is the romanization of the Sindhi language. This is a new step in the history of the Sufi legacy among the Hindu Sindhis, and already it has been started by California Hindu Sindhis. The Marchandanis have been the pioneers since they already published Sufi anthologies in Roman script, these especially targeting the young English-speaking generation.

The hinduization of Indian politics and society has often been referred to as a main factor explaining the withdrawal of the Sufi legacy in India. In Pakistan, despite the mass migration, the Sindhi Hindus number several millions, with a majority of them belonging to the so-called scheduled castes, mostly Menghwars, Bhils and Kohlis. The country has undergone, since the late 1980s, different steps of islamization, a process that would better be called sunnization. The goal of leaders such as Ziya al-Haqq was to gradually impose the *sharia*, a legal system in which the religious minorities are officially discriminated against. In this South Asian context marked by a rigidification of religious affiliation and representation, it is now relevant to wonder how the Hindu Sufis of Pakistan deal with the Sufi legacy of Sindh. How do the Hindu Sufis of Pakistan face the increasing islamization of the country, not to speak of how they face the increasing violence towards them, including such practices as forced conversions mostly implemented by alleged Sufi *murshids*? The next chapter aims at providing a survey of the Pakistani Hindu Sindhis in relation to the Sufi legacy. The final goal of this project aims to provide a kind of mirrored perspective, intermingling the Sindhi Hindu Sufis of India with those of Pakistan.

The Sufi paths and the Hindus
of Sindh in Pakistan

The Hindu Sindhis who migrated to India from 1947 onwards created new Sufi *darbar* shrines in their new country. The Sufi shrines were among the other paths which were transferred to India, and there was no uniform policy, so the Sufis had to find a place to stay just like thousands of other Hindu Sufis. Every Sufi path has been built by a saint who was the core of the veneration, expressed through poetry as well as through rituals. But despite the diversity of the paths, a general process did impact the Hindu Sufis of India. This process imposed a shortage of a number of rituals seeming 'too Muslim' inside the growing hinduization dynamics of the country. For example, the *dhamal* was stopped once Mulchand's shrine was settled in the classic Hindu pilgrimage city of Haridwar. But in the Sindhi-dominated environment of Ulhasnagar, it is still performed in Rochaldar's *darbar*. Consequently, as expected, the Sufi paths have been reshaped in the context of the local and regional set-ups.

The Hindu Sufis of India have many challenges to deal with, some of them being no different from those which all of the Hindu Sindhis of India have to face. The first challenge was obviously the issue of language, coupled with that of the script. The Sindhi language had long been written in several scripts, but in India and among the diaspora, not only has the Arabic Sindhi almost been lost but also the Devanagari is becoming problematic for young Western-settled generations. As we saw in the previous chapter, a trend seems to be more and more dominant: to publish the Sindhi devotional literature, including the Sufi poetry, in a romanized Sindhi script.

Although a large majority of Hindus have migrated to India from 1947 onwards, Sindh is the province of Pakistan with the most significant Hindu population. The province of Sindh now belongs to Pakistan, a country that has been through different steps of islamization. Despite the islamization, though, and despite the spread of Islamist terrorism in Sindh as in other parts of Pakistan, I argue that the Sufi culture still pervades Sindhi society. Seventy years after partition, it is fruitful to mirror the situation of the Hindu Sufis from Sindh against those in India. This comparison will facilitate an underscoring of the particular feature of the Sufi legacy among the Hindu Sindhis of India. Furthermore, it will allow us to balance the representation suggesting that the integrative function performed by Sufism is currently weakened in Sindh. Here again, the situation is far more complex than the current depiction we can find in the media. Sufism does not organically imply tolerance towards other religions. For example, the most active people working for the conversion of young Hindu girls to Islam are well-known Sufi *pirs*.[1] The ideology of the *wahdat-e wujud* stating that there is only one God, and that rather there is no prerequisite related to the religious belonging of a Sufi, is not accepted by all of the Sufi *tariqas*.

What is presently the relationship that the Hindus of Sindh have with Sufism in Sindh? Do they visit the Sufi shrines, and above all, are they involved in the Sufi institutions? Are there Sufi Hindus in Sindh, meaning Sindhi Hindus living like Sufis? This last chapter will address all of these issues, with the primary purpose of deciphering if a process of distinction is at work between the Hindu Sufis of Pakistan and those of India. Consequently, the final goal is to see if the circulation of the *Sindh ji Sufiyyani saqafat* still permeates the two 'national sides' of Sindhiyyat, in Pakistan and in India.

Sindhi encounters between Sufism and Hinduism

As we saw in the introduction, the encountering which has occurred between Islam and Hinduism is a widely studied topic in the field of South Asian studies. In the field of Sindh studies, however, there is no published research related to Sufism and the Hindu Sufis in Sindh. The publications on the issue, as we saw in the introduction, always deal with India. In Sindh, there are different ways through which the Hindus are related to Sufism, according to which three categories of encountering can be distinguished. Most of the time, the encountering process is attached to a place. The first category is the most common: a sacred place is a Sufi tomb which is visited both by Muslims and Hindus. For example, this is the case with Shah Abd al-Latif's *darbar* in Bhit Shah. The religious identity of the saint is not challenged: he was a Muslim, a Sayyid, who was a *wujudi*, preaching throughout his poetry the Oneness of God. The Hindus belonging to different paths and castes come every day and for the annual *urs*. They go to the tomb, circumambulating around it, touching it, and then attend the *Shah jo rag*, the singing of Shah's poetry by the local *faqirs*.

The second category is also relatively common. It is a sacred place hosting one or two tombs and catafalques, and the saint has a double identity, Muslim and Hindu. The best example is the *darbar* of Udero Lal. The Hindus worship Jhulelal, who they claim to be an *avatar* of the Vedic God Varun. The Muslims venerate a Sufi, Shaykh Tahir, who could have been a Sohrawardi. In this case, this is a shared space, but only the Hindus pay a visit to Shaykh Tahir's tomb. The Muslims do not go to the space devoted to Jhulelal.[2] The annual fair is performed separately, and there is a *gaddi nashin* for the Hindus and a *sajjada nashin* for the Muslims. Such a scenario should not be idealized since the groups interact very little, and many disputes arise regularly. In other places, there is only a tomb, but the Hindus give the saint a distinct identity. In Sehwan Sharif, Lal Shahbaz Qalandar is said to be Raja Barthari, or Raja Vir. Many years back, it is said that there was a *lingam* inside the *dargah*. In this configuration, there is only one annual fair, in which the Hindus play a leading ritual role. Sehwan will be one of the case studies in this chapter.

The third category is a place where a Sufi *darbar* is managed by the Hindus. A significant example is that of Pithoro Pir, located between Mirpur Khas and Umerkot. Pithoro Pir, to which I shall return in the last part of this chapter, was initiated to the Sohrawardi *tariqa* by Baha al-Din Zakariyya. Thus, nobody challenges the fact that the saint was a Sufi. Notwithstanding, the shrine is managed by Hindus claiming to belong to the Rajputs. These would be the descendants of Pithoro's brother, since he was himself a renunciant who never married. The followers of Pithoro Pir are mostly Hindus but also include Muslims. The Hindus are almost all from Dalit castes, with a huge amount of Menghwars. But despite the Sufi identity of Pithoro, which is expressed in the devotional songs, the *darbar* exhibits a Hindu identity in the architecture and inscriptions. The 'Sufi' shaped tomb of Pithoro Pir is surmounted by a huge

Om. There is also in the courtyard an altar devoted to Shiva. Apparently, this does not prevent local Muslims from attending the annual fair in September every year.

While the Hindus of Sindh visit the Sufi shrines, there is also the case of the Hindu Sufis who did not migrate to India as followers of the Sindhi Sufis. For example, Mukund Bhatia was close to the Sufi poet, Kojhi, which is the pen name of Muhammad Bakhsh Shaikh (1891–1959), whose Sufi *kalam* is still much appreciated among the Sindhis in India and in Pakistan. He became one of the closest followers of the *sajjada nashin* of Daraza at the point when he became his *khalifa*. While his brothers left Sindh for India, he decided to stay. Another Hindu Sufi decided to stay in Pakistan: Sobhraj Faqir (1901–81). He belonged to the Harjani family who fully migrated to India. He was often in company with Mulchand Faqir and they were both fond of *dhamal*, as they used to perform together. Sobhraj wanted to stay for the ending of his life in Sehwan Sharif, which he did. His *kalam* was published in India in 1997 (Sobhraj 1997). Interestingly, his brother Gidumal Khatanmal Harjani, who had migrated to Ulhasnagar, was the publisher of Dalpat Sufi's *kalam* in 1965 (Dalpat Sufi 1965).

Turning back to the issue of encountering, and of the places where this process occurs, we see that the basic typology presented in the beginning of the chapter has excluded some elements that cannot fit into these categories; in other words, there are some exceptions. Nonetheless, this chapter is based on the study of three different cases. The first case is that of Sehwan Sharif, a main Sufi pilgrimage centre of Sindh, where the *darbar* of Lal Shahbaz Qalandar is located. The second case is a Sufi shrine ran by the Lohana Hindus in a small village named Tando Ahmed Khan. The third case study that we should now examine is how the Sufi legacy is managed in the lower castes of the Hindu community.

The Hindus and the Sehwan system

Sehwan Sharif is a small town located in central Sindh, between the Indus River and Lake Manchhar, coiled in the Aral Wah and linking both. Before partition, the Hindus made up about half of the total population, and the town hosted two main Hindu temples. The first one was devoted to Shiva and settled in the north-eastern part of the town. The other one was devoted to Jhulelal and was established on the north-western side of the town. From 1947 onwards, almost all of the Hindu population migrated to India. All the Thakurs, the priestly caste of Jhulelal, left Sindh to settle in India, especially in Bombay and Ulhasnagar. In Sehwan, they could have been the most powerful Hindu group, and in Bombay, there is still a Sehwani *panchayat* which has published several directories of the Sehwanis in India and overseas since partition. For some time now, the Sehwani *panchayat* has had a Facebook page.[3]

As could be said of many other Sufi *dargah*s, the Hindus use to come to pay homage to Lal Shahbaz Qalandar. But in Sehwan they are integrated into the system of the *kafis*, what I call the Sehwani system.[4] The Sehwani system is made up of a number of Sufi lodges, settled all around Lal Shahbaz Qalandar's *darbar*. There are complex relationships of authority and dependence between the different holders of the Sufi lodges. Nonetheless, two lineages dominate the system, both being Sayyids. The Lakkiyaris are usually accepted as being the head of the system, but the Sabzwaris also share the symbolic power since the shrine itself came under government control in the 1960s.

Two *kafis* are currently managed by Hindus. The first is the *kafi* of Lal Das and the second is that managed by Ramdas (or Ramchand), which is Mulchand Kafi. Mulchand Kafi is situated to the east of the *darbar* of Lal Shahbaz and it adjoins the *kafi* of Doda Mard Haqani. Although Hindus are very few in number in Sehwan today, it should be noted that Mulchand Kafi works to a certain extent as a place of community worship. Concerning the cult of Lal Shahbaz proper, although it is true that the *kafi* is open to the public mainly on the occasion of the *urs*, certain ceremonies of the cycle of life are always realized there. The centre of these ceremonies is a cubic building composed of a single room. In its centre is a brick construction that is the *qabr* (tomb) of Mulchand Faqir. This construction is four or five times the size of an ordinary grave. No decoration or inscription appears, but it is covered, as is the tradition, with a chador. Additionally, the *kafi* shelters the cremation ground of the Hindus of Sehwan.

Lal Das was a Hindu from Kashmir who came to make the pilgrimage to Sehwan Sharif. He devoted nearly forty years of his life to serving Lal Shahbaz Qalandar. He was in charge of lighting the lamps (*chiraghi wala*) before extinguishing himself 'in the smell of sanctity' in 1993. He himself had disciples who raised a small *dargah* not far from his Master's. His devotees regularly receive his blessing, whether Hindu or Muslim. His alleged son, Lal Gul, performs the *mehndi* during the *urs*. Before the procession, there is a musical session in a house, with the presence of the head of the Lakkiyyaris, Murad Shah. Therefore, there are three *mehndi* processions organized for the *urs*: on the 18th of Shaban, it is the procession led by the Lakiyyaris, on the 19th it is the one led by Ramchand and on the 20th is that of Lal Gul.

For all categories of people involved in sharing the charisma, the *urs* is also a moment of prime importance. It is at this moment that the position of each one is reaffirmed. These positions, be they honorary or real, can be watched during the implementation of a protocol imposed by the State. This protocol, as well as the distribution of tasks between confessions, has not undergone fundamental change since the partition, with one exception. In the middle of the nineteenth century, Richard Burton mentioned the following custom: 'Every year, a daughter of the Khonbati caste (saffron flower dyers) was married to the grave, with music, dance and all the solemnities due to her' (Burton 1851: 211).

This custom, known as Lal Kunwar (the fiancée of the red), disappeared during the partition in 1947. Here we find the symbolism of marriage, but Burton specifies, however, that the bride was released after a year, though she had to remain forever unmarried. The caste of Khuhnbatis was a caste of dyers specializing in dyeing with the flower of saffron. Their name comes from the Sindhi word *khuhnbo*, which means saffron. *A priori*, this term is reserved for Hindu dyers. In South Asia, dyers are one of the most impure castes, and their status is therefore the lowest. Yet, in the case of the Khuhnbatis, the situation was different because of their specialization. The colour saffron, which corresponds in Sindh to a bright red, is both a religious symbol and a symbol of marriage for the Daryapanthis, the two being related. It should be understood that, in reality, the red (*lal*) and the saffron are one and the same colour. The Khuhnbatis, as saffron specialists, were attributed a priestly function in the ceremony of the mystical nuptials of Lal Shahbaz Qalandar.[5] In the traditional marriage of the Daryapanthis, one of the preparatory ceremonies of marriage is known as the *khuhnbo* ceremony (Thakur 1959: 176). A few days before marriage, members of the caste as well as seven women who are happily married (*sohagan*, which means they are not widows) prepare the saffron colour to dye ceremonial wedding clothes.

That said, according to other sources, the young Lal Kunwar belonged to the caste of Kanungos. The origin of the custom comes from the fact that a young woman of the caste had fallen in love with Lal Shahbaz. The latter being a renouncer, she threw herself from a balcony at his feet, thus sacrificing her life for him. Lal Shahbaz would have been touched by this sacrifice and he would have authorized that, after his death, a young virgin of the caste should be married to his grave. The Lal Kunwar lived for a year in a room where she was venerated as a *devi*, a goddess. When she was released, she was forced to accept celibacy. Despite a relatively thorough investigation, with Pakistani and Indian informants, both Muslim and Hindu, it was not possible to obtain evidence of this chain of events.

Is there a link between this marriage ceremony carried out by the Kanungos, or the Khuhnbatis, and the fact that Hindus are also 'bearers of henna' (*mehndibardars*)? The protocol of the *urs* reflects the balance at which the communities involved in the distribution of the charisma have arrived. Each procession is organized upon the same pattern. It is composed of singers, musicians and dancers. A designated person wears the silk chador, which is deposited on the tomb of the *qalandar*, and places a tray on which the henna (*mehndi*) is located. It is said that the act of depositing the *chador* on the grave

Figure 7.1 Asan Gul, a Hindu *sajjada nashin* in Sehwan Sharif.

amounts to putting the fiancée in her wedding clothes. It is also said that, the next morning, palms and fingerprints are visible in the henna that was deposited the day before. This suggests that, during the night, the qalandar coated his hands with henna and is therefore ready to be united to his divine lover.

Before partition, the first procession was led by Gul Muhammad Lakkiyyari. On the second day, it left the house of the 'Meranis' and 'Nevanis' under the direction of Mulchand Faqir. Finally, on the third day, it started from the house of the Kanungos. Now, the eldest son of Gul Muhammad, Murad Shah, has replaced him to lead the *mehndi* of the first day. The two groups leading the following *mehndi*s have changed. After the death of Mulchand Faqir in 1962, the duty of the *mehndi* was transmitted to his cousin, Mohan Lal, who then passed it on to his son, Ramchand, in 1981. The Kanungos migrated to India in the same year and the burden fell to Lal Das, a Hindu from Kashmir. It is today his son Lal Gul who fulfils this obligation.

No timetable is given for the custom of *mehndi*. It proceeds according to the document of the Awqaf manager in relation to the procession of the *matamis*. The procession is the reproduction of the classic procession of marriage. Each time, the procession runs through the narrow streets of the town while the 'clients' of each party grow more and more numerous. The roofs of the houses are filled with onlookers who do not want to miss this show. In any case, the celebration of the wedding will be repeated on each of the three days of the feast. The only difference will be that, each time, the officials will be different.

In a Pakistan under the pressure of Islamist extremists, it may seem surprising that Hindus can still play a ritual role in the Sufi set-up of Sehwan Sharif. This resilience can be explained primarily by the desire to preserve a historic heritage. But beyond this integrative dynamic of Sufism, it must be understood that the Hindus do not exercise this function as Hindus, but as Hindu Sufis. This is obvious from the fact that the Hindu processions cannot be distinguished from the Muslim ones, and furthermore, nothing especially Hindu can be observed in these devotional events. The Hindu processions are quite similar to all of the processions that take place in the Sufi mausoleums.

One can claim that the Sehwan system is an exception in Pakistan. It may be that it is, indeed, but this does not prevent us from stating that it is still at work. Furthermore, even if it reflects a specific situation, we saw that the Hindus of Sindh are coming to the Sufi mausoleums since the nineteenth century. The interaction between Muslims and Hindus through Sufism can be observed through other perspectives, as well. I shall now focus on a singular case, a shrine located in the Kohistan, in Sindh, which is named the 'Hindu *dargah*'.

The 'Hindu *dargah*' of Tando Ahmad Khan

In April of 2016, I started a new research project on the *darbar* of Udero Lal, the huge sanctuary close to Hyderabad where Hindus and Muslims worship a dual figure: Jhulelal/Shaykh Tahir. With a team, we toured in Southern Sindh to map out the different shrines devoted to Jhulelal in Southern Sindh. Because I had heard for years that Thano Bula Khan hosted many Hindu temples, I asked a Hindu in a village if there was a temple of Jhulelal in the town. He said no, but that there was one in the neighbouring village of Tando Ahmad Khan. I decided to go to the village. There, a number of Hindu shrines belonged to different paths, and I passed by a sanctuary whose golden dome should have shown it was a Sufi *dargah*. In fact, it was the Jhulelal temple, but was not devoted to Jhulelal, the famous god of the Hindu Sindhis. A local follower told me it was a 'Hindu *dargah*' devoted to Lal Shahbaz Qalandar, here worshipped as Jhulelal. Indeed, the sanctum sanctorum was but a replica of the *darbar* of Lal Shahbaz Qalandar in Sehwan Sharif, though settled in a different religious environment.

This unexpected 'discovery' roughly challenges our usual categories. According to them, a *dargah* is a Muslim place, but the Hindu *dargah* of Tando Ahmad Khan hosts Lal Shahbaz Qalandar's tomb, surrounded by Hindu temples, also Sufi *astanas*, and with many inscriptions referring to an array of religious traditions, including the Nanakpanth. I have to confess that there is a scarcity of information about Thano Bula Khan. It is located in the Kohistan, the western part of Sindh that stands close to Baluchistan. It is in the Jamshoro district and the seat of a *taluka*. We learned during our visit that Thano Bula Khan is rich in minerals, and that there are beautiful Burgat tombs in the vicinity. Before visiting the village, I had never heard about any of this, as was the case for many of my Sindhi friends.

Tando Ahmad Khan is a small village, but it hosts important Hindu temples. Near the Hindu *dargah*, about 100 metres away, there is a compound with several

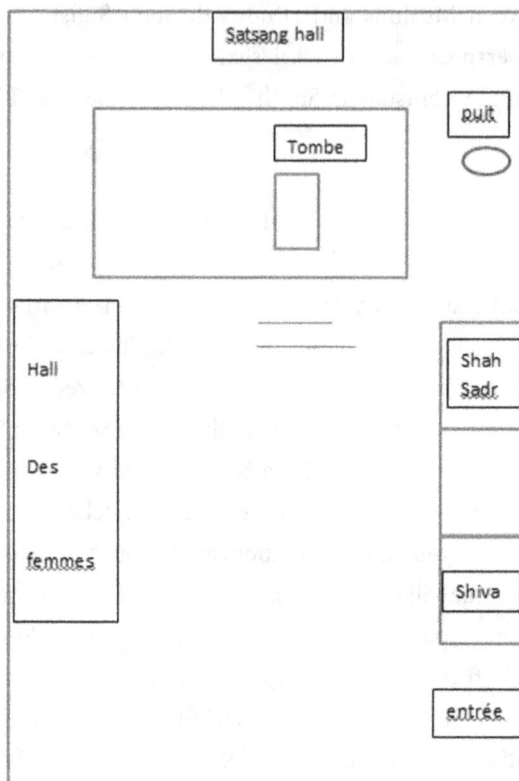

Figure 7.2 Map of the Hindu *dargah*, Tando Ahmad Khan.

Shivaite temples. There is another temple devoted to Raja Vir Vikramaditya. And, about 200 metres from it, there is a *gurdwara*. Consequently, the religious environment is especially varied and Hindu dominated. The local Hindus mostly belong to the Lohana caste, who are also those who built the Hindu *dargah*. It is located in a compound of about 60m × 25m. Before investigating what this Hindu *dargah* told us about the relation between Sufism and the Hindu Sindhis, let us start with a brief description of the shrine's agency.

As we can see on the map, the entrance is followed by a shrine devoted to Shiva, another one to Raja Vir and still another one to Shah Sadr, who is said to have been the Sufi Master of Lal Shahbaz Qalandar in Sindh. The main building where the catafalque is looks like a 'classical' Sufi *dargah*. The tomb is under the dome with a *taj* put on the head of the dead saint. Also, there is a well (*kuh*) on the right side, and a 'satsang hall' behind the *dargah* proper, and I here use the name given there in an inscription. Furthermore, the most amazing point to be made is regarding the different inscriptions. Above the tomb, there are many inscriptions pertaining to different religious traditions. Nonetheless, the biggest one is: *Sab ka malik ek hai*, 'There is only one Master (God)'. This formula has for some years been very popular among the Hindus of Sindh. It could be of Sikh origin, but it was mainly popularized by Sai Baba of Shirdi (1838–1918), the famous Indian saint.

Most of the other inscriptions across the sanctuary refer directly to Jhulelal, the Hindu god, like for instance *Jhulelal bera par* (May Jhulelal safely guide our nave). Furthermore, the presence of a well is also strongly reminiscent of Jhulelal, since he is said to have disappeared in a well set up in the *darbar* of Udero Lal. In this *darbar*, during the annual fair in April of 2016, there was a huge poster staging Shah Abd al-Latif and Jhulelal, with the epigram: *Sab ka malik ek hai*. I would argue this is a renewed version of the *wahdat-e wujud*, expressed in a more 'modern' language, but with a Hindu flavour overall, and bridging the Sindhi figures with the popular Shirdi Sai Baba. Here, 'modern' means that it is a formulation which will be understood by as many people as possible. It is true that this formula fits particularly well with the religious agency of the Hindu *dargah*. It can be framed as a spiritual pilgrimage from Shiva to Lal Shahbaz, who is finally merged through the space's agency in Jhulelal. The phrase *Sab ka malik ek hai* signifies a new policy implemented by the Hindus of Sindh.

What is the final message of the Hindu *dargah*? Do the Lohanas of Sindh want to recapture their Sufi legacy? Or formulate it through a new shape? Or do they want to exhibit a more Islamic setting in the Muslim environment? The first argument seems more relevant since the phrase is notoriously linked to a Hindu context. Furthermore, since the Sufi *dargahs* are now targets of Islamist terrorism,[6] one can wonder about the future of the Hindu *dargah*. More pragmatically, it is difficult not to think that the Hindu *dargah* would have been temporarily closed after the terrible terrorist attack which occurred in Sehwan Sharif in February of 2017. Does it mean there is an opposite process in India and in Pakistan? It is tempting to see the Hindu *dargah* as the reverse of the Sufi *mandir* mentioned above. The latter is located on a small lane of the Sindhi colony in Sion, Mumbai. For someone who is not aware of it, it is almost impossible to find. Contrarily, the Hindu *dargah* is located in a rural area, and one can see it exhibits an accepted relationship between Hinduism and Sufism.

Notwithstanding, and even if it is an isolated scenario, the Hindu *dargah* shows that the Hindus of Sindh are strongly related to their Sufi legacy. Beyond this case that concerns the middle and high Hindu classes of Sindh, a final element is to be examined in relation to the Hindus of Sindh and Sufism. As a matter of fact, the lower groups in the hierarchical system of Brahmanical Hinduism were known under many different names. In Sindh now, there is a debate among the Hindus to determine if the term 'Dalit' is relevant. However, I shall use it for convenience.

Neither Hindu nor Muslim: The Sufi-related cults of the Sindhi Dalits

In Sindh, we already know that a number of sacred figures have a dual religious identity, Muslim and Hindu. The Muslim identity is always related to Sufism, while the Hindu side usually belongs to the Nathpanth. During British colonization, there was much evidence of the flexibility of religious belonging in Sindh. In his famous book on the populations of Sindh published in 1851, Richard Burton stated that different populations of Sindh were 'neither Hindoos nor Moslems'. Burton's statement was explicitly applied to two groups: the Shikaris and the Dheds, while other authors consider the Shikaris as Muslims, and the Dheds as Hindus (Burton 1851: 307, 323).

In this respect, an interesting case study is that of Pithoro Pir. Before coming to the hagiographic legend of the saint, however, it is necessary to wonder about the name that is allotted to him: Pithoro Pir. In the Sindhi context, there are some examples where a Hindu saint can be described as a *shah* and also as a *pir*. That said, nobody disputes that Pithoro Pir was himself a Muslim: neither Burton, nor the present *gaddi nashin*, nor people of any other group. The name of Pithoro, comes from the Sindhi word *pithu*, which means a piece.

A historical character, however, bore the name of Rai Pithora in Muslim sources. Sometimes named Prithvi Raj, he was the last sovereign of the Chauhan dynasty, which was overcome in 1192 by Muhammad Shihab al-Din of Ghor in the second battle of Tarain. This character is the focus of several legends. Amir Khwurd reports in his *Siyar Al-Awliya* (Biographies of the Saints) that Muin al-Din Tchishti, the famous Sufi of Ajmer, captured Prithvi

Raj alive thanks to a miracle before delivering him to the sultan of Ghazni, Muizz al-Din. Rai Pithora appears in another legend relating to Goga Pir. According to another version, Gorakhnath would have sent an invisible army to help Goga Pir against Rai Pithora.

The legend of Pithoro Pir can be summarized as follows. One Madan had asked for the intercession of Baha al-Din Zakariyya (d. 1267) to obtain a son, when the famous Sufi of Multan was touring in Sindh. Baha al-Din offered him a small end (*pithu*) of a dried date. At the moment his wife tasted the blessed piece, she became pregnant. The son whom they had was named Pithoro, or the name of the date end. Thereafter, Pithoro became the disciple of Baha al-Din. The legend of his birth is always identical, except that sometimes, as for example the case with the *gaddi nashin*, the Sufi Master was not Baha al-Din Zakariyya, but Shah Rukn-e Alam (d. 1335), another later saint of Multan. It should, however, be stressed that both Sufis were members of the Sohrawardi order, and that Shah Rukn-e Alam was none other than the grandson and successor of Baha al-Din Zakariyya.

The local tradition adds another episode to the hagiography of Pithoro Pir. The area of Umarkot where he lived had been a place of rough combat between two groups of Rajputs, the Somras and the Sodhas. In 1439, the *rano* (local version of *raja*) Hamir Sodho inflicted a defeat to the Somras. At this time, Pithoro was already a venerated saint who had many *murids*. Their number increased day after day. Hamir Rano was convinced that the final objective of Pithoro Pir was to seize his kingdom. Consequently, the *rano* raised an army and he decided to attack Pithoro Pir. But a miracle turned the situation in Pithoro Pir's favour, and the *rano* did not have any option but to pay homage to him and to require forgiveness. One will notice that the topic of the miraculous victory enclosed already the confrontations which opposed Muin al-Din Tchishti and Goga Pir to Rai Pithora.

From this moment onwards, the subjects of the *rano* made consequent gifts to the *pir*, while the *rano* himself paid a tribute to the same *pir*. The topic of the confrontation of the saint with the representative of the temporal power is consequently a redundant trope of the regional hagiography. Another trope very frequent in Sufi narratives does not appear in the tradition of Pithoro Pir: the confrontation of the Sufi with the yogi. What is the place of Pithoro Pir with respect to the representatives of the religion? The official representation of the saint shows him arriving on a horse near a character who raises his hand. In the Kutchi version, the inscription indicates that this character is a Brahman. It is difficult to draw conclusions regarding the respective positioning of the two characters, but one thing is certain: the Brahman is not in any case the disciple of Pithoro Pir.

If it is not possible to specify the historical circumstances of the life of Pithoro Pir, one can observe that the period when he lived was turbulent. The area of Umarkot was at the centre of conflicts of local, regional and central interests. On the local level, it passed under the successive control of the Somras and the Sodhas. At the regional level, this period was that of the transition between the Somras and the Sammas. Although the latter officially took power from the first in 1351, the Somras had preserved their control of certain outlying areas of Sindh, including, precisely, the area of Umarkot. In 1351, the sultan of Delhi, Muhammad Shah Tughluq, arrived in Sindh in pursuit of a rebel. The sultan died shortly afterwards in Sonda on the banks of the Indus, and he was buried in Sehwan Sharif, near Lal Shahbaz Qalandar's shrine. In 1367, his successor, Firuz Shah Tughluq, returned to lay siege to Thatha; Jam Juna I Samma would have to ask for the intercession of a saint of Multan, Sayyid Jalal al-Din Bukhari, better known under the name of Makhdum Jahaniyyan Jahangasht (d. 1383). Then, in 1397, Pir Muhammad was in Multan, and the following year, his father Timur Lang (Tamerlan) put an end to the sultanate of Delhi. Jam Juna II, who controlled Sindh then, sought alliances with the sultan of Gujarat.

As a saint of the importance of Pithoro Pir cannot be born as a common person, it cannot die either like common people. Actually, the saint does not die: he disappears, which means that he will re-appear. Pithoro Pir disappeared under the ground and in his sanctuary, and the place where he disappeared is the subject of a particular veneration. A small altar is there and the *puja* is performed on a daily basis. The tomb of Pithoro Pir is located in the hamlet of Pithoro, between Mirpur Khas and Umarkot, on the railway line which formerly connected Hyderabad (Sindh) to Barmer and Jodhpur, in Rajasthan. As for many other saints, the site of their sanctuary bears the name of the saint.

Like all of the renunciants, Pithoro Pir did not marry: he transmitted his knowledge and his authority to his brother, Bhanwarji, whose tomb is in a small temple located in the lower part of his tomb. The current *pir* of Pithoro,

Figure 7.3 Pithoro Pir's tomb with the *Om*.

Hathesingh, is the direct descendant of Bhanwarji, and he is the twenty-second *pir* of the line. His authority as *pir* comes only from this filiation. The other descendants of the brother of Pithoro Pir form a kind of sacerdotal caste in the sect. Known under the name of Pithoro Pota Pir – that is, descendants of Pithoro Pir, which is not exact since they come down from his brother's lineage – they are the priests (*gurara*) of the sect. They officiate in the altars of villages, especially in Thar Parkar. In the temple of Bhuj, the *pujari* is a Pithora Pota Pir, whereas the singer of *bhajans* is a Sodha Rajput.

Interestingly, the Pithoro Pota Pirs are compared with Sayyids rather than with Brahmans. In the middle of the nineteenth century, Burton had mentioned already that they were much respected. This respect certainly came from their filiation with the family of Pithoro Pir as well as from the knowledge which they had in the interpretation of their scriptures. As a matter of fact, Burton mentions they have scriptures known as *pothis*. According to the current *pir*, the tradition of Pithoro Pir is mainly oral, and his version has been confirmed by many disciples I met in various places. Nonetheless, the Pirpanthis could have *pothis*.

Hathesingh claims being a Thakur,[7] that is, a Lord, a Master, which is an honorary title given to the Rajputs. Rajputs are subdivided into many subgroups: the *pir* belongs to the subgroup of Sodhas. This assertion is surprising when it is known that Pithoro Pir was Muslim. The priest (*pujari*) of the temple of Bhuj affirms for his part that the *pir* of Pithoro is a Meghwar. Burton made the same thing clear. The Sodhas form the dominant group among Rajputs of Sindh and, according to their tradition, they would have come from Ujjain, in Malwa, in 1226. Their chief, Parmar Sodha, would have been established as king (*rano*) at Umarkot. The majority of them became landowners and farmers. The *Gazetteer* of 1907 describes them as worshippers of Shiva. No mention of Pithoro Pir appears there.

In Pithoro, the *pir* officiates each evening towards 6.45, after the sunset. The ritual is a form of *puja pat*, which is divided into three principal sequences: (1) the preliminaries (*arti*) during which the *pir* lights the candles, and where *bhajans* are sung without instrumental accompaniment, (2) the invocatory prayer (*dua*) and (3) the ritual of communion (*piyalo*). The *pir* performs this last rite only with his disciples (*murids*) and apart from the sanctuary. The text of the *dua* is simple: *Dado bhali kundo!* 'Dado will bring only good to you!'

Who are the disciples of Pithoro Pir? When the question is asked, the *pir* enumerates about fifteen groups. One can divide them into three principal categories: the untouchable ones, the Muslims and the Sodhas. Among the untouchable ones, three groups are prevalent: Meghwars, Bhils and Kohlis. Among the Muslims of Sindh, one can take note of Sindhis like Sammas, Panhwars and Baluchs like the Maris and the Legharis. In Kutch, the devotees are mainly Meghwars, Bhils, Kohlis, Sutars (carpenters) and Sodhas, whereas it does not seem that the Muslims venerate Pithoro Pir. Other Rajputs, such as Jarejas of Kutch, can come to make a request in the temples, but they are not strictly speaking disciples of Pithoro Pir, and they do not make the *puja*. Another distinction must be mentioned: the disciples of Pithoro Pir mix in Sindh, whereas in Kuch, the untouchable ones practise separate worship, which is different from that of the Rajputs in different temples.

One can wonder about the role Pithoro Pir plays within Meghwars as well as about his relationship with the other saints and divinities that they venerate. The fact that Burton considers them to be neither Hindu nor Muslim indicates that they have their own religion. In Sindh and Kutch, Pithoro Pir is associated with two charismatic figures: the pan-Indian divinities and the regional divinities. The first category is limited to various representations of Devi, the wife of Shiva. Pithoro Pir is most of the time associated with soteriological figures. In this category, the saint most venerated is Ramdeo Pir, still known in Sindh as Rama Pir. Ramdeo Pir is also the object of widespread worship in Gujarat and Rajasthan. Although he is very present for the untouchable ones, he is also venerated by the Nathpanthis of Gujarat. In Sindh, he is today integrated into the temples dedicated to the pan-Indian divinities. In Karachi, for example, a painting of Ramdeo Pir stands in the temple of Lakhshmi Narayan.

The worship is not exclusive: the majority of Meghwars who venerate Pithoro Pir also venerate Ramdeo Pir. On the other hand, the reverse is less sure. The *pir* of Pithoro does not mention Ramdeo Pir among the companions with whom Pithoro Pir travelled. He quotes the names of the Lal Shahbaz Qalandar, Puran Bhagat and Jhulelal. A most interesting point is the convergence of certain elements within these methods of worship, starting with the iconography. The figures of the two saints seem to draw with them a common model of holiness based on the renouncement. The other divinity with whom Pithoro Pir is very frequently associated is the Devi. The most frequent forms are Sitala Mata, the very powerful goddess of smallpox, and Kali.

Following the examination of the cult of Pithoro Pir, one can see the variety of the negotiations between Sufism and Hinduism in Sindh. Pithoro Pir's figure shows the complexity of the religious context. In this case, there is only one concrete link with Sufism: Pithoro Pir would have been initiated to Sufism by Baha al-Din Zakariyya. Such an element is incorporated into an oral tradition, and it can be related to a kind of legitimization of Pithoro's charisma.

Conclusion

The purpose of this chapter was to provide a brief survey of the relationship between the Hindus of Sindh and Sufism. It has established that the Hindu Sindhis of Pakistan have a different relationship to Sufism than what we find if we compare them with the Hindu Sindhis of India. Nonetheless, the large majority of the Hindus used to pay a visit to the Sufi shrines, but does it mean they are Sufi? Of course not. It does mean that, for them, the Sufis are a part of their religious legacy. A tentative typology was also proposed, and it shows that the Sufi legacy is managed by the Hindu Sindhis in a number of different ways. Mostly, the reverence they have for the Sufis belongs to the charismatic realm, in which people ask a saintly figure to help in curing a disease, providing a job, the giving of a son, and so on.

The discussion of the Sufi legacy among the Hindu Sindhis of Pakistan has furthermore been deepened through three case studies: Sehwan Sharif, Tando Ahmad Khan and Pithoro Pir. The first case is related to a probably old tradition, pre-partition situation, where the Hindus were associated with the performance of the main rituals. Sehwan Sharif hosts about twenty *kafis*, or Sufi lodges, of which two are Hindu. Already, we know about the Mulchand Kafi, but it does not play a ritual role for the Hindu community, although it is used for cremation. Nonetheless, the *sajjada nashin* is Ramchand, Mulchand's nephew, and he performs the *mehndi* ritual every year, leading a procession from Mulchand Kafi up to Lal Shahbaz Qalandar's *darbar*. There is another 'Hindu *kafi*' whose *sajjada nashin* also leads a *mehndi* procession. Due to the situation in Sehwan, a capital question arises: is Sehwan an exception? Does the system with the Hindus reflect an ancient order in the city, where the dominant elites shared the symbolic power? All in all, it is relevant to think the involvement of the Hindus is a remnant of an old past, but whatever the explanations can be, it is in any case remarkable that it has survived in a post-partition context.

The second case is of more recent, probably post-partition, situation, and it resulted from a Lohana agency. The Lohanas, once the dominant Hindu community in pre-partition Sindh, are still mostly involved in trade. Many Lohanas, especially those belonging to the subcaste of the Amils, have played a leading role in integrating Sufism as a main component of Sindhi identity. In the small town of Tando Ahmad Khan, there is a rich Hindu religious market, so it is not a coincidence the Hindu *dargah* was built here. As Pakistani citizens, the local Lohanas could have reacted to the growing fame of the saint of Sehwan Sharif, especially since Bhutto's rule in the 1970s. Interestingly, the local Hindus have integrated the Hindu *dargah* in the Hindu religious environment, but they have also set up a new agency in organizing the space of the *dargah* itself. While the figure of Lal Shahbaz is dominant, insofar as the shrine is a replica of the Sehwan one, he has been given the identity markers usually attributed to Jhulelal. But even this merging of the two figures is finally united through the formula of *Sab ka malik ek hai*.

Since partition, the majority of the Pakistani Hindus of Sindh have belonged to the low castes. They are Dalits, as they are named by some, and some even claim they are not Hindu. They worship different saints and gods, but a category of divinized heroes is relevant for study since it builds a link between them and Sufism. Pithoro Pir is said to have been initiated onto the Sohrawardi path by Baha al-Din Zakariyya. While most of his followers are Hindu, nobody challenges the fact that he was a Sufi *pir*. In this case, and although one can hardly find Sufi rituals in the worship, we are given further evidence of how the Sufi legacy is still alive among the Dalits of Sindh.

Consequently, the Hindus of Sindh in Pakistan incorporate the Sufi legacy into their religious beliefs and practices. The incorporation nonetheless operates through an array of processes which themselves depend on the social milieu, the caste system and the urban/rural context. It is thus relevant to claim that Sufism can be a challenge in the competition between dominant groups for the social control. The relationship built with Sufism also depends on the historical context of the place where it is implemented.

General conclusion

The scholars involved in Sindhi studies have often depicted Sindh as a hub of religious encountering, ignoring the fact that such a situation was not prevalent only in Sindh. It is amazing to see the extent to which scholars, be they Sindhi or not, approach the issue as if the complex processes at work in the region could be constructed as an isolated, specific identity marker, as if comparable dynamics were not implemented in other regions, be they neighbouring Sindh, such as Punjab, Rajasthan or Gujarat, or elsewhere, such as Bihar or Bengal. There are numerous academic studies providing templates where we can observe that comparable processes have worked in these regions. During the Pax Britannica imposed by the colonial rule, the exchange of goods and products was reinforced between the different regions of the north-western Indian subcontinent, including Punjab, Rajasthan, Gujarat and Sindh. Beyond the networks developed by the merchants, there had been networks of circulating knowledge, and especially religious knowledge. The issue of religious encounters was rarely addressed through the issue of circulation.

Furthermore, the difficulty of grasping the fluidity of such religious belonging is mirrored by the variety of terms used by scholars, mostly Westerners, trained in Western universities or in 'Eastern' universities following Western patterns which are, more or less, the heir of Orientalist constructions. This pattern means that most of the concepts come from a Christian intellectual environment, and that they were built by colonizers who were often involved in religious predication. Many concepts or notions have been used, such as liminality, hybridity or maybe the most controversial, syncretism. Other scholars have rooted their studies in the translation theory – especially Finbar B. Flood, Rita Kothari for Sindhi studies and Tony Stewart, who also wrote with Carl Ernst a very critical note on the notion of syncretism (Stewart and Ernst 2003: 586–8). Obviously, it is a tremendous issue to select a term to be used to describe and analyse the socio-religious facts at play here. Another issue is that of the emic and etic, which questions if it is more relevant to use categories built by outsiders, mainly Western scholars. But what about the non-Westerners who use Western categories?

Due to the interaction between the colonial state and a new intelligentsia, Sufism has now become focused on the principle of Unity in the realm of mysticism. To understand the *darbar* culture, it is necessary to look at the religious ideology which underlies the poetry, itself the main vehicle of the religious culture: the oneness or unity of God, *wahdat* or *advaita* (literally non-duality), which can be called the *wujudi* ideology. This *wujudi* ideology is the foundation of the devotional performance at work in the *darbars*. Furthermore, the ideology was framed in the nineteenth century during British colonization, and reinforced by new Western spiritualities, especially the Theosophical Society, whose motto was: 'Nothing is higher than Truth.'

For the users, the *darbar* culture is framed as a system so that, for them, their religious belonging or affiliation, in beliefs as well as practices, is not an issue, since they represent their own religious culture as an organic tradition. The adjective 'organic' is meant to highlight that the religious construction of people makes a system – that is, a coherent complex of beliefs and values where the contradictions, discrepancies and other fallacies are not visible on the surface because they are subsumed in the *wujudi* ideology. This set-up results from a process of inclusiveness which has been implemented by particular social groups at given historical periods. The organic theory allows for the addressing of the issue of religious encountering without representing it as a mixture, or any other blending, because, from the users' perspective, it shapes a meaningful system through this cohesiveness. Furthermore, devotion is the core of the system, and it also responds to daily commitments related to the basic elements of life, such as health, happiness and eating.

Nevertheless, the study of the encounter between Islam and Hinduism, and surely among other religions, is to decipher very intricate processes involving not only religious matters but also primarily social factors, as well as political and economic factors. The elaboration of an organic tradition results from a body of elements, which were ultimately aggregated throughout different historical circumstances, with main agents belonging to the dominant classes of different groups organized in a hierarchical society. However, one can also find processes which allow more or less marginalized populations to be integrated in the encounter framework, as we saw with the Menghwars and the cult of Pithoro Pir. In a varied array of encounters between Sufism and Hinduism, a main issue is understanding the relations they have between them, since the Hindu Sufis never gave up their Hindu belonging.

In the case of the Hindu Sindhis, how was it possible for them to construct a path between their Hindu belonging and Sufism? If it was possible for them to bridge Sufism and Hinduism, why is it that all of the Hindus do not integrate the Sufi legacy, since it is so widespread in South Asia? Beyond religions, how can we understand such a construction which is still at work in India, as well as in Pakistan, more than seventy years after the Great Divide, which was followed by mass exile with no possible return? This study proposes some analytical explanations which are based on a limited framework. The data collected reflects the situation of three main Sufi paths among the Hindu Sindhis of India, with a survey of contemporary Sindh. Thus, the following comments are grounded in a specific historical and cultural context, that of post-partition Sindh, but they also have a universal echo since such encounters can be, and have already been, observed in other parts of the world.

The keystone of the set-up was that Hinduism was providing the social framework through which the Hindu Sufis were able to perform rituals for birth, weddings and deaths, while Sufism was addressing the mystical quest: both religious systems were working at different levels, in a kind of continuity. To some extent, one can state that Sufism was the inner meaning of Hinduism, which was the outward religion. Furthermore, in the case of the Sindhicate environment, the Hindu Sufis were in touch with a Sufi legacy built in pre-partition Sindh. For all of them, their Sufi masters were Muslim, but at the same time, they could also have followed Hindu masters. All in all, it is interesting to observe that the Hindu Sufis belonged to a Hindu context impacted by the Bhakti, and especially by Krishna's Bhakti. Krishna and Radha were represented as the embodiment of mystical love, and a number of Sufis from nineteenth-century Sindh, such as Sachal, Qutub Ali Shah and Bedil, themselves include Krishna in their Sufi poetry. In this case, it is worth observing that, despite the fact that Sindh was Muslim dominated, the Krishnaite Bhakti was influential among *wujudi* Sufis.

Nevertheless, as early as the 1930s, N. J. Narsain claimed that Sufism was particularly well adapted to the life of the Amils, the Hindu caste employed by the British for administration. This is true, but it does not really explain why the Amils preferred to take a Sufi (Muslim) Master, instead of the many Hindu *guru*s who were as attractive as the Sufis, since the Amils were also Nanakpanthis or Daryapanthis. In terms of religious practice, there were of course differences between following a Nanakpanthi Master or a Sufi Master, just regarding the beliefs, for example. But the religious practice itself was built on the same pattern: a direct relation with a spiritual Master, and a very flexible religious practice, of which a main part could be performed alone, as an individual. The best example in this respect is the practice of meditation. Consequently, the objective factors obviously played a leading role in the process of becoming affiliated with a Sufi Master instead of any other spiritual Hindu Master.

But before proposing further arguments, it is important for us to remember that Sindh was a largely Muslim-dominated country, making up about 75 per cent of the whole population, where the power had been in the hands of Muslims for centuries. Therefore, there was a kind of 'cultural islamization' working beyond the religious affiliation itself, to which the Hindus were automatically and unconsciously surrendering. Turning back to the objective factors, this means that, first, the Muslim Sufi market was far more developed than the Hindu market. As a hypothesis, one can consider that to be a Sufi for a Hindu could allow him or her to escape the very strict rules pertaining to the caste system. Another objective factor is related to the building of a modern Sindhi identity, of which Sufi poetry was the core. Finally, to be a Sufi for a Hindu was to participate fully in the process of building a modern Sindhi province, so far as the Sufi poetry was itself very open, if not integrative, through the vernacularized ideology of the *wahdat-e wujud*.

Simultaneously, Sindh was submitted to a religious recomposition in the late nineteenth century and early twentieth century, as is attested by the building of many new Nanakpanthi *darbar*s all over Sindh. On the Sikh side, in the late nineteenth century, the Singh Sabha was to open a new era in patiently constructing a distinct and separate Sikh identity, which would culminate with the Gurudwara Reform Act of 1925, this determining who had the right to manage *gurdwara*s and who was their legal owner. A main result of this process was that all non-Sikh worship, such as related to the Hindu gods or Sufism, were banned form the religious practice of the Sikhs. The Sikh religion focused on the ten Sikh *guru*s, and the Guru Granth Sahib. It was the final step towards the creation of a separate religious identity. The Sindhi Nanakpanthis were thus not included in the Sikh community, and they identified themselves as being a Hindu religious sect.

A main factor in the religious renewal in Sindh was the new formulation of Hinduism that spread all over India in the late nineteenth century: the Neo-Vedanta as built by Ramakrishna. The Vedanta philosophy was transformed into a universal message claiming there was only one God. In his memoirs, Sadhu Vaswani clearly shows how influential the Neo-Vedanta was, stressing the non-duality of God, a conception that perfectly matches with the Sufi concept of *wahdat-e wujud*. In this climate of universalism permeating the religious market, which coincides with the apex of European colonization across the globe, and the socio-economic upheaval left by the Industrial Revolution, the modalities of Sufi affiliation were renegotiated. A new dialectic between universalism and locality was emerging. From one side, there was the claim that the *wahdat-e wujud* was universalism, and from the other side, the *tariqas* did not display their affiliation to the 'great' pan-Indian *tariqas* and rather highlighted through their names their local rooting. In this new context, while the Hindus who became Sufis belonged to given Hindu paths or schools, it is also clear that the Sufis with whom they were in touch, including their masters, mostly belonged to two regional *silsilas*: the Darazi *silsila* and the Jahaniyya *silsila*.

Contrary to the Hindu Sufis studied by Dahnhardt, one cannot count a single Naqshbandi. This said, and although some of these Sufi masters have claimed a relation with the Qadiriyya, the Qalandariyya or the Sohrawardiyya, the ties with the order were flexible, at least: in Sindh, Sufi practice was more based on a personal allegiance with an individual than any affiliation with a Sufi *tariqa*. Furthermore, Sufis could be affiliated with several different *tariqas*.[1] This topic is one of the numerous ones that deserves to be studied further in Sindh. However, the Darazi and the Jahaniyya *silsilas* share a main feature: they were staunch *wujudi silsilas*. Their two major poets, Sachal Sarmast and Qutub Ali Shah, frequently mentioned in their *kalams* Hindu deities, especially Krishna, going further than Shah Abd al-Latif, for whom the *jogi*, the Nathpanthi renunciant, was already the pattern of the mystic path. Another referent figure is Lal Shahbaz Qalandar, the Sufi saint of Sehwan Sharif who is worshipped by the local Hindus as Raja Barthari, a main character of the Nathpanth.

Since partition, Hindu Sufism of Sindh has undergone major changes which have followed the main political evolution of South Asia. A watershed occurred in the 1980s with the Ayodhya Affair. In this new context, the Sufi paths among the Hindu Sindhis adopted different strategies of resistance. Nonetheless, the main impact was the retreat and/or disappearance of major Sufi rituals, especially the *dhamal*, the *alam* and the *mehndi*. The broader hinduization following Ayodhya was differently negotiated according to the various regional contexts. In Ulhasnagar, the *dhamal* is still performed in the *darbar* of Rochaldas, while it is not in the Haridwar *darbar* devoted to Mulchand and Gehimal. The *mehndi* procession is performed inside Rochaldas's *darbar*, while previously, at the time of the Kanungos, it was made from the *darbar* to the river.

The weakening of the Sufi legacy is also clear throughout the literary references used for prayers and other rituals. Sometimes the Muslim Sufi authors are not the most used, and thus, the core of the sung poetry is that authored by the *silsila*'s members who are Hindu. For example, in Vadodara, Sachal has declined, and now Nimano is at the forefront. Also, the present *gaddi nashin*, Nirmal Jani, has succeeded in centralizing his followers as focused on his own person. This process could be the result of how Nirmal Jani took power among the followers of Nimano, a topic that was hardly addressed by my informants.[2] However, in this case, it is uncertain whether this shifting was due to the broad 'hinduization' of public life in India. I argue that it reflects a 'communalization' of the Sufi path rather than hinduization, although both can be coupled together. What does it mean? It means that there was a will from the Master, maybe meeting that of the group, to identify the path with a leading character reflecting the very local identity of the path.

To speak of a possible communalization in process is like addressing the issue of community: in other words, do the Hindu Sufis make up a community? And if this is the case, what kind of a community is it? Mostly, this study has shown that the struggle in which the Hindu Sufis are involved is mainly that of the preservation of the Sufi legacy as a main part of the Sindhi identity. With the spread of the Jhulelal's apotheosis, room for the Sufi legacy was reduced among the Hindu Sindhis. In this respect, as we saw, Panjwani's trajectory is exemplary, and influential. Thus, the challenge faced by the Hindu Sindhi Sufis of India is twofold: to face the challenge inside the Sindhi group, and to face the hinduization of the Indian society. To find how the Sufis represent themselves as a group, it is necessary to turn back to the vocabulary they use.

In the broad Sufi context, the Sufi brotherhood, or order, is called *tariqa*, an Arabic word for a path, a way. The Hindu Sufis do not use it frequently, or, I mean to say, in a current discussion. Nonetheless, one can find it in the books they publish. In the copious glossary provided in his *Sufi Galaxy*, S. L. Gajwani translates it as 'discipline, methodology, system' (Gajwani 2000: 307). Another frequent word used in Sufism is *silsila*, or the chain, a reference to the chain of transmission throughout the succession of the different masters. It can be an equivalent of *tariqa*, for naming the Sufi community, thus emphasizing the transmission of the tradition, and the succession as authority. It is hardly used by the Hindu Sufis, and absent from Gajwani's glossary. Several Hindu Sufis, such as Nimano Faqir, Molchand Kripalani and Jogi Sain, refer to the group made by their followers as the *sangat*.

The Hindu Sufis prefer to use the term *sangat* instead of *panth*, as is the case with the Nanakpanth and the Daryapanth. This does not mean they want to distinguish themselves from Hinduism: they are Hindu! In fact, the *sangat* is the usual term used by the Sikhs to name the community they form. It came into use when the *gurus* wanted to put emphasis on the community and give great importance to congregational worship. Due to the spread of the Nanakpanth in Sindh, the Hindu Sufis were very familiar with Sikh terminology, but they did not use the term *sangat* as the Sikhs did. As a matter of fact, in Sindh, the groups of Sufis and Nanakpanthis did not have a central organization ruling an encompassing body of followers. Thus, the process of communalization is very fragmented and is unconducive to creating a community including all of the Master's followers, a *sangat*. Another perspective regarding an answer to the issue of community involves scrutinizing how the concept of authority is framed.

We saw that authority among the Hindu Sufis is traditional, with many convergences with the authority as conceived in the Hindu paths where there is no central authority, contrary to the organization among the Sikhs. The Sufi Master has spiritual knowledge and he can only initiate disciples, in giving them the *nam* and teaching techniques of meditation. The Sufi path is made of different degrees and the first one aims at breaking the Ego. It requires a total submission to the Master. In the first step, the follower has to clean the stable and the toilets, and carry out other tasks which are looked upon as being degrading according to the common standards of local society. This conception is shared by many spiritual paths in India. The exercising of traditional authority was disturbed by the social change following colonization and independence. The Amils had to move often because of their jobs, so that they could hardly be regularly in touch with their Master. In this context, the *sangat* was a community to the extent that it gathered as a body no more than once a year, for the *urs* or the *versi*. In this case, it would be more relevant to call it a *communitas* instead of a *sangat*.

In the process of communalization at work, another issue is related to how the *silsila* still keeps in touch with the Sufi legacy. The link is still preserved through different channels. First, there is the 'living' link with the Master who stays in Sindh, nowadays in Pakistan. Still, the Pakistani *sajjada nashin* travels to India to meet his followers. Another channel to claiming the link with the *silsila* is to exhibit the images of the masters. First, they are widely hung on the walls, in different parts of the *darbar*. Also, they are copiously included in the publications. It would be fallacious to think the function of the book's photographs or paintings is illustrative: it is much more than a decoration. For the followers, it is a visual proof of the rooting of the *silsila* in continuity. Furthermore, since the Master is supposed to be the most powerful, the follower can even be bestowed with a vision through the visualization of his Master's image.

While nobody can deny that the Sufi paths are still at work among the Hindu Sufis of India, it would be erroneous to claim there is not a vanishing interest among the young generation, not to speak of the growing hostility from the mainstream Hindus, for whom there is no room for an alleged 'mixed' religion. The issue of the preservation of the Sufi legacy among the young Sindhi generation is linked to that of Sindhi culture, first of all the language. The matter is not easy to deal with since, beyond the use of Sindhi language, a minority language, there is that of the script, both being closely related. A growing trend is to claim that the romanization of Sindhi will allow for a preservation of the Sufi legacy and Sindhi culture. In this respect, the pioneers could have been Hindu Sindhis from the diaspora – meaning the overseas diaspora. Since this initiative is still recent, it is too early to know if it is successful.

As stated before, the Sufi legacy among the Hindu Sindhis is partly shared with other South Asian cultures, but it also possesses its own specifics. I shall summarize a number of points that illustrate, according to my own research, what I shall call the Sindhi touch. But before I make this point, it is necessary to go back to how the Sufi legacy was constructed in Sindh. Broadly speaking, the Sufi culture is a part of the *darbar* culture, but with a main distinction which can perhaps be called the Sindhi touch: sometimes, it can be a place where not only the Hindus, or non-Muslims, come for the pilgrimage (*ziyarat*) but also a place where the Hindus still play a ritual role. In her book on ambiguous sacred places in South Asia, Bellamy did not really examine the 'conditions of possibility' – that is, what makes this encounter possible. In Sindh, it was possible thanks to an ideological framework provided by the *wujudi* ideology, reformulated in the Theosophical perspective through its congruence with *advaita vedanta*. Consequently, this construction was expressed in the late nineteenth century. Two factors determined the spread of the *darbar* culture: locality and social agents. The *darbar* culture provided answers to local challenges, either urban or rural, as related to competition for domination involving different social classes.

Furthermore, in the introduction, I quoted Anita Thapan as being perhaps the first scholar to address a central issue regarding Sufism and Hinduism in the Sindhicate context: what does it mean for a Hindu to be a Sufi? She stated that a Hindu who calls himself a Sufi was normally one who had taken initiation from a Sufi *pir*. But, this said, a number of clues we have been through in this study would lead us to wonder if this statement is still relevant in 2017, seventy years after partition, and furthermore, when we note that, after the process of hinduization, all of the Sufi paths had to be within India, especially. Consequently, I shall address the issue with other words: is it still relevant to speak of a Hindu Sufism in early third millennium India? And, if this is the case, what does it mean now to be a Hindu Sufi?

More than ever, the core of Sufism is the singing of poetry: I would argue it is the essence of Sufism, especially since, most of the time, other rituals have been in their majority hinduized. In the Maqbul Manzil in Ulhasnagar, for example, Sachal's devotees started the *satsang* with an *arti*: nothing distinguishes it from any other *arti* performed in a Hindu temple. We saw that, in the Nimanal Sangam, the reference to Sachal has even been suppressed. But Nimano Faqir's verses still embodied the very spirit of Sindhi Sufism, and especially that of the Darazi *silsila*. The *versi* at Rochaldas's *darbar* deserves to be mentioned also since this could be presently the only place where a *dhamal* is performed, and an *alam* exhibited.

Singing Sindhi Sufi poetry is not only a matter of keeping a link, through language and music, with Sindh as a fatherland. It is also the opportunity to praise a vision of society and religion, a vision of the world and humanity, in which love plays a fundamental role, and where it is said that the final message of all of the religions, here mostly Islam and Hinduism, is, if not the same, convergent to the principle of the unity of God: *wahdat-e wujud* and *advaita*. It can be expressed as unity or non-duality. This belief is a compulsory prerequisite for the one who seeks out divine vision, *didar* or *darsan*, and finally divinization, although this exalted goal is not really the one shared by the Sindhi Hindu middle classes.

In this respect, it is still relevant to distinguish two main groups among the Hindu Sindhis: the shopkeepers and businessmen on one side, the ex-Bhaibands, the civil servants working in Indian administration, including education, and the ex-Amils on the other side. Although it is difficult to conduct a systematically sociological approach, it is obvious that the Amils are more involved in Sufism than the Bhaibands. If we want to be even more precise, it is relevant to claim that the 'real' Sufis, to be distinguished from the devotees who attend the rituals, belong to this category in their majority. While in pre-partition Sindh, there are many stories where businessmen decided to give up all of their worldly goods and activities to become renunciants, and not only in relation with Sufism, I have never heard such a story in independent India.

As we saw, the backbone of the transmission and spread of Hindu Sufi poetry is still in the publication of books. This does not mean the Hindu Sufis are not involved in the internet and social networks. Most of them have a website, and they can sell through it different items, including books. Nonetheless, although it would be fascinating to enquire into this virtual Sufism, it will take some more years to know the real impact of this new communicative world. In fact, the main question now is to know if it will help the young generations of Hindu Sindhis, all over the world, to keep in touch with the Sindhi Sufi paths.

Nevertheless, among the followers, the process of transmitting Sufi poetry still works through the books, and actually, the main issue is related to the script that is to be used. It seems there is a growing consensus to use the Latin script. While most of the Hindu Sindhi middle classes are able to read it, another interesting aspect is that it could even attract non-Sindhi people. But, such a scenario will be possible only if the Sindhi Sufi poetry is also translated into English. This could be a wonderful duty for the globalized Sindhi youth.

Notes

Introduction

1 On the Sindhi Community House in London, see Nimrita Rana's dissertation (Rana 2014). For a brief mention, see also Falzon 2004: 71.

2 See Markovits 2000, David 2001, Thapan 2002, and Falzon 2004. Regarding the issue of diaspora, Rita Kothari does not agree with my view on this issue and claims that the Sindhis of India belong to the larger Sindhi diaspora. See Kumar and Kothari 2016.

3 Hodgson provides a long explanation for why he was compelled to use a new word such as 'Islamicate': 'There has been, however, a *culture*, centred on a lettered tradition, which has been historically distinctive of Islamdom the *society*, and which has been naturally shared in by both Muslims and non-Muslims who participate at all fully in the society of Islamdom' (Hodgson 1974: 58).

4 There are innumerable books devoted to Sufism. See Ernst 1999, Suvorova 1999, and Green 2012.

5 See below. On the different phases of the vernacularization process, see Boivin 2016: 12–29.

6 The use of the term 'classical' means that two main functions have been attributed to a body of poetry. The first function is that this poetry is represented as being the apex of the relevant aesthetics, an unsurpassable expression of the core of the Sindhi identity. The second function is related to the fact that it is represented as the pattern for the field, in terms of both poetry and literature, as well as culture at large.

7 On the Nathpanthis, see Briggs 1938.

8 The Mughal emperor Akbar (1542–1605) would have 'invented' a new religion, known as *din-e illahi*, or the Divine Religion, mostly inspired by Sufism. This religion was open to all his subjects, whatever their creeds.

9 On the role played by the Ismaili Shias in the 'encountering' between Islam and Hinduism, see the pioneering work by Dominique-Sila Khan (Khan 1997). For a study on the de-hinduization process and the islamization process among the Ismaili Shia Khojas, see Boivin (2013).

10 The first generation is that of the migrants; the second generation is the first to be born in independent India.

Chapter 1

1　Regarding shrines and spaces in devotional Islam, see my introduction to the volume devoted to the topic (Boivin and Delage 2016).

2　For a detailed analysis of the Muslims of Sindh and their classification during the colonial era, see Boivin 2005.

3　The Ashrafs (sg Sharif) constituted the nobility among Indian Muslims. They were descendants of Arab, Turkish, Persian and Afghan immigrants. The Indian converts form the group of Ajlafs whose status could be diverse, from honourable to impure. It depends usually on their professional activities.

4　See also the two lithographed editions of the same treatise in its Sindhi version in Bombay at the beginning of the twentieth century (Baloch 1992: 102–3).

5　From a Polish word, the intelligentsia appeared in mid-nineteenth century and it was first used in the Russian Empire to designate the intellectual elite whose efforts were to modernize the society. Soon in late nineteenth century, the word spread in Western Europe.

6　Interestingly, Narsain's analysis meets Max Weber's typology, according to which a given profession fits a given type of worship.

7　It is noteworthy that the activities of the society stopped in Karachi after the 2007 assassination of the society's president, the late Dara Feroze Mirza (1937–2007).

8　This book was reprinted in 1963 by the Sindhi Sahit Sangat, Bombay.

9　In Arabic alphabet, when a word starts with the long vowel 'o', it is written with 'a'.

10　The Udasis of Sindh are coined as being a heterodox Sikh tradition, in one of the very few, if not the sole, academic papers devoted to the Nanakpanth in Sindh (Jatt 2016).

11　Unfortunately, the lack of sources does not allow us to state that Dalpat Sufi really followed a Sufi path during his lifetime. Apparently, he used to stay in a place in Hyderabad which can be called a *darbar*. On Dalpat Sufi and his samadhi in Mumbai, see Chapter 5.

12　I draw upon different hagiographers (sometimes anonymous) who are themselves Rochaldas's followers (Gajwani 2000). This biographical sketch thus draws upon the official tradition of Rochaldas's *darbar*, hereby the tradition.

13　Vasan Shah (1847–1927) was a popular saint from Rohri, in Northern Sindh. He became famous for his singing of Guru Nanak's *banis* as well as Sufi *kalams*. He was a follower of Sai Parul Shah (1820–90). Vasan Shah's *darbar* is located in Ulhasnagar, while another one is in Rohri, on the bank of the Indus River.

14　During the first ten days of the Muslim month of Moharram, the Shia Muslims commemorate the martyr of their third imam, Husayn, the grandson of

Prophet Muhammad. He was slaughtered with his family in 680 at Karbala, in Iraq. Different events are organized in commemoration, especially including processions of réplicas of his tomb, known as *tazia*. Many non-Shias participate, such as Sunni Muslims and Hindus.

15 On Qutub Ali Shah and the Jahaniyyan lineage, see the master's thesis by V. J. Matai submitted in 1972, recently reprinted by the Institute of Sindhology (Matai 2003).

16 The death of a Sufi saint is commemorated as his wedding with God. The Sufi is represented as the bride and God as the bridegroom. In South Asia, the bride is decorated with henna for her wedding.

17 Ulhasnagar was mostly populated by Sindhi refugees but throughout the years, other populations from India and beyond migrated to the city and today, the Sindhis would be about 35–40 per cent of the total population. Nonetheless, Ulhasnagar probably hosts the most numbers of Hindu Sindhi shrines compared to rest of India.

18 The *dhamal* is an ecstatic dance performed every day before the sunset in the precinct of Lal Shahbaz Qalandar's *darbar*, in Sehwan Sharif.

19 Haridwar (the Gate of God) is one of the most famous places of pilgrimage for the Hindus. It is located in North India where the Ganga breaks through the last range of the Himalayas and enters the plains. It is one of the four places where the kumbhamela, a major religious gathering when the sun stands in the Aquarius, is held every twelve years.

20 About the Manzilgah Affair, see Khuhro (2000), and also the detailed timeline provided by the Gul Hayat Institute's website, based on official British data and media reports (gulhayat.com).

21 The Mohajirs were the Urdu-speaking Muslims who had migrated from India in the wake of partition. They were mostly from the Delhi area and also from Hyderabad Deccan. They had left all of their belongings in India, and many thought they were legitimate to take over the goods left by the Sindhi Hindus, or even they had the right to seize their properties.

Chapter 2

1 The last book is Raj Daswani's *Shattered Sindh Scattered Sindhis* (Daswani 2017).

2 The word *silsila* is an Arabic word very often used in Sufism. While it can be employed as an equivalent of *tariqa*, or path, and brotherhood, the first meaning is chain. Thus, it refers to the idea of transmission and legacy.

3   The *gaddi nashin* is the one who sits on the throne, the *gaddi*. The *gaddi* symbolizes
    the *darbar*, and the *gaddi nashin* is thus the one who rules on it. The expression is
    used by both Muslims and Hindus. Nonetheless, in the Sufi context, the Muslims
    also use the word *sajjada nashin*, this meaning the one who sits on the carpet.

4   In Sehwan Sharif, the place where the *faqirs* stay, usually known as a *khanaqah*,
    is named *kafi*. The origin of the use of this word is unknown, but maybe that it is
    related to the fact that it signifies a place where poetical verses, or *kafis*, are sung.

5   For instance, the pre-partition temples devoted to Jhulelal in Sindh were built with
    a dome, as were some Sikh *samadhis*. The main site known as the *darbar* of Udero
    Lal hosts many domes (Boivin and Rajpal 2018).

6   The Thakurs were the priests of Jhulelal. In Sindh, they were settled in different
    cities but they migrated to India from 1947 onwards. Here, the Thakurs came
    from Sehwan Sharif.

Chapter 3

1   Ajwani even uses the expression 'Vedantism-Bhakti' (Ajwani 1970: 52).

2   Born in the Muslim caste of the weavers, Kabir (1440–1518) was one of the
    leading medieval India poets using a vernacular language. He belongs to the *sant*
    tradition. His poetry is like a synthesis of Sufism and the Bhakti. Mirabai (1498–
    1547) was the princess of Mewar and her poetry makes her an exponent of the
    Krishnaite Bhakti.

3   Motwani could have borrowed the expression 'great integrators' from a book
    where it is used for the *sants* of the Bhakti (Raghavan 1966). For G. Allana, a
    fourth poet belongs to this category: Shah Inat (1623–1712). His complete name
    was Sayyid Inayat Allah Rizvi, and was probably a Shia Muslim, initiated in the
    Qadiriyya brotherhood of Sufism (Allana 1983).

4   Mohanlal Matlani labelled them as *asasi Sindhi shairi*, or 'Classical Sindhi poetry'
    (Matlani 2001).

5   Jalal al-Din Rumi (1207–73) is known as one of the greatest Sufi poets all over
    the world. He has composed one of the most influential Sufi poetical works, the
    Masnavi, in Persian. Also, he claimed in his poetry that music and dance are the
    best method of meditation (*zikr*) to reach God. Hence, the Sufi brotherhood he
    created is known as the Whirling Dervishes.

6   A *marsiyyo* is a dirge devoted to the martyrdom of the third imam, Husayn, the
    grandson of Prophet Muhammad, with his family and companions.

7   Though he is usually noted as being one of the greatest poets of Sindh, Sami's work is still understudied. See the pioneering work by Vadana Ramwani (Ramwani 2000).

8   Abu ʾAbd Allah al-Husayn Mansur al-Hallaj (d. 922), known as Mansur Hallaj in South Asia, is one of the most important Sufis who is known all over the world, and he was very popular in Sindh. He has claimed in his poetry: 'Ana al-haqq', a formula usually translated as: 'I am God'. Because of this, he was condemned by *ulemas* to death, and was finally hanged in Bagdad (Schimmel 1986).

9   Unfortunately, I was not able to find the original text in Dalpat's Sindhi *kalam*, in any of the three editions that have been completed. It could imply the poem was included in his Siraiki *kalam*, a piece of poetry that has never been published, and which is therefore known only through oral transmission. Thus, I used two printed versions, one in the Ladkani's *Siraiki kalam al-sufiyya* (Ladkani 2000: 58) and the other by Sakhi Qabool Muhammad Faruqi (Faruqi 2002: 35). The slight differences between them would argue in favour of an oral transmission.

10 Bedil has authored *kalam*s in different languages in addition to Sindhi, such as Siraiki, Hindi, Urdu, Persian and Arabic. On his Siraiki *kalam*, see Shackle 1981.

11 The Quraysh is the name of the clan to which Prophet Muhammad belonged.

12 Ibn al-Arabi was born in Murcia in 1165 and died in Damascus in 1240. He is one of the most acclaimed Sufi authors, whose influence spread all over the world.

13 The work authored by Shah Abdul Latif was 'canonized' by the British in the middle of the nineteenth century, and later on re-appropriated by the Sindhi intelligentsia. Since the latter wanted all of the Sindhi classes to understand Shah properly, they started to publish glossaries and lexicons to explain the difficult words and expressions, or to translate them into Sindhi, knowing that most of them were Arabic expressions. See Boivin 2014.

14 Muhammad Iqbal was a poet born in Lahore, who was granted a PhD by the University of Munich. He is one the greatest Muslim poets in the Indian subcontinent, and one of the founding fathers of Pakistan.

15 On the figure of Hallaj in Sindhi Sufi poetry, especially in Sachal's verses, see Schimmel 1986: 96–149.

16 Ahmed, a name of Prophet Muhammad.

17 Diwali is the Hindu festival of lights, celebrated upon the anniversary of Ram's victorious return home.

18 Ayodhya is today one of the seven ancient holy cities of Hinduism. A place of pilgrimage, it was used as a target by the extremist Hindu political parties, such

as the BJP, for mobilizing Indians in the context of elections. They claimed the Babri Masjid had been built on a temple devoted to Rama. After years of political actions, the Babri Masjid was demolished by Hindu activists in December of 1992. It provoked the worst Hindu–Muslim rioting since independence all over India, as well as in Pakistan and Bangladesh.

19 The many wall paintings of Krishna in the Hindu temples could mean there was a kind of Krishnaite revival in the nineteenth century among the Sindhi Hindus (Kalhoro 2014: 238–44). Otherwise, on the variety of cults devoted to Krishna, see Beck 2006.

20 Schimmel wrongly claimed they were all Rohal Faqir's sons (Schimmel 1974: 21).

21 On the Kandri school, and especially Darya Khan, see Baloch 1959, 1: 41–66 and Baloch 1966: 455–7.

Chapter 4

1 All the data I have mentioned is available on the website http://www.sufidar.org. What I refer as being the 'official narrative' comes from the website.

2 I shall not go further into this issue since it was already addressed by Frédérique Pagani's thesis on how philanthropy is constructed as a path for salvation in a Sindhi temple located in Bhopal (Pagani 2007). In this respect, there is no major difference between a Sufi Sindhi *darbar* and any other Sindhi religious institution in India.

3 Dasserah is a famous Hindu festival commemorating the victory of the god Rama over the demon Ravan in Lanka, on the tenth day of the waning moon in the month of Asu, running from the middle of September to the middle of October. This festival is the time when the Sindhi children perform the tonsure ceremony (Thakur 1959: 140).

4 It would be tedious to give details for every Sufi mentioned in the *Dil kusha*. Let it suffice to give a few comments. There is a notable absence: Shah Abd al-Latif, the king of the Sufi poets of Sindh. In fact, no Sufi from Sindh, including those who are much-acclaimed poets in Sindhi, as for instance Sachal Sarmast, is enumerated. Despite his fame, Lal Shahbaz was not Sindhi since he was born in Persia and his alleged *diwan* is composed in Persian.

5 On Shia iconography, see the comprehensive study by Ingvild Flaskerud, who thinks the first portrait of Ali was first drawn in Sindh and then brought as a gift to Fath Ali Shah (d. 1824), the shah of Persia who had friendly relations with the Talpurs, the emirs of Sindh, who were themselves Shia (Flaskerud : 25).

6 On this 'paradoxical' terminology, see also the discussion on the 'dargah mandir' devoted to Pir Baba Ratannath in Delhi (Bouillier and Khan 2009: 571 *passim*).

7 I pronounce his name as Molchand, for him not to be confused with Mulchand Faqir.

8 I have been unable to find any information on this Sufi. However, his name gives evidence that he was a Qadiri. Nevertheless, he goes unmentionned in the chart of the Qadiris as provided by Eaton in his work on the Sufis of Bijapur (Eaton 1978: 298–9).

9 Bijapur is a historical city known for being the capital of the Adil Shahi sultanate, conquered in 1686 by the Mughal emperor Aurangzeb. Also, it is a city where many Sufis came to settle.

10 The Amils were a subcaste of the Lohanas. Since the eighteenth century onwards, they specialized in becoming the official scribes in the administration of the Kalhoras and the Talpurs.

11 On 9 November 2011, three Hindus from Shikarpur were assassinated because they had invited a dancer woman who was Muslim. See *Dawn*, 10 November 2011, http://www.dawn.com/2011/11/10/three-hindu-doctors-shot-dead-in-s hikarpur.html.

Chapter 5

1 Here, 'radical' designates the different Hindu groups who claim that the Hindus are the true and authentic – if not the sole – inhabitants of the Republic of India. In fact, it could be understood as an equivalent of the hindutva.

2 I have been unable to identify the provenance of this representation of Ali.

3 Steven Ramey briefly refers to Rai Rochaldas (Ramey 2008).

4 The followers of the Pushtimarg founded by Vallabhacharya (1479–1531). He belonged to the Bhakti and was a Vishnuite underscoring the pure Advaita, or non-Dualism. His worship was mostly devoted to Krishna.

5 Personal communication, Haridwar, 26 April 2012.

6 The story of Manjnun and Layla originated in seventh-century Arabia, and it spread all over the Muslim world in many different versions. It symbolizes the absolute love, at a point where Majnun became crazy since Layla's father did not allow him to marry his daughter.

7 See, for example, the study on the issue of breathing techniques as borrowed by the Naqshbandis from 'the Indian Yogis' (Paul 1996: 210).

8 Baloch quotes six *kafis* by Roshan Ali Shah (Baloch 1959 1: 487–90).

9 Sathya Sai Baba was born in Andhra Pradesh, in a poor peasant family. Beyond his teaching, he was also deeply involved in charity works, and he had, for example, hospitals built (Srinivas 2012).

10 Shirdi Sai Baba is the most popular saint in present-day India. His origins and early life are unknown, but he settled in Shirdi, a town of Maharashtra, where he lived in a mosque, although his official tradition claims he was born a Brahman. For him, there was no religion but only one God, hence his famous epigram *Sab ka malik ek hai* (there is only one God). His teaching and religious practice combined elements from Islam and Hinduism (Pandia 2014).

11 I warmly thank Manu Bhatia for providing this information through the mail we exchanged in September of 2017.

Chapter 6

1 According to the official website, Rajnish Chandra Mohan Jain, better known as Osho (1931–90), published eleven books on Sufism, which are mostly with a compilation of his conferences on Sufism. See http://www.oshorajneesh.com/osho-books-on-sufi.htm.

2 According to his website, Ram Panjwani also published a book on Sachal Sarmast's poetry, with the title *Sachal jyun kafiyun*. See http://prof.rampanjwani.com/books/.

3 A double CD was published in 2006, with the title *Sufyani Chownki ain pallaw*, with no listed location or publisher.

4 With the expression 'non-migrant Sindhis', I want to speak of the young generations of Sindhis born in India. The use of the Arabo-Sindhi script quickly faded away. The key issue of the interplay between the chosen scripts and access to the Sufi legacy will be addressed in the last section of this chapter.

5 Ramey devoted some pages to literature in Rochaldas's movement (Ramey 2008: 90–4).

6 The term 'hinduized' refers to the process of hinduization, which has already been mentioned. Although it is out of the scope of the present study to give depth on this perspective, suffice to say that in this broad and complex issue, a category of religious communities have been especially targeted by the pro-hindutva organizations, such as the Arya Samaj or the RSS, and including political parties such as the BJP or the Shiv Sena. These communities have been differently named by the scholars as 'syncretic' or 'liminal', a nomenclature I have

already discussed the introduction. In these communities, 'Islamic' referents have been suppressed and replaced by Hindu referents, in terms of religious figures and concepts, as well as rituals. Thus, it is relevant to locate the evolution of the Sindhi Hindu Sufis in this broader context in which a similar process has been observed, such as the Imamshahis or the Pranamis (Khan 2001; Sikand 2003).

7   A composition by Guru Nanak that is recited by the Nanakpanthis and the Sikhs every morning. This is the most commonly known Sikh liturgical prayer.

8   Ajiz or Aijaz, whose complete name was Akhund Haji Faqir Muhammad Aijaz (1846–1918), was a Sufi poet from Northern Sindh (Memon 2005: 450–5). Baloch quotes a *kafi* without any information on the poet (Baloch 2 1959: 902).

9   On Kamal Faqir, a Sufi from Nawsharo Firoz, see Baloch 1959 1: 355 and Baloch 1966: 320–3. As we saw before, all the other Sufi poets belonged to the Kandri school, and they were all related.

10 On the *bhagat*, see Jyoti Garin's pioneering doctoral thesis written in French (Garin 2005).

11 The Siraiki language is mainly spoken in Southern Punjab, with Multan as capital. Interestingly, this area was a part of Sindh during the Middle Ages. On the Sufi poetry of Sindh in Siraiki, see Shackle 1981.

12 There is no standard transliteration of Sindhi language in Roman script, as is the case for many non-Roman scripts all over the world. Nonetheless, Western scholars have commonly used the transliteration provided by the University of Chicago. In Sindh, there is another official transliteration, which is also different from that of Ahmedabad.

Chapter 7

1   About this controversial issue, see the documentary *Thrust into Heaven* (Schaflechner 2016). One of the involved *pir*s, the *pir* of Bharchundi, is the descendant of the one who was accused of having ordered the assassination of Bhagat Kanwar Ram (1885–1939).

2   The reason behind this is not clear. According to some Hindu informants, the Muslims are forbidden to visit.

3   See https://fr-fr.facebook.com/Sehwanis/.

4   The word *kafi* is locally used instead of *khanaqa*, the Sufi lodge.

5   It is tempting to think of a connection, or even of a fusion, between Lal Shahbaz Qalandar and Jhulelal, but none of the sources allow for us to go that far. That said, both are today called Jhulelal.

6 While the terrorists have targeted Sufi places in Pakistan for years, a huge terrorist attack took place in the *darbar* of Lal Shahbaz Qalandar in Sehwan Sharif on 16 February 2017. It was during the *dhamal* and ninety people were killed; more than 300 were injured.

7 Not to be confused with the Thakurs, the priests of Jhulelal. In Sindhi, the Rajut Thakur is written with a long 'a', while the Jhulelal Thakur is written with a short 'a'.

General conclusion

1 Furthermore, it is amazing to observe that the Chishtiyya was not widespread in Sindh, while it is dominant in Punjab and North India. The *sajjada nashin* of Daraza alluded to a possible link with the Chishtiyya, while he is not explicit regarding the formal affiliation of Daraza with a *tariqa*. On the one hand, he claims that, unlike the Qadiriyya, the masters of Daraza loved and promoted poetry and singing (Faruqi 2002: 94). But on the other hand, the genealogy he provides clearly shows an allegiance to both the Qadiriyya and the Sohrawardiyya (Faruqi 2002: 120–1).

2 In fact, there is a suspicion that Nirmal Jani was not designated as the successor of Nimano, or of her own successor. I could not establish a relevant and convincing version of the narrative regarding how Nirmal Jani won access to the *gaddi*. However, both the reluctance of the followers to talk about it, and the contradictory narratives I heard, would lead us to think it was not a 'legitimate' succession.

Glossary

Abd al-Qadir Jilani (d. 1192): A famous Sufi from Baghdad, the founder of the Qadiriyya Sufi Brotherhood; his death anniversary, known as Yarhen, the 11th, since he passed away on the 11th of Rabi al-Sani, is a popular festival in South Asia.

Abdul Sattar: the name of several Sufi masters at the *dargah* of Jhok Sharif.

Advaita: non-duality.

Alam: the standard that is raised for stating the beginning of a Sufi ritual.

Ana al-Haqq: 'I am Truth' or 'I am God'; see Mansur Hallaj.

Arti: worship of a deity accompanied by the waving of lights. Often it is the first part of the *puja*.

Astano: a Sufi place.

Atma: the God Infinite; the Hindu Sufis make it the equivalent of *haqq*.

Bairagan: a crooked stick, a kind of a forked stick on which the *bairagi* that is the renouncer places his head when meditating.

Baqa bi Allah: the Sufi stage that comes after *fana fi Allah*, it is the stage of ultimate union of the conscious with the super conscious.

Baraka: the divine grace; the spiritual power of a Sufi Master.

Bhandaro: food distributed to the people during the *versi*.

Chownki, chowki: a session during which Sufi *kalam*s are sung.

Dam: breath; it has a special significance in Sufi practice. When a disciple is initiated, he is given a chant along with which he is told about the posture he is to be in when chanting and also about the manner in which he is to breathe. See *pranayama*.

Daraza: the name of a town in Northern Sindh where Sachal's *dargah* is.

Darbar: literally meaning 'court', it connotes the place of worship of a Sufi. In India, the Sindhi *darbar* is a place of interest where one may find pictures of saints and gods, from all religions, and at times the Guru Granth Sahib.

Dargah: shrine of a Muslim saint, a destination for worship.

Dard: pain, agony. This is an essential experience all Sufis apparently go through. It is not the physical pain, which in fact is bearable, in contrast to which the emotional agony is torturous. This pain teaches valuable lessons in patience, sabr, tolerance, and so on.

Darsan (darshan): sight, seeing, showing; for Sufi context, see *didar*.

Darvish: a saint, one who is close to the One.

Dastarbandi: ceremony of 'enthronement' of the Sufi Master.

Dham: a Hindu sacred place of pilgrimage.

Dhamal: a Sufi ritual where a dance is performed with drums.

Didar: literally seeing; in Sufi context, it may mean blessed by the vision of the One. See *darsan*.

Dua: prayer.

Fana fi Allah: a stage of the Sufi where the disciple and God are one; the mystical meeting of both; the merging of the self with the super conscious.

Faqir: one who is lost in thoughts of One and is therefore penniless.

Gaddi nashin: literally, the 'keeper of the throne'. A name given to a Sufi Master who heads a *darbar*.

Gunbaz: the dome of a Sufi shrine; in Sindhi, the tower of any temple, Hindu or Sikh, thus the equivalent of *shikara*.

Gurdwara: the Sikh place of worship.

Hama ust: the Persian equivalent of the *wahdat-e wujud*.

Haqq: Truth, a term for God.

Havan: an oblation to gods made in fire.

Ishq: mystical love. In the Sufi context, it is love of the seeker for the sought. Among Sindhi Sufi poets, the Sufi often writes in the feminine mode, assuming the sought to be masculine. The Sufi sees himself as the bride of God.

Ishq haqiqi: love of ultimate Truth that is, Divine Truth.

Ishq majazi: according to the Sufis, this is a step towards *ishq haqiqi*. In *ishq majazi*, the seeker meditates upon something beautiful in creation as a reflection of the ultimate Truth.

Jabarut: see *malakut*.

Jap: the repetition of a sacred name, or *mantra*.

Jhando: a Sindhi word for the *alam*.

Jhok Sharif: a village with an important Sufi Centre in Taluqa Mirpur Bathoro in Southern Sindh where Sufi Shah Inayat's *dargah* is.

Jind faqir: the *faqir* who has reached the divine.

Jogi: wandering Shivaite ascetics who meditate on One, usually affiliated with the Nathpanth.

Kafi: a piece of poetry; in Sehwan, the name of the Sufi lodge.

Kalam: a piece, or a verse, of Sufi devotional poetry.

Katha: narrative; anecdote. A narrative used for explaining a Sufi concept.

Lahut: see *malakut*.

Madah: a composition in praise of the *murshid* or God.

Malakut, jabarut, lahut: three different stages in Sufi experience, each more intense than the other.

Mansur Hallaj: a Sufi from Iraq. He claimed 'Ana-ul-Haqq' that is 'I am Truth' equivalent to 'I am God', for which he was beheaded in Baghdad in the year 922. He visited Sindh in 905.

Mantra: a sacred word or formula for meditation.

Marifat: the mystical knowledge; a stage of the Sufi path.

Mast: drunk, mad, whimsical; intoxicated with Divine Knowledge. Among Sufis, it is one who, forgetting his own self, is lost in thoughts of the One, ecstatic; drunk on Divine drink.

Mujavar: the one who is in charge of a *dargah* or a *darbar*.

Munajat: a poetical praise to God.

Murid: an officially initiated disciple.

Murshid: a Sufi Master; one who initiates the disciple officially.

Murti: the statue or image of the God or of the Master.

Nabh kanwal: literally meaning the lotus of the navel. The lotus is the traditional symbol of spirituality in the Indian subcontinent. To channel the breath so as to begin it from the navel is important in Sufi practice.

Nam: literally meaning name, *nam* is the word given to the disciple by the Master, during the initiation. It is believed to be a secret. The regular chanting of the *nam* is a basic practice in Sufism. Meditation centres around the *nam*. See *shabd*.

Nam vathan: to take the name; to be initiated to the Sufi path.

Nazar nihal: literally meaning to immerse another with one's sight.

Nur: divine light.

Pir: a Sufi Master.

Pohtal: a name given to the one who has reached the divine.

Pranayama: breath control as being a basic technic of yoga, as expressed by Patanjali (second century BC). The word *pranayama* is already used in the Bhagavad Gita.

Prasad: food or drink that is offered to a deity, and thus distributed among the devotees.

Puja: the basic Hindu worship, especially of an image of a god, including a minimum number of sixteen ritual acts.

Ruha rihan: 'spiritual conversations'; conversations about God.

Sab ka malik ek hai: 'There is only one God'; a formula attributed to Baba Sain of Shirdi, which has spread among the Hindu Sindhis.

Sajayo: spiritual reward.

Sajjada nashin: 'spiritual master'; a common Persian title for the head of a Sufi order; head of a particular *darbar* or *dargah*.

Sakhi: honorific title literally meaning generous. Sakhi also refers to several Sufi masters of Daraza, especially Nimano Faqir's *murshid*, Sakhi Qabool Muhammad II of Daraza Sharif.

Sama: the musical session of the Sufi; the performance when Sufi poetry is sung with musicians. See *satsang*.

Samadhi: a shrine; a place where the ashes of a saint are preserved.

Samaran: remembrance. Another term for *zikr*.

Sant: saint. A term given especially to Bhakti saints, such as Kabir and Mirabai.

Satchidanandra: 'the Indivisible and Eternal Being'. A concept of Ramakrishna's Neo-Vedanta.

Satgur/u: sat+guru= Truth+Master, Master who is Truth.

Satsang: literally associated with the Truth; name given to a musical session in which devotional Sufi songs are sung. See *sama*.

Shabd: see *nam*.

Shikara: the tower of the Hindu temple. In Sindhi, it is called the *gunbaz*.

Siraiki: a language spoken in Northern Sindh and Southern Punjab. Several Sufi poets from Sindh, such as Sarmast and Bedil, composed poetry in Siraiki.

Sur: a Sindhi word with the meaning of chapter in Shah Ab al-Latif's work; it is also the equivalent of *rag*, the musical mode in Indian music.

Urs: the annual fair organized for commemorating the demise of a Sufi saint.

Versi: see *urs*.

Wahdaniyyat: the unity (of God).

Wahdat-e wujud: the Oneness of God; the equivalent of *advaita*, or non-duality, uniqueness.

Wujudi: a Sufi who is a follower of the *wahdat-e wujud*.

Zikr: the Sufi meditation.

Annexes

1. Abstracts of Sufi poetry in Sindhi and English translation

DALPAT SUFI
(Ladkani 2000)

Sufi so jo sachu panchhani	The Sufi is the one who knows the Truth
Ap ganwai murshid kunani	Loses his Ego and merges in the guru
Mata mazhab man tahen ani	Knows no religions,
Sabh gahti eko atam jani	Sees one in all
Berah agan ka machu machavi	Kindles the fire of love and burns his Ego
Deh abhman jai jalawi	Transforms with word and thought
Ranji ranjavi kismun nanhen	Neither hurts, nor is hurt
Apna ap peki sabh manhen	Finds the self in everyone
Bir akar men sada samawi	Transforms Ego into Self
Jism jahan dolu bhal janhen	Forgetting the manifestations
Andar bahar safi rahe	Outer inner lives so pure
Such such tun sam kar sahi	Pain and pleasure feel the same
Apna ap, ap men lahi	Speaks of the Unseen
Agana nagama de batan kahi	Abandoning Ego becomes unattached
Denhan sat sumri sacho khaliq	Always remains in devotion
Ap ganavai rahe be taluq	In everyone sees one God, Friends and foe treats as one
Har bandi de vach tyani eko malik	Happy unhappy he never is
Dalpat so sufi sacha salik	Dalpat the true Sufi is

DALPAT SUFI
(53)

garaq thiya gareban mein
    ke gabar giyaani
vijhi valorho vajud mein
    mahabat maandhani
juda kayaun jism jahan khon
    makhan masaani
	They immersed in themselves,
	    a few able ones who knew;
	They did turn their existence,
	    retaining love filtered!
	They separated their body from this world,
	    smearing dust of the graveyard!

chaane khaadaun kheer khe
    pare kare paani
dalpat thiyo dil mein tin
    alakh ayaani
aashiq aasaani,
    naath muliyo tin nenhan saan
	Filtering, they did take the milk,
	    doing away with the water![1]
	Dalpat, in their hearts did they find,
	    the One Truth!
	With love easily,
	    did they find God with their eyes!

---

[1] In Eastern philosophy, a true saint is a swan – who can separate the milk from the water, the truth from the illusion.

QUTUB ALI SHAH

Sakhi sabhajal

Sakhi sabaajhal baajh karyo
   fazal karyo avheen haane
haadi rehem karyo avheen haane.

Generous, Merciful One!
   Grant thy blessings![2]
Master, favour with thy grace now!

1. Dar tuhinje te kaye savaali
   dar tuhinje taan ko na viyo khaali
   hia ba ta hik nimaani.

1. Numerous seekers come to Your door,
   none goes unblessed from Your door,
   this too is a humble devotee[3]

2. Dard muhinje jo daarun tunhi
   bye dar ji maan naahyaan soonhi
   haal sabhiyo tho jaane.

2. You alone the medicine for my pain are.
   This small boat belongs to no other door,
   You O Holy one everything know!

3. Charakh falakh je ghano aa sataayo
dukh katan jo kariyo avheen saayo
   murshid thi achi saan.

3. The wheel of Heaven[4] enough has harassed
To ease the affliction make an endeavour
   come be with me my Guide now!

4. Karam qutub te kart un khaalik
   to bin byo naahe ko maalik
dukhda kateen tun paan hi .

4. Accept Qutub's plea O Creator!
   None but You is the Master!
Come soothe the pain Yourself!

ishq budho aa haraam
geet ana ul haqq gaayin tha.

Love I've heard is vain
they sing songs of I Am Truth!

1. taalib mard mazkar asali
   paan vinjaaye paatayun tasali
   ihe sandan ahkaam
   har dum chit saan chaiyan tha.

1. Disciples the real heroes are,
   destroying themselves, they find peace,
   this their work is,
   every moment with conscious do they love.

2. vahadat vang vajudi paaye
   vetha mahbat mach machayi
   vathi gurua ja ahakaam
   darsan dil saan paayin tha.

2. Non-duality of existence do they don,
   lighting the flames of love,
   following the Master's precepts,
   the Vision with their hearts they see!

3. taalib nobat nenhen vinjaye
   sar surea te aaya sambhaye
   aha paroriyaun maam
   paan vinjaye naam khe paayin tha.

3. Disciples witness ruining their self,
   to the cross they come with heads ready!
   deciphering reflections around,
   themselves perishing find the name!

4. Qutub ishq asraar allah jo aahe,
   jenhen sar aayo soyi tho gaaye
   kare aayo dhoom dhaam
   naazuk nenharo chchipaayin tha.

4. Qutub love is a mystery of God,
   whoever falls into it sings,
   comes enjoying the splendour,
   delicate the attachment they veil!

---

[2] Blessings: the first three lines have three different terms for blessings – baajh, fazal and raham – here translated as blessings, grace and mercy. With each term, the intensity of the desire to be blessed increases.

[3] Humble devotee: Qutub Ali Shah uses the feminine term for himself in the original. This is common in Sufi verse, where the seeker sees himself as the feminine surrendering to the higher power that is masculine because the values of devotion, dedication and so on are associated with the feminine. Surrender is believed to be easy for the feminine.

[4] Wheel of Heaven: reference to Time, fate and so on.

DADI GANGA[5]
(Dadi Ganga 1988: 22)

aashiqan je dard ji,
   gaalh kaje kehi!
athai pahar alakh saan,
   rihaan kan vehi,
deedaar kan dilbar jo,
   manjhaan manjeehi,
paan pehi,
   rochal reedha rahan ranul saan.
duniya sande daur khe,
   samjh tun mashal khwab,
aado ajeeban je,
   kehrho deendein jawab,
kareeban je kurb saan,
   kusi thije kabaab,
jehenjo nenhan nawab,
   rochal sei nanga gaddiya nath khe.

Of the lover's pain,
   what can one say!
All eight segments of Time with the One,
   they sit conversing,
Visions of the Beloved do they see,
   inside their own self!
Within they go,
   Rochal[6] in union with Ranul
The world with its journeys,
   know you is instance of illusion!
To curved mysterious ways,
   what can be your response?
For the love of the Dear ones,
   get slaughtered to meat!
Those whose king is affection,
   Rochal those naked faqirs met God!

[5] Dadi Ganga was the mother-in-law of the famous Indian Sindhi politician L. K. Advani, who was Home Minister and Deputy Prime Minister in the second term of the BJP government (1998–9). It can sound amazing that a member of a party for which the Hindus only are true Indians proudly mentions in his memoirs that his wife Kamla with her sister Sarla published Dadi Ganga's Sufi poetry. In fact, only the name of Sarla is quoted in the publication.

[6] Rochal: though the pen-name 'rochal' is used in this composition, it is actually one composed by Dadi Ganga compiled in *Gaibi Awaz*. Dadi Ganga believed that it was Dr Rochaldas who visited her in sleep and made her write these poems; hence, his name. In *Gaibi Awaz*, some verses are Dadi Dhan's. It is not possible to know who the real composer is.

NIMANO FAQIR
(174)

aaun mangandarh savali aahiyan   A seeker seeking am I
daataar aaheen tun.   You the Giver be.

1. shaan tuhinjo aali aahe   1. Your glory divine is,
   sada jeeaeen tun.   immortal are you.

2. sakha tuhinji jaari aahe,   2. Yours the compassionate flowing current is,
   met madaayun muhinjyun.   of clay are the flaws all mine.

3. panbarheun saan angan buhaariyan,   3. With leaves and twigs shall I the
                                           courtyard sweep
   je ghar acheen mun.   if only you were to come home.

4. ranjhan tokhe rijhaayan lae,   4. Ranjhan to please you,
   nachi paayan feriyun.   will I dance and whirl around.

5. punhal to saan pech peerho,   5. Punhal[7] with you am I fastened,
   muhinjo asul khon.   from the Beginning.

6. nimani taan meher pehenji jo,   6. Let your hand of grace,
   lah na hath mathun.   on 'Nimani' be.

---

[7] Punhal= Punhu+al. Punhu is a Sindhi folk hero and 'al' is a suffix of endearment.

GEHIMAL MOTWANI

ach murshid ach vav yaar,
tuhinjo vichorho tho maare.

1. royi roz nihaariyaan,
   vaat pandh puchaayaan,
man khe ghanoi maariyaan,
        josh jigar t

2. dei dilaaso dil khase,
   haane vetho aahin baalam bani,
jan baanhi asul na sunjaani,
     baahe birah ji baare.

3. turt milanji kar tayaari,
    mataan mout na kare vaari,
poi aansu vahaaindei jaari,
     ki samjh surhai seaani

4. balka khan tun vikh vadhaaye
   muhabit sandi maam malaae,
bhural eendo bhaal bhalaaye,
       pai aahin jehnje panaare.

Come Master, come, alas, Friend,
separation from you kills me!

1. Every day I weep and wait,
   seeking the path, the way!
How I try the desire to restrain,
            my heart the passion does tear.

2. Giving comfort you stole my heart,
   now you sit hostile, indifferent!
This slave as if you don't know at all,
     having the fire of separation lit.

3. Quick, to meet, get ready,
   what if death comes earlier!
Then will you weep, shedding tears,
     understand O brave compassionate one!

4. Balka, take your steps ahead,
   with love will unveil all secrets,
Beloved will come with good tidings,
     in whose refuge you lie!

2. Hindu Sufis' *silsilas* in Sindh

DARAZI (QADIRIYYA)
Nimano Faqir   Radha Kishin   Pratap Rajani

JAHANIYYA (SOHRAWARDIYYA)
Rochaldas

JALALANIYYA (QADIRIYYA)
Jogi Sain

SAINDAD (QALANDARIYYA)
Mulchand Kripalani

SEHWAN SHARIF (QALANDARIYYA)
Rochaldas   Dalpat Sufi

JHOK SHARIF (QADIRIYYA)
Dalpat Sufi   Mulchand Faqir (via Rakhiyyal Shah)   Molchand Kripalani

The chart above clearly shows that three main Sufi *tariqa*s were dominant among the Hindu Sufis of Sindh (Boivin 2015). The Qadiriyya is the most influential, as is the case in the whole Indian subcontinent.[8] The Qalandariyya is not so widespread over it, but in the case of Sindh, it reflects the radiation of Lal Shahbaz Qalandar and the pilgrimage centre of Sehwan Sharif (Boivin 2012). The third *tariqa* is the Sohrawardiyya (Al-Huda 2003), the oldest Sufi order that settled in Multan and was predominant in the Indus Valley from the thirteenth century onwards. In this chart, there are two significant absences: the Chishtiyya and the Naqshbandiyya. The Chishtiyya is usually considered to be one of the most powerful Sufi orders in Northern India and Punjab. Most of the scholars accept that the order was instrumental in using the *sama*, the musical devotional session, to spread their Sufi ideology, as well as Islam in the Middle Ages (Bruce and Lawrence 2002). Maybe because of the Sohrawardiyya's hold on Sindh, the Chishtiyya could not spread in Sindh as it

---

[8] Amazingly, while all of the specialists are aware of the situation, there is a lack of academic studies devoted to the Qadiriyya in South Asia. Yet, there are monographs on the Sohrawardiyya, the Naqshbandiyya and the Chishtiyyas, the three other important Sufi *tariqas*. As of today, the best academic reference is the synthesis written by Arthur Buehler (Buehler 1999).

did in the rest of South Asia. Notwithstanding, music appeared very early in the Sufism of Sindh.

The case is different for the Naqshbandiyya (Buehler 2008). It came to Sindh from the sixteenth century onwards, with the coming of the Tarkhans and the Arghuns, two Central Asian dynasties that ruled Sindh. The Naqshbandis have several important centres in Sindh, especially that of Lowari Shari located in Southern Sindh, near Badin. From the end of the seventeenth century onwards, different Naqshbandis were prolific authors, and after the beginning of the eighteenth century, they composed treatises on Islam, especially to explain how to follow the Islamic rules properly, such as how to pray. Deduction shows that the Sindhis, even when they were officially Muslim, did not practise 'Orthodox Islam'. Unfortunately, the lack of sources does not allow the researcher to know more on the topic.

All over South Asia, the Naqshbandis are orthodox Sufis since they give great importance to following *sharia*. No Muslim Sufi, at any level he could have reached, is exempt from submitting himself to the prescriptions of Islamic law. As we saw in the introduction, this does not mean that a Hindu cannot be a Naqshbandi follower. Thomas Dahnhardt has studied a Hindu branch of the Naqshbandiyya (Dahnhardt 2002). Nonetheless, it is hardly the case in Sindh. Furthermore, the majority of the Naqshbandis in Sindh are strongly opposed to music and to the singing of devotional songs: these are strictly forbidden. This opposition can explain why the Hindu Sindhis did not look after spiritual masters belonging to the Naqshbandiyya. But, here again, there are exceptions. For example, the official book devoted to the Naqshbandis of Lowari Sharif was written by a Hindu follower.

Bibliography

1 Corpus and references

Advani, Kalyan, *Shah jo Risalo – risalo shah Abdul Latif Bhittai Jo*, Bombay, Smt Liladevi C. Vaswani, 1955.

Aitken, E. H., *Gazetteer of the Province of Sind*, Karachi, Mercantile Steam Press, 1907.

Allana, G., *Four Classical Poets of Sind: Minyoon Shah Inat, Shah Abdul Latif, Sachal Sarmast, Sami*, Jamshoro, Institute of Sindhology, University of Sindh, 1983.

Baloch, N. A. (ed.), *Madahun ain munajatun*, Volume 1–2, Hyderabad, Sindhi Adabi Board, 1959.

Baloch, N. A., *Sindhi Script and Orthography*, Karachi-Hyderabad, Sindhi Language Authority, 1992.

Baloch, Nabi Bakhsh Khan, *Kafeeyun*, 2 volumes, Jamshoro, Hyderabad, Sindh, Sindhi Adabi Board, 1985–87.

Baloch, Nabi Bakhsh Khan, *Sindhi Lughat*, Volume I–V, Jamshoro, Hyderabad, Sindh, Sindhi Adabi Board, 1960–88.

Bedil, Abd al-Qadir, *Ahwal wa athar Abd al-Qadir Bedil Sufi al-Qadiri*, ed. Doctor Abd al-Ghaffar Somro, Hyderabad, Sindhi Adabi Board Kitab Ghar, 2012.

Beg, Mirza Qalich, *Lughat-e Latifi: Shah ji risali mushkil lafzan ji mana*, Hyderabad, Sindhi Adabi Board, 1913.

Blumhardt, J., *Catalogue of the Hindi, Panjabi, Sindhi and Pushtu Printed Books in the Library of the British Museum*, B. Qaritch, London, 1893.

Blumhardt, J., *Catalogue of the Marathi, Gujarati, Bengali, Assamese, Orya, Pushtu and Sindhi Manuscripts in the Library of the British Museum*, London, 1905.

Boivin, Michel, *Historical Dictionary of the Sufi culture of Sindh in Pakistan and in India*, Karachi, Oxford University Press, 2016.

Chawla, Paru (ed.), *Chund Sindhi kalam ain dohira*, Bombay, Sindhi Art Printers, 1992.

Dadi Dhan, see Samtani, Dadi Dhan, *Thus spake: Pravachan ain kalam Sain Daktar Rochaldas Sahaban ja*, Ulhasnagar, 1991.

Dadi Ganga, see Jaghtiyyani, Shrimati Ganga Devi, *Ghani awaz*, Bombay, 1988.

Dalpat Sufi, *Deewan Dalpat*, Volume 1, Compiled by Harjani, Gidumal Khatanmal, Kalyan Camp, Gidumal Khatanmal Harjani, 1965.

Gajwani, S. L., *Sindhi Sufi Literature in Independent India*, Delhi, Sindhi Akademy, 1997.

Gajwani, S. L., *A Sufi Galaxy. Sufi Qalandar Hazrat Sai Qutub Ali Shah, His Spiritual Successor and Select Disciples – Sufi Saints of the Present Times*, Ulhasnagar, H. M. Damodar, 2000.

Hari, R. M. (ed.), *Ke saitun sajnan san urf Sain (Daktar) Rochaldas Sahib ji satsangi rihan*, 4 volumes, Ulhasnagar, H. M. Damodar, 1959–65.

Hari, R. M., *Shrimad Bhagwad Gita (Ilm ludani va-tawhid)*, Bombay, H. M. Damodar, 1982.

Hari, R. M., *Sri Yoga Vasishtha. The Spiritual Dialogue between Sri Ramchandra and Sri Vasishtha*, Ulhasnagar, H. M. Damodar, 1992.

Hari, R. M. (ed.), *Some Moments with the Master. Spiritual Dialogues with the Sufi Saint Sai Rochaldas Sahib*, Ulhasnagar, H. M. Damodar, 1995.

Harjani, Sobhraj Faqir, *Diwan Sobh*, Ulhasnagar, S. J. Chandrani, 1997.

Hazrat Sain Raaz Peer Wah, *Diwan Hazrat Ishq Mijaaz Ein Hazrat Ishq Haqeeqi (Madaah Samet)*, New Delhi, B.K.A. Publications, 1980.

Hazrat Sain Raaz Peer Wah, *Deewan Saain Raaz, Rindi Kalaam Al- Sufiyya*, New Delhi, B.K.A. Publications, 1999.

Hazrat Sain Raaz Peer Wah, *Musings of a Mystic*, New Delhi, B.K.A. Publications, 2001.

Hughes, A. W., *Gazeeteer of the Province of Sind*, London, George Bell and Sons, 1872.

Isarlal, *Isar ja Sufiyana kalam*, Ed. Lachhman K. Bhatia, Ahmedabad, 2012.

Jaghtiyyani, Shrimati Ganga Devi, *Ghani awaz*, Bombay, 1988.

Jogi Sain, Parsuram Keswani, *Dilkusha*, ed. Daulat Keswani, Mumbai, Sufi Sangat, 1996.

Jotwani, Seth Premchand, *Puj Sain Paru Shah Sahib ain Puj Sain Vasan Shah Sahib*, Ulhasnagar, Sain Vasan Shah Darbar, 1968.

Kripalani, L. M., *Sai Mulchand Kripalani jo jivan charitra*, Bombay, Sufi Trust, 1986.

"Krishin", Faqir Radhakrishin Lal Sahib Darazi, *Kalam*, Ulhasnagar, Hari R. Kataria, 1986.

Ladkani, Sognaram Mangaldas, *Siraiki kalam al-sufiyya*, Adipur, Indian Institute of Sindhology, 2000.

Mallick, Gurdial, *Divine Dwellers of the Desert (Mystic poets of Sindh)*, Baroda, Nalanda Publications, 1949.

Mewaram, Parmanand, *Sindhi-English Dictionary*, Hyderabad, The Sind Juvenile Co-operative Society, 1910.

Mewaram, Parmanand, *A New English-Sindhi Dictionary*, New Delhi, Sahitya Akademi, 1981.

Mirchandani, Manju (Jaya) Kamal, *Roohani Choond Sindhi Kalaam. Roman Script with Meaning*, Fremont (CA-USA), Fremont Printing, 2008.

Mirchandani, Manju (Jaya) Kamal, *Roohani Choond Sindhi Kalaam (Part Two). Romanized Script with Meaning*, Fremont (CA-USA), Fremont Printing, 2012.

Motwani, Gehimal Bhojraj, *Manzil-e-ilahi*, New Delhi, Gehimal Bhojraj Motwani, 1969.

Motwani, Gehimal Bhojraj, *Jivan charitra Sufi Darvish Faqir Mulchand Sahib Sehwan Navesi*, 1965; translated from Sindhi to Hindi by Kiku Motwani Bhalla, 2012.

Nasir Faqir, Muhammad, *Sufi sunhun: Hazrat Nasir Muhammad Sahab Faqir Sufi al-Qadiri jan ji hayat ain hidayat*, ed. R. R. Kirpalani, Bombay, 1972.

Nimanal Maan. Pooj Nimanal Sai jin ja Kalaam, Bheta, Dua Salaam, 2011.

Nimano Faqeer, *Haq mawjud*, Baroda, Nimanal Shah Yaadgaar Trust, 1997 (Second edn).

Nimano Faqir, *Nimanal Man Sain Nimani Faqir Sahaban ja kalam*, Baroda, Sakhi Kuthia, 1977.

Paniker, Ayyappa K. (ed.), *Medieval Indian Literature: An Anthology*, Volume IV, New Delhi, Sahitya Akademi, 2000.

Panjwani, Ram, *Latif*, Bombay, Bharat Jivan Sahita Mandal, 1981 (1st edn, 1945).

Panjwani, Ram (Compiled by), *Sik ji sogat*, Bombay, Doulat Printing Press, 1959.

Panjwani, Ram (Compiled by), *Sahit Malha, Pushp-1*, Bombay, Bharat Jeevan Saahiti Mandal, 1960.

Panjwani, Ram, *Sindhi ain Sindhyat*, Bombay, Mahalaxmi Printers, 1987.

Parsram, Jethmal, *Sind and Its Sufis*, Madras, Theosophical Society, 1924.

Premchand, Lilaram and Jethmal Parsram, *Sufī sagura*, Hyderabad, 1921.

Qazi *Qazan jo kalam*, ed. Hiro Thakur, Delhi, Pooja Publications, 1978.

Qutub Ali Shah, *Faqeer Qutub Ali Shah Sahib jin jo Kalaam Mubarak*, Compiled by M. K. Jhuremalani, 1985 (1st edn, 1964).

Rakhiyyal Shah al-Qadiri, *Bahar al-ishq*, Jacobabad, 1923 (5th edn, 2005).

Rakhiyyal Shah al-Qadiri, Chandiyo, Hakim Eijaz Hasan (Compiled by), *Rakhiyyal Shah Jo Kalam*, Kandiyaro, Roshni Publications, 2007.

Roshan Ali Shah, *Munajat Sai Roshan Ali Shah Sahib Roshan*, ed. P. L. Kirpalani, Ahmedabad, Kavita Printing Press, no date.

Sachal Sarmast, *Risalo Sachal Sarmast*, ed. Ashman Ali Ansari, Karachi- Hyderabad, Sindhi Adabi Board, 1958.

Sachal Sarmast, *Sachal jo risalo. Siraiki kalam*, ed. Mowlana Muhammad Sadiq Ranipuri, Kandiaro, Roshni Publications, 1997.

Sachal Sarmast, *Sachal Sarmast Jo Kalam*, Delhi, Sindhi Akademy, 1997.

Sami, *Sami ja slok*, Karachi, Prem Sagar Publications, 2002.

Samtani, Dadi Dhan, *Thus spake: Pravachan ain kalam Sain Daktar Rochaldas Sahaban ja*, Ulhasnagar, 1991.

Shah Abd al-Latif Bhittai, 1985, *Shah jo risalo alias Ganje Latif*, 3 volumes, Revised, Annotated and Translated by Muhammad Yakoob Agha, Hyderabad, Shah Abdul Latif Bhitshah Cultural Centre Committee.

Shah Karim Bulri wari jo kalam bayan al-arifin va tanbiyya al-ghafaliyyan, ed. Doctor Omar Muhammad Daudpota, Bombay, Qayyimah Press, 1937/1356.

Shirt, George, Udharam Thavurdas and S. F. Mirza, *A Sindhi-English Dictionary*, Karachi, Commissioner's Printing Press, 1879.

Sindilo, Abd al-Karim, *Lughat-e Sachal*, Khairpur, Sachal Chair, Shah Abdul Latif University, 1984.

Sufi Darvish Sain (Doktor) Rochaldas Sahaban jo mukhtasar jivan charitra, Mumbai, Wrown Printery, no date.

Vaswani, Ranjit Premchand, *Darvishan jo dawr ain hek chor jo sidiqu*, Ajmer, 1955.

Vaswani, Sadhu T. L., *Sufi Saints of East and West*, Edited with an Introduction by J. P. Vaswani, New Delhi, Sterling Publishers, 2002.

Vaswani, Sadhu T. L., *Ecstasy and Experiences: A Mystical Journey*, translated from Sindhi by Aruna Jethwani, New Delhi, Sterling Paperbacks, 2011.

Venti ain prarthna, 2009 (no publisher, no place).

2 Studies

Aggarwal, Saaz, *Sindh: Stories from a Vanished Homeland*, New Delhi, Black-and-White Fountain, 2012.

Ajwani, L. H., *History of Sindhi Literature*, New Delhi, Sahitiya Academy, 1970.

Ansari, Sarah F. D., *Sufi Saints and State Power. The Pirs of Sindh, 1843–1947*, Lahore, Vanguard Books Ltd., 1992.

Asani, Ali, 'The Bridegroom Prophet in Medieval Sindhi Poetry', in A. Entwistle and F. Mallison (eds), *Studies in South Asia Devotional Literature: Research Papers 1989–1991*, Paris-Delhi, EFEO-Manohar, 1994.

Bartley, Christopher, 'Vedanta: Modern Vedanta', in Knut R. Jacobsen, Helen Basu, Angelika Malinar and Vasudha Narayana (eds), *Brill's Encyclopedia of Hinduism*, Leiden, Brill, 2009, pp. 733–44.

Beck, Guy L. (ed.), *Alternative Krishnas: Regional and Vernacular Variations on a Hindu Deity*, New York, State University of New York Press, 2006.

Belani, Dipchand, *Jethmal Parsram*, Delhi, Sahitiya Akedemi, 1990.

Bellamy, Carla, *The Powerful Ephemeral: Everyday Healing in an Ambiguously Islamic Place*, Berkeley and Los Angeles, University of California Press, 2011.

Bhatti, Rashid, *Tasawwuf ain Classical Sindhi shaeri*, Sindhi Adabi Sangat, 2010; trans. into English by Saleem Noorhusain, *Sufism and Classical Sindhi Poetry*, Karachi, Culture Department, Government of Sindh, 2012.

Bhavnani, Nandita, *The Making of Exile: Sindhi Hindus and the Partition of India*, New Delhi, Tranquebar Press, 2014.

Bigelow, Anna, *Sharing the Sacred: Practicing Pluralism in Muslim North India*, New York, Oxford University Press, 2010.

Boivin, Michel, 'Remarques sur les stratifications sociales et les solidarités chez les Musulmans du Sindh colonial', *Revue du Monde Musulman et de la Méditerranée*, 105–6, 2005, pp. 153–73.

Boivin, Michel, "Sufism, Hinduism and Social Organization in Sindh: The Forgotten Tradition of Pithoro Pir", in M. Boivin and Matt Cook (eds), *Interpreting the Sindhi World: Essays on Society and History*, Karachi, Oxford University Press, 2010, pp. 117–32.

Boivin, Michel, 'Murshid Mulan Shah (1883–1962): A Sufi itinerary from Sehwan Sharif in Pakistan to Haridwar in India', *Oriente Moderno*, XLII:2, 2012a, pp. 289–310.

Boivin, Michel, 'The Sufi Centre of Jhok Sharif in Sindh (Pakistan): Questioning the *ziyarat* as a Social Process', in Clinton Bennett and Charles M. Ramsey (eds), *South Asian Sufis: Devotion, Deviation, and Destiny*, New York, Continuum, 2012b, pp. 94–109.

Boivin, Michel, *L'âghâ khan et les Khojah. Islam chiite et dynamiques sociales dans le sous-continent indien (1843-1954)*, Paris, IISMM-Karthala, 2013.

Boivin, Michel, 'Shah Abd al-Latif's *Risalo* and the Reshaping of Sufism in Nineteenth-Century Sindh: Imperial Policy and the Impact of Printing in British India', in Rachida Chih, Denis Gril, Catherine Mayeur- Jaouen and Rudiger Seesemann (eds), *Sufism, Literary Production and Printing in the Nineteenth Century*, Wurzburg, Ergon Verlag, 2014, pp. 99–120.

Boivin, Michel, 'Migration et soufisme chez les hindous sindhis de l'Inde: d'après l'exemple du *darbar* de Sain Rochaldas à Ulhasnagar (Maharashtra)', in Mathieu Claveyrolas et Rémy Delage (dir.), *Territoires du religieux. Parcourir, mettre en scène, franchir*, Paris, Editions de l'EHESS, 2016, pp. 275–302.

Boivin, Michel and Bhavna Rajpal, 'From Udero Lal in Sindh to Ulhasnagar in Maharashtra: Partition and Memories across Borders in the Tradition of Jhulelal', in Churnjeet Main and Anne Murphy (eds), *Partition and the Practice of Memory*, New York, Palgrave Mcmillan, 2018, pp. 43–62.

Boivin, Michel and Rémy Delage (eds), *Devotional Islam in South Asia: Shrines, Journeys, and Wanderers*, London and New York, Routedge, 2016.

Bouillier, Véronique and Dominique-Sila Khan, 'Hajji Ratan or Baba Ratan's Multiple Identities', *Journal of Indian Philosophy*, 37, 2009, pp. 559–95.

Bourdieu, Pierre, *Choses dites*, Paris, Editions de Minuit, 1987.

Bourdieu, Pierre, *Les règles de l'art : genèse et structure du champ littéraire*, Paris, Seuil, 1992.

Briggs, George Weston, *Gorakhnath and the Kanphata Yogis*, New Delhi, Motilal Banarsidass, 1998 (1st edn, 1938).

Buehler, Arthur, 'The Indo-Pakistani Qadiriyya: An Overview', *Journal of the History of Sufism*, 1, 1999, pp. 339–60.

Buehler, Arthur, *Sufi Heirs of the Prophet: The Indian Nasqhbandiyya and the Rise of Mediating Sufi Shaykh*, Columbus, University of South Carolin Press, 2008.

Burton, Richard F., *Sindh and the Races that Inhabited the Valley of the Indus*, Karachi, Indus Publications, 1988 (1st edn, 1851).

Certeau, Michel de, *L'invention du quotidien. I. Arts de faire*, Paris, Gallimard, 1990.

Cheesman, David, *Landlord Power and Rural Indebtedness in Colonial Sind, 1865–1901*, London, Curzon, 1997.

Chittick, William, *Rumi and Wahdat-e Wujud*, London, Cambridge University Press, 1997.

Dahnhardt, Thomas, *Change and Continuity in Indian Sufism: A Naqshbandi-Mujaddidi Branch in the Hindu Environment*, New Delhi, D. K. Printworld (P) Ltd., 2002.

Daswani, Raj, *Shattered Sindh, Scattered Sindhis*, London, 2017.

David, Maya Khemlani, *The Sindhis of Malaysia: A Sociolinguistic Account*, London, Asean, 2001.

Digby, Simon, 'Encounters with Jogis in India Sufi Hagiography', Seminar on Aspects of Religion in South Asia, SOAS, University of London, document ronéotypé, 1970, 35 pages.

Dirks, Nicholas B., *Castes of Mind: Colonialism and the Making of Modern India*, Princeton and Oxford, Princeton University Press, 2001.

Eaton, Richard M., *The Sufis of Bijapur: Social roles of Sufis in Medieval India*, Princeton, Princeton University Press, 1978.

Ernst, Carl, *The Shambala Guide of Sufism*, Boston and London, Shambala, 1999.

Ernst, Carl, *Refraction of Islam in India. Situating Sufism and Yoga*, Los Angeles/New Delhi, Sage/Yoda Press, 2016.

Ernst, Carl W. and Bruce B. Lawrence, *Sufi Martyrs of Love: The CHishti Order in South Asia and Beyond*, New York/Basingstoke, PalgraveMacmillan, 2002.

Falzon, Mark-Anthony, *Cosmopolitan Connections: The Sindhi Diaspora, 1860–2000*, Leiden, Brill, 2004.

Faruqi, Dr. Sakhi Qabool Muhammad, *Study of Mysticism in Darazi School of Sufi Thought*, Karachi, Culture and Tourism Department, Government of Sindh, 2002.

Flood, Finbarr Barry, *Objects of Translation: Material Culture and the Medieval Hindu Muslim Encounter*, Princeton and Oxford, Princeton University Press, 2009.

Foucault, Michel, *L'archéologie du savoir*, Paris, Gallimard, 1969.

Fuller, Christopher, *The Campor Flame: Popular Hinduism and Soceity in India*, Princeton, Princeton University Press, 1992.

Garin, Jyoti, *Le bhagat, une tradition orale sindhie*, thèse de doctorat, INALCO, Paris, 2005.

Geertz, Clifford, *The Interpretation of Cultures*, New York, Basic Books, 1968.

Gidumal, Dayanand, *Hiranand, The Soul of Sind*, Karachi, Diwan Metharam Dharmada, 1932.

Green, Nile, *Sufism: A Global History*, Oxford, Balckwell, 2012.

Hawley, John Stratton, *A Storm of Songs: India and the Idea of the Bhakti Movement*, Cambridge-London, Harvard University Press, 2015.

Hiranandani, Popati, *History of Sindhi Literature (post-Independence: 1947 to 1978)*, Bombay, Anuradha Publications, 1984.

Hodgson, Marshall G. S., *The Venture of Islam: Conscience and History in a World Civilization*, Chicago and London, The University of Chicago Press, 1974.

al-Hudda, Qamar, *Striving for Divine Union: Spiritual exercises for Suhrawardî sûfîs*, Londres and New York, RoutledgeCurzon, 2003.

Hughes, A. W., *Gazetter of the Province of Sindh*, Karachi, Indus Publications, 1996 (1st edn, 1876).

Jatt, Zahida Rehman, 'Heterodox Traditions of Udasipanth in Sindh: Case Study of Sri Chand Darbar, Thatta', in Sajid Mahmood Awan and Rhat Zubair Malik (eds), *Asian History, Culture and Environment: Vernacular and Oriental Paradigms*, Islamabad, National Institute of Historical and Cultural Research, Quaid-I Azam University, 2016, pp. 975–97.

Jotwani, Motilal, *Sufis of Sindh*, New Delhi, Ministry of Information and Broadcasting, 1975 (1996).

Kalhoro, Zulfiqar, *Art and Architecture of Sindh*, Karachi, EFT, 2014.

Kent, Eliza B. and Kassam Tazim (eds), *Lines in Water: Religious Boundaries in South Asia*, Syracuse, Syracuse University Press, 2013.

Khan, Dominique-Sila, *Conversions and Shifting Identities: Ramdev Pir and the Ismailis in Rajasthan*, Delhi, Manohar, 1997.

Khan, Dominique-Sila, *The Pranami Faith: Beyond 'Hindu' and 'Muslim'*, Yoginder Sikand, Bangalore, 2001.

Khuhro, Hamida, *The Making of Modern Sindh: British Policy and Social Change in the Nineteenth Century*, Karachi, Indus Publications, (2nd ed. 1998).

Khuhro, Hamida, *Mohammed Ayub Khuhro: A Life of Courage in Politics*, Karachi, Oxford University Press, 2000.

Kothari, Rita, *The Burden of Refugee: The Sindhi Hindus of Gujarat*, Chennai, Orient Longman, 2007.

Kothari, Rita, 'Being-in-translation. Sufism in Sindh', in Judy Wakabayashi and Rita Kothari (eds), *Decentering Translation Studies: India and Beyond*, Amsterdam/Philadelphia, John Benjamin Publishing Company, 2009, pp. 119-31.

Kumar, Priya and Rita Kothari (eds), '"Sindh, 1947, and Beyond: Introduction", "Partition and Sindh: Dispersals, Memories and Diasporas"', *South Asia: Journal of South Asian Studies*, 39:4, 2016, pp. 773-89.

Lalwani, L. W., *The Life, Religion and Poetry of Shah Latif: A Greatest Poet of Sind*, Lahore, Sang-e Meel Publications, 1994 [1890].

Leghari, Abdul Jabbar Abid, *Sindh ja Sufi sha'ra' karam*, Hyderabad, Sindhi Adabi Board, no date.

Lorenzen, David (ed.), *Bhakti Religion in North India: Community Identity and Political Action*, Delhi, Manohar, 1996.

Manghnani, Shri Murij J. (ed.), *Prof. Ram Panjwani 70th Birthday Commemoration Volume*, Bombay, Felicitation Committee, 1981.

Markovits, Claude, *The Global World of Indian Merchants, 1750-1947: Traders of Sind from Bukhara to Panama*, Cambridge, Cambridge University Press, 2000.

Matai, V. J., *Jahaniyyan khandan*, Jamshoro, Institute of Sindhology, 2003 (M. A. Thesis 1972).

Matlani, Mohan, *Asasi Sindhi shairi*, Departemnt of Sindhi, University of Mumbai, 2001.

Memon, Muhammad Sadiq, *Sindh adabi tarikh*, Shikarpur, Mehran Akademi, 2005 (1st edn, 1944).

Mir, Farina, *The Social Space of Language: Vernacular Culture in British Colonial Punjab*, Berkeley and Los Angeles, University of California Press, 2010.

Motwani, Motilal, *Shah Abdul Karim – A Mystic Poet of Sind*, Karachi, Sindi Kitab Ghar/Indus Publications, 1986.

Mubarak Ali, Dr., *Sindh Analyzed. Mc Murdo's & Delhouste's Account of Sindh*, Lahore, Takhleeqat, 1994.

Narsain, S. J., *Amil Community of Hyderabad, Sind*, Unpublished Ph.D., University of Bombay, 1932.

Oberoi, Harjot, *The Construction of Religious Boundaries: Culture, Identity and Diversity in the Sikh Tradition*, New Delhi, Oxford University Press, 1994.

Pagani, Frédérique, *'Servir les hommes, c'est servir le Seigneur': le salut par la philanthropie: étude d'une association de bienfaisance sindhie (Bhopal - Inde Centrale)*, thèse d'anthropologie sociale, Université de Paris X-Nanterre, 2007.

Pandia, Samta P., 'Syncretism and Pilgrimage in India : Nuances of Devotion to Saibaba of Shirdi', *South Asia Research*, 34:1, 2014, pp. 31-46.

Paul, Jürgen, 'Influences indiennes sur la naqshbandiyya d'Asie centrale ?', *Cahiers d'Asie centrale*, 1-2, 1996, pp. 203-17.

Pollock, Sheldom, 'Introduction', in S. Pollock (ed.), *Literary Cultures in History. Reconstructions from South Asia*, New Delhi, Oxford University Press, 2003, pp. 1–36.

Pollock, Sheldon, *The Language of the Gods in the World of Men: Sanskrit, Culture, and Power in Premodern India*, Berkeley, Los Angeles, London, University of California Press, 2006.

Raghavan, V., *The Great Integrators. The Saint-Singers of India*, New Delhi, Ministry of Inforation and Broadcasting, Government of India, 1966.

Raikes, S. N., *Memoir on the Thurr and Parkur Districts of Sind*, Karachi, Indus Publications, 1977 (1st edn, 1856).

Ramey, Steven, *Hindu, Sufi, or Sikh Contested Practices and Identifications of Sindhi Hindus in India and Beyond*, New York, Palgrave Macmillan, 2008.

Ramwani, Vandana, *Sami hek Vedanti shar*, Ulhasnagar, Runaq Enterprises, 2010.

Rana, Nimrita, *An Exploration into the Holy Mission of Guru Nanak, Sindhi Community House in Cricklewood, North London*, M. A. Dissertation, Department of African Studies and Anthropology, University of Birmingham, 2014.

Sadarangani, H. I., *Persian Poets of Sind*, Sindhî Adabi Board, Jamshoro/Hyderabad, 1987 (1st edn, 1956).

Schaflechner, Jürgen and Sarah Ewald, *Thrust into Heaven*, Heidelberg University, 76 min., 2016.

Schimmel, Annemarie, *Sindhi Literature*, Wiesbaden, Otto Harrassowitz, 1974.

Schimmel, Annemarie, *Pearls from the Indus: Studies in Sindhi Culture*, Jamshoro, Sindhi Adabi Board, 1986.

Schimmel, Annemarie, 'Ana al-haqq', in *Encyclopedia Iranica*, Vol. I, Fasc. 9, Leiden, Brill, 1989, pp. 1001–2.

Shackle, Christopher, 'Styles and Themes in the Siraiki Mystical Poetry of Sind', in Hamida Khuhro (ed.), *Sind through the Centuries: Proceedings of an International Seminar Held in Karachi in Spring 1975 by the Department of Culture Government of Sind*, Karachi, Oxford University Press, 1981, pp. 252–69.

Shaikh, Muhammad Ali, *Sindh Madressah's Roll of Honour: Linaries of the Land: Lives of Sixteen Great Men*, Karachi, Sindh Madressatulislam, 1999.

Sikand, Yoginder, *Sacred Spaces. Exploring Traditions of Shared Faiths in India*, New Delhi, Penguin Books, 2003.

Sooklal, Anil, 'The Neo-Vedanta Philosophy of Swami Vivekananda', *Nidan*, 5, 1993, pp. 33–50.

Srinivas, Tulasi, 'Articles of Faith: Material Piety, Devotional Aesthetics and the Construction of a Moral Economy in the Transnational Sathya Sai Movement', *Visual Anthropology*, 25, 2012, pp. 270–302.

Stewart, Tony K., 'In Search of equivalence, Conceiving Muslim-Hindu Encounter through Translation Theory', *History of Religions*, 40:3, 2001, pp. 260–87.

Stewart, Tony K. and Carl Ernst, 'Syncretism', in Margaret A. Mills, Peter J. Claus and Sarah Diamonf (eds), *South Asian Folklore: An Encyclopedia*, New York and London, Routledge, 2003, pp. 586–8.

Suvorova, Anna, *Muslim Saints of South Asia: The Leventh to Fifteenth Centuries*, Oxon, Routledge, 2004 (first edn, 1999).

Thakur, U. T., *Sindhi Culture*, Bombay, University of Bombay, 1959.

Thapan, Anita Raina, *Sindhi Diaspora in Manila, Hong Kong, and Jakarta*, Honolulu, University of Hawai Press, 2002.

Thapan, Anita Raina, 'Sufism and Sikhism. Understand the Dynamics of Tradition and Change in the Religious Beliefs and Practices of Sindhi Hindus', in Satish Saverwal and Supriya Varma (eds), *Traditions in Motion: Religion and Society in History*, New Delhi, Oxford University Press, 2005, pp. 205–29.

Walker, Benjmin, *Hindu World: An Encyclopedic Survey of Hindism*, New Delhi, Munshiram Manoharlal, 1983 (1st edn, 1968).

Weber, Max, *The Religion of India. Sociology of Hinduism and Buddhism*, trans. and ed. Hans H. Gerth and Don Martindale, Glencoe (Illinois), The Free Press, 1958.

Westphall-Hellbusch, Sigrid and Westphall Heinz, *The Jat of Pakistan*, Berlin, Duncker & Humblot, 1964.

Zamindar, Vazira Fazila-Yacoubali, *The Long Partition and the Making of Modern South Asia: Refugees, Boundaries, Histories*, Karachi, Oxford University Press, 2007.

Index

advaita 75, 76, 78, 86, 89, 96, 184, 191, 192
Advani, Bhagwan 157
Advani, Hiranand 90
Advani, Kalyan 111
Aggarwal, Saaz 53
Aijaz, Akhund Haji Faqir Muhammad 153, 203 n.8
Ainani, Gehimal 62
Aitken, E. H. 34
Ajlafs 25, 196 n.3
Ajmer 55, 143, 174
Ajmer Sharif 110
Ajwani, Bhagwan K. 156
Ajwani, L. H. 77, 82, 94
Akbar, Ali 28–9, 195 n.8
akhanda satchidananda (indivisible and eternal being) 90–1
akhaniyyun (folktales) 35
alam 67–8, 130, 136, 139, 188, 192
Alam, Shah Rukn-e 175
al-Arabi, Ibn 86, 199 n.12
al-Farabi 89
al-Ghazzali, Abu Hamid Muhammad 111
al-Hanafiyya, Muhammad 29
al-Haqq II, Khwaja Abd 61
al-Husayni, Shah Karim 11
Ali 119
Ali, Ghulam 94
al-Jilani, Abd al-Qadir 84, 102, 107–11, 116, 119–20, 157
al-Karim, Shah Abd 78
al-Kindi 89
Allana, G. 198 n.3
al-Latif, Shah Abd 1, 4, 21, 35–7, 48, 55, 75, 78–80, 81–2, 87, 92–3, 107, 142, 143, 144, 145, 147, 148, 152, 153, 165, 173, 187, 199 n.13, 200 n.4
alms *(zakat)* 102
al-Qadiri, Rakhiyyal Shah 46

al-Qonyawi, Sadr al-Din 86
al-Sani, Rabi 110
Amar Lal 41
Amils 14, 17, 23, 27, 30–7, 41–2, 47, 90, 122, 180, 185–6, 190, 192, 201 nn.9–10
Amritsar 81
amulets *(tawiz)* 113
ana al-haqq (I am God) 81, 89, 123, 199 n.8
antiquity, ideology of 8
Arabic alphabet 20, 65, 135, 159, 161, 196 n.9
Arabic language 28, 39
Arabic-Persian mystic culture 36
Arabic Sindhi script 56, 142
Aroras 30
arti 102, 128–30, 136, 138, 159, 178, 191
Asardas 105
Ashrafs 25, 26, 196 n.3
astano (Sufi place) 57, 105
Attar, Farid al-Din 108, 111, 147, 157
attendants 1
avatar
    Krishna 76
    of Shiva 64, 166
    of Vedic god Varun 165
Ayaz, Shaykh 148
Ayodhya 93, 188, 199 n.18

Baba Sadhuram 55
Baba Sukhdev Sahib 55
Badho (month) 107
Baghavad Gita 125
Baghdad 89, 110, 157
Bakhsh, Faqir Qadir *see* Bedil
Bakhsh, Hadi 44, 85, 120, 153, 154
Balani, Dada Ishwar 1
Baloch, Nabi Bakhsh 5, 46
Baluch 26
Baluchistan 37, 46, 171
Bambridge, Reverend 33

*baniya*s, cast   17
baraka   60
Baroda *see* Vadodara
bayragins   80, 106–7
Bedil   55, 69, 84–5, 91–2, 108,
      135, 142, 143, 145, 153, 155,
      185, 199 n.10
Beg, Mirza Qalich   36, 82, 87
Bekas   69, 135, 142, 148
Bellamy, Carla   12, 37, 191
Besant, Annie   33–4, 35, 142
bhagats   157, 203 n.10
Bhagavad Gita   34, 128, 150, 153
Bhagti   38, 119
Bhai, Jivat   61
Bhaibands   27, 192
bhajans   55, 131, 148, 153, 159, 177, 178
bhakti   38, 74–7, 81–2, 94, 119, 122, 143,
      151, 185, 198 nn.2–3, 201 n.4
Bhakti movement   75–7, 78
Bhalla, Kiku Motwani   160
bhandaro   131
bhang (narcotic beverage)   46
Bhatia, Lachhman   156, 159
Bhatia, Manu   156, 159, 160, 161
Bhatia, Mukund   166
Bhatias   27
Bhats   27
Bhavnani, Nandita   53
Bhils   27, 162, 178
Bhraspativar *arti*   130
Bhuj   44, 177, 178
Bijapur   100, 110–11, 115, 201 n.9
*Biography of Mulchand Faqir Born in
      Sehwan* (Motwani)   154
Bistami, Bayazid   108
BJP, political party   20, 139, 157,
      199–200 n.18
Blavatsky, Helena   33–4, 35, 142
Blavatsky Printing   35
Blavatsly, Tibet   37
blessing *(fazal)*   83
Bodlo Bahar, renunciants *(faqirs)* of   127
Bohrah (Muslim group)   26
Bombay *see* Mumbai (Maharashtra)
Bourdieu, Pierre   6
Brahma (God)   125
Brahmans   13, 23, 26, 27, 28,
      123, 176, 177
Brahmo Samaj   90

breath *(dam)*   118, 124
British colonization, impact of   4,
      17, 23, 24, 31, 39, 50, 51,
      106, 174, 184
Bubak   105
Buddha   35
Buddhism   36
Burton, Richard   6–7, 28, 38, 168,
      174, 177, 178

Calcutta *see* Kolkatta
canonical prayer   10
caste musicians *(manghanar/mirasi)*   40
castes   23–5, 27, 29, 30, 31, 48, 137, 162,
      165, 166, 168, 181
Central Hindu College   34
Certeau, Michel de   4
chadors   113
chakriyun (sandals)   106–7
Champra   113
Chand, Shri   40
Chander, Master   148
Chandrani, Chandmal   112
chang   79
charan   79
char dham   65
Chaudhry, Daulatram   62
Chawla, Paru   148–9
Chawla, Thakur   145, 148–9
Cheesman, David   31
Chennai   102
Chishtiyya   204 n.1
Chittick, William   86
chownki   131, 148
Chund Sindhi kalam ain dohira
      (Chawla)   148
Colaba, Mumbai   104, 105, 106, 107
concentration *(dhyan)*   126
Creator *(khaliq)*   83
culture   4
      Arabic-Persian   36
      darbars (shrine)   17, 24, 37–41
      religious   10, 78, 148
      Sindhian   40
      Sufi   4–7, 23–5, 36
      Sufis of Sindh   4–7

Dada Ratanchand Sahib   102
Dada Sain Kuthir, Haridwar   66, 68–9,
      70, 119, 121

Dadi Dhan *see* Samtani, Dadi Dhan
Dadu Dayal 76
Dadupanthi monastery, Haryana 158
Dahnhardt, Thomas 12–13,
    126, 149, 187
daily rituals 118, 127–31
Dalits 165, 174–9, 181
Dalpat Sufi 7, 14, 18, 35, 36, 47,
    59, 61, 78, 80–2, 84, 85, 88–9,
    91–4, 96, 104–8, 118, 119, 123,
    129, 130, 136–9, 142, 143, 145,
    147, 148, 153, 155, 185, 187–8,
    191, 200 n.4
dam (breath) 118, 124
Damodar, H. M. 60, 134, 136, 149–50
Daraza 47
    dargah of 54
    Faruqi *silsilo* in 47
    sajjada nashin of 14, 59, 61, 80, 83–4,
        122, 130, 138–9, 166, 204 n.1
    silsila 54, 59, 61, 65, 80, 187, 188,
        189, 190, 192, 197 n.2
Darazi
    Nimano 122
    Sakhi 122
    satsangs 137–9
    silsila 80
darbars (shrine) 24–5, 54, 118
    activities 102–4, 127–31
    al-Latif 165
    architectural styles 66–71
    authority 59–64
    building in India 54–9
    culture 17, 24, 37–41
    Daryapanthi 25, 40
    duty 102–3
    extensions 100–4
    Halani 41, 55, 103
    of Haridwar 121
    Hindu 23, 42
    Hindu Sufi 42, 57, 82, 97, 127
    of Imam Shah (Pirana,
        Ahmedabad) 12
    Indian 60, 64–7, 102–3
    Jinda Pir 41
    Kathwaro 55
    legitimacy 59–64
    naming in India 64–6
    Nanakpanthi 25, 40–1
    Nimano's 54, 57–9, 61–2, 65–6

as pilgrimage 12
Pithoro Pir 38, 165–6
Qalandar's 120, 166, 167,
    171, 176, 180
Rochaldas (Shantinagar,
    Ulhasnagar) 1–2, 65–9, 99, 102–3,
    118–22, 136, 139, 149, 159, 163,
    188, 192, 196 n.12
of Sain Vasan Shah 55
of Shantinagar 154
Sindhi 55, 118, 121, 131,
    138, 200 n.2
succession 59–64
Sufi 18, 24–5, 42, 57, 59, 82, 96, 97,
    99, 102, 104, 127, 163, 165
of Udero Lal 165, 198 n.5
in Ulhasnagar 1–2, 55, 65–8, 99,
    102–3, 118, 121–2, 136, 139, 149,
    159, 188, 192, 196 n.12
dargah(s) 24
    of Daraza 54
    of Fatehpur 46
    of Jalalani *tariqa* 109
    of Jhok Sharif 46, 111, 115
    of Qutub Ali 154
    of Sachal Sarmast 18
    of Sindh 119
    of Tando Ahmad Khan 110, 171–4
darsan (divine vision of God) 93, 94,
    117, 124, 192
Darvesh Asthan, Delhi 102
darvish 57
Darvishan jo dawr 143
Daryapanths 25, 29–30, 168, 189
Dasserah, Hindu festival 107, 200 n.3
dastarbandi (coronation) 60–1, 113,
    132–3, 136, 154
Dattaramani, Chainrai Bachomal 81–2
Dayaram Jethmal Science College 34
death anniversary 69, 131–7, 157, 161
    Dalpat 107
    Daulatram's wife 101
    Hari, R. M. 60–1, 138
    Isarlal 161
    Mulchand 63, 69, 70
    Rochaldas 154, 192
    Sachal 138
Delhi 29, 62, 101
Deva, Jaya 77
Devanagari script 56, 142, 163

Devi (goddess) 30
devotional supplication *(munajat)*
134
dham
char 65
Rohri 65, 71
dhamal 47, 197 n.18
Qalandar's *darbar* 127
Rochaldas's *darbar* 118, 127
Dhunjishaw 34
dhyan (concentration) 126
Diach, Rao 79
Dibgy, Simon 7–8
Dictionary of Sindhi Literature
(Jotwani) 94
didar (divine vision of Sufi Master) 55,
82, 117, 124, 192; *see also darsan*
(divine vision of God)
Dil Kusha 108–9, 200 n.4
Dirks, Nicholas 7
Diwali (Hindu festival) 93, 199 n.17
Diwan Dastgir 111
Doda Mard Haqani Kafi 109
Dukh Bhanjan Darbar, Kolkatta 102
Dwarka 79

Ego 84, 108, 126, 147, 189
ektara (one-string guitar) 46
English language 31, 142
episteme of Sindh 39
equivalence, in encounter of
religions 9, 151
Ernst, Carl 8, 183

fana fi'llah 73, 97
fanai (absorption) 91
faqeeri dhamal 57
faqih (religious agent) 28
Fara'iz al-islam (Hashim) 28
Farid, Ghulam 78, 148, 158
Faruqi, Sakhi Qabul
Muhammad 83–4, 199 n.9
Fathepur 46
fazal (blessing) 83
Flaskerud, Ingvild 200 n.5
folktales *(akhaniyyun)* 35
Foucault, Michel 19, 39
Freemasonry 33
Frere, Bartle 31, 50
Fuller, Christopher 30, 123

gaddi nashins 55, 67, 69, 114, 119, 120,
122, 132, 136, 174, 175, 198 n.3
Baba Sadhuram 55
Hindus 165
Indian 55
migration 55
Nimanal Sangam 159
Nimano 61, 100
of Rochaldas's *darbar* 99, 149
Shah, Vasan 57
of Tando Saindad 110
Gajwani, S. L. 1, 60, 83, 153–4, 156, 158
Ganga 93
Gazetteer (Aitken) 34
Geertz, Clifford 4
ginan 10
Gobindram 135
God 83
Gorakhnath 8, 64, 107, 175
grace *(rahim)* 83
Great Integrators 38–9
Guga Pir 30
guide *(murshid)* 83
Gujarat 11, 20, 40, 59
Gujarati 39
gunbaz 66
Gurbuxani, Gopi 69, 70, 71
gurdwaras 72, 172, 186
Gurmukhi script 41, 81
Guru Granth Sahib 108, 120, 122
guru (master) 14, 54
Guru Nanak 40, 41, 55, 76, 77, 78, 90,
120, 121, 128, 138, 143, 147, 159,
196 n.13, 203 n.7

Ḥafiẓ, Khwaja Muḥammad 80
Halani clinic 103
Halani *darbar* 41, 55, 103
Hallaj, Mansur 81, 89, 108, 123,
153, 199 n.8
hama ust (all is he) 36
Hanuman (god) 94
haqq mawjud 47, 88–9, 90, 96
Hari, H. M. 83–4
Hari, R. M. 44, 45, 57, 60, 84, 124, 126,
149–55, 161
Haridwar 47, 63, 64, 100, 101, 130,
163, 197 n.19
hari (landless farmers) 26
hari om 123

Harjani, Gidumal Khatanmal   166
Hasan   108
Hasan, Mian Abu'l   28
Hashim, Makhdum Muhammad   9, 28
havan ritual   101, 123
Hawley, John Stratton   75, 76
hekal   88
hek nimani (humble devotee)   83
Hindi   39
Hinduism   36, 95
    iconography in   117, 118–22
    vs. Islam   8, 9, 11, 12, 16, 164–6
    in Sindhicate area   14–16
    Sindhis encounters   164–6
    vs. Sufism   12–13, 20, 24, 164–6
    as universal religion   32
hinduization process   11, 13, 20, 147,
        157, 160, 162, 163, 188, 189,
        191, 202–3 n.6
hindu momin nahyan   7
Hindu mythology   93
Hindu Sindhi
    castes   27
    identity   2, 142, 147
    of India   1, 2, 19, 20, 57, 83, 116,
        128, 139–41, 143–5, 154, 157, 160,
        163–4, 179, 185
    migration   18, 21, 30, 42, 48–50,
        51–2, 53, 55
    in Pakistan   163–81
    panchayat system and   27–8
    religion of   15–16
    religious legacies   32
    representations   15
    social sciences, issue in   7–13
    Sufi paths   2, 12, 13, 16, 20–1, 24, 40,
        41–8, 47, 61, 85, 95, 100–2, 104,
        110, 111, 117–18, 124, 154, 159,
        163–81, 188–9
    syncretism of   15–16
    traditions   1, 13, 20, 116, 145, 146
Hindu spirituality   151
Hindus
    Naqshbandis   13, 125–6
    and Sehwan system   166–71
    Sufi paths   13, 24, 40, 41–8, 61, 85, 95,
        100–2, 104, 110, 117–18, 124, 154,
        159, 163–81
    Sufis   14–15, 17–18, 20–1, 23, 47
    worship, categories of   37–8

Hinglaj   37, 79, 93
Hiranandani, Popati   131, 148
History of Sindhi Literature
        (Ajwani)   82, 94
Hodgson, Marshall   3, 195 n.3
Hong Kong   61, 101
humble devotee *(hek nimani)*   83
Husain   108
Husayn (Shia imam)   79–80, 196 n.14
Hussein Tikri, sanctuary   12
Hyderabad   17, 34, 35, 41, 47, 65, 105,
        106, 110, 154, 171, 176

iconography   117
    in *darbar* of Rochaldas   120
    and genealogy   119
    in Hinduism   117
    as idiom of transference   117–22
    role of   118–19
    set-up   119
    Shia Muslims   200 n.5
ideology   8, 74
idol *(murti)*   136, 138, 139
Ilaiah, Kancha   7
Ilhya ulum al-din (al-Ghazzali)   111
illusion *(maya)*   81, 94
Ilm al-laduni va towhid   150
Imam   10
*imambara*s   18
Inat, Shah   92, 198 n.3
Inayat, Shah   36, 94, 111
Indian National Congress   34
indigenization   15
influences   8
    non-christian religions   8
    Yogic   8
initiation, Sufi   123–7
insal kamil (perfect man)   43
intelligentsia of Sufism   30–4, 196 n.5
Iqbal, Muhammad   89, 199 n.14
Iraq   28
Isarlal   156, 157
ishq (Sufi love)   122, 152–3
    haqiqi   153
    majazi   153
Islam
    vs. Hinduism   8, 9, 11, 12, 16, 164–6
    practices   29
    South Asian   39
Islamicate   3, 37, 195 n.3

Ismailism   10, 11
ism-e azam (expression/word)   36

Jacobabad   46
Jagat ja netaun   35
Jaghtiyyani, Dadi Ganga
    Devi   85, 96, 150
Jahan, Shah   11
Jahangasht, Jalal al-Din Bukhari
    Makhdum-i Jahaniyyan   43
Jahaniyya   60, 82, 85, 99, 132, 154, 187
Jainism   36
Jajiks   27
Jalalani Sharif   108
Janamashtmi   153
janeo   93
Jani, Nirmal   61, 159, 188, 204 n.2
jap sahib (repetition of name of
    guru)   93, 152
Jats   26
Jesus   35
Jethmal, Dayaram   34
Jethwani, Basant   34, 63, 64, 101,
    121, 122, 130
Jethwani, Sonu   63, 66, 69, 70, 71, 121
jhando   132, 136
Jhangara, Sehwan   62
Jhok Sharif   46, 47, 105, 106, 111, 128
Jhulelal   41, 57, 58, 70, 128, 140, 143–8,
    157, 161, 165, 167, 171, 173, 179,
    181, 188, 198 n.5, 198 n.6
Jindani, Pushpa Tilly   61
Jinda Pir   41
jiva   44
*Jivan charitra Sufi Darvish Faqir
    Mulchand Sahib Sehwan navesi*
    (Motwani)   154
jogis   7, 8, 10, 78, 79, 107
Jogi Sain   100, 107–10, 119
Jotwani, Motilal   38–9, 75, 78, 87
Junagarh   79
Junaid   108, 109

Kabir   78, 147, 153, 198 n.2
Kabirpanth   13
kafi   203 n.4
*kalam*s   7, 43, 46, 47, 55, 61, 69, 85, 102,
    105, 106, 108, 109, 120, 128, 130–6,
    138, 139, 145, 148–9, 154, 156–61,
    166, 187, 199 n.9

Kalhoras   25, 26
Kali (goddess)   91
Kalyan   44
kamach   79
Kamal Faqir   203 n.3
Kandri   94
Kaniyya *see* Krishna (god)
Kanungos   45, 134, 188
Karachi   13, 31, 33, 34, 43, 44,
    49–51 54–55, 57–8, 65, 81, 90,
    102, 143, 179
Karachi riots   53
Karbala   79, 80, 196–7 n.14
kardar (tax collector)   31
Karim, Shah   92
Kashefi, Husayn Va'iz   29
Kashi (Banaras)   93
Kataria, Soni   129
katha (stories)   76, 128
Kathwaro Darbar   55
Katwara Sahib   101
Kayasht community   12–13
*Ke saitun sajnan san urf Sain
    (Daktar) Rochaldas Sahib ji
    satsangi rihan*   151
Keswani, Daulat   108, 109
Keswani, Parsuram   107
Khairpur   13, 18, 55, 80, 109,
    137, 156
Khalsa   30, 40, 90
Khalsa Sikhs   40
Khan, Darya   94, 155
Khan, Dominique-Sila   195 n.9
Khan, Liaqat Ali   49
Khetrapal, (festival of disciple
    of Shiva)   30
Khizr, Khwaja   41
Khojah (Muslim group)   26
Khudabadi Amils   90
Khudawadi script   41
Khuhnbatis   168–70
khuhnbo ceremony   168
Khuhro, Hamida   49
Khuhro, Muhammad Ayyub   49
Khusraw, Nasir-e   11
Khwaja Khizr (sanctuary)   18
kishti   80
Kohji   148
Kohlis   27, 162, 178
Kolkatta   90, 102

Kothari, Rita   15, 53, 195 n.2
Kripalani, Molchand   100, 110–11, 115, 119, 189
Krishna (god)   32, 35, 44, 76, 77, 81, 93–4, 121, 122, 200 n.19
Krishna (Sufi)   119, 120, 122
kuthiyya   62, 65, 70

Ladkani, Sugnaram Mangadas   158
Lakki   48
Lakkiyyari, Gul Muhammad   170
Lakkiyyaris   168
Lal, Isar   156, 157
Lal, Kanya   112
Lal, Mohan   112
Lal Das   114, 134, 167–8, 170
Lal Gul   168
Lal Kunwar   168–9
Lal Shahbaz Qalandar   7, 36, 37, 43, 45–7, 58, 62, 67–8, 67–9, 105, 108, 109, 112, 113, 120, 127–8, 132–4, 153, 165, 167–9, 171–3, 176, 179–80, 187, 198 n.5, 200 n.4, 203 n.5
Lalwani, Lilaram Watanmal   87
landless farmers *(hari)*   26
landowners *(zamindar)*   26, 31
Laxman (god)   94
Layla   122, 152, 153, 201 n.6
learning
    imperial centres of   8
    regional centres of   8
legacy, Sufi   2, 17, 18–21, 30, 85, 108, 116, 140, 141–61, 162, 164, 166, 173–4, 180–1, 185, 188, 190–1, 202 n.4
    diaspora role in transmission   157–60, 195 n.2
    non-poetic chains for transmission   149–56
    other networks of transmission   156–7
    Panjwani, Ram and   142–9
    post-partition transmission, challenge of   142–9
The Life and Teaching of Muhammad (Besant)   34
The Life, Religion, and Poetry of Shah Latif (Lalwani)   87
linguistic translation   10

Literary Cultures in History: Reconstructions from South Asia (Pollock)   5
Literary Society   33
Lohanas   27, 29, 30, 31
Lorenzen, David   74
Lowari Sharif (Badin, Sindh)   9
Lucknow   44

Madras   36
*madrasat*s   28
Maharaj, Ramchandraji   12–13
Maharashtra   20
Mahdi, Imam   108
Majma' al-bahrayn (Shikoh)   11
Majnun   122, 152, 153, 201 n.6
Malaga   61, 101
malfuzats (Sufi Master and his disciples, dialogues between)   8, 152, 154
Mallik, Gurdial   142
mandir (temple)   93, 110–11, 115, 173
manghanar/mirasi (caste musicians)   40
manqullat (religious sciences)   28
Mansharamani, D. K.   108
Mansharamani, Rochaldas   42–5, 57–8, 60
mantra   123
    jap   93, 152
    of Vedantists   36
Manu   35
Manzil-e illahi (Motwani)   154
Manzilgah Affair   48, 58, 197 n.20
maqallat (rational sciences)   28
maqbaro (tomb)   62, 66, 100
maqtal nama   29
marifat   147
Markovits, C.   195 n.2
marsiya (devotional literature of Shiite origin)   29
marsiyyo genre   80, 198 n.6
mastan   27
Master *(guru/malik)*   8, 14, 17, 23, 38, 42–3, 46, 47, 54, 57, 59, 83, 85, 88, 99, 105, 107, 110, 111, 114, 115, 117–19, 122, 141, 155, 160, 172, 175, 185–7, 189
Matlani, Mohanlal   198 n.4
maya (illusion)   81, 94
meditation   36, 118, 123–7
mehndi (henna)   45, 132, 197 n.16

procession   134, 136, 139, 168–70, 180, 188
    Qalandar, ceremony of   45, 47, 58, 105, 112–14
    in Ulhasnagar   136
    wedding and   131
mehndibardar   44, 113, 134, 139, 169
Memon (Muslim group)   26
Menghwars   27, 30, 162, 165, 184
Merani, Nandirani   32
Meru   45
middle class   41–8
Mir, Farina   5, 6
Mirabai   76, 78, 136, 147, 198 n.2
Mirchandani, Kamal   159–60
Mirchandani, Manju   159–60
Mishra, Brahmashankar   13
Mohajirs   49, 58, 197 n.21
Moharram   80, 196 n.14
Motwani, Daulatram   101, 115, 131
Motwani, Gehimal   57, 58, 60, 62, 64, 66, 69–70, 85, 100, 101, 112, 122, 154–5
Motwani, Kiku   158
Motwani, Tirthdas   62, 70
mufti (religious agent)   28
Mughal Empire   11, 13
Muhammad II, Sakhi Qabul   45, 47, 119, 122, 137
mujaddid (renovator)   111
mukhthyarkar (revenue officer)   62
Mulan Faqir jo asthan   62
Mulchand Faqir   23, 42, 45–7, 51–3, 57–8, 60, 62–6, 69–71, 85, 88, 96, 100–1, 105–6, 111–14, 118, 120, 122–4, 130–1, 136, 154–5, 156, 158, 160, 161, 163, 166–7, 170, 180, 188
Mulchand *kafi, Sehwan*   66, 100, 111–14
Mul Kutiyya, Ulhasnagar   63, 66, 70, 101, 130
Mumbai (Maharashtra)   12, 14, 44, 50, 55, 61, 62, 68, 69, 101, 102, 110, 131, 135, 143, 144, 167, 196 n.4
munajat (devotional supplication)   134–5, 159
Muqaddimat al-Salat (Hasan)   28
Murad Faqir   94–5, 143
murshid   45, 50, 51, 52, 59, 60, 62, 66, 80, 83, 85, 119, 121–3, 128, 136–7, 162
murti (idol/statue)   136, 138, 139

Muslims
    identity   9, 174
    Master   42, 54, 66, 186
    *murshid*s   45, 50, 51, 52, 59, 60, 62, 66, 80, 83, 85, 119, 121–3, 128, 136–7, 162
    pirs   14–15
    refugees   49
    religious legacies   32
    Shiites   28
    Sindhis   1, 9, 25–6, 75, 178, 196 n.2
    of Sukkur   48
    Sunnis   28
    worship, categories of   37–8
mystical poetry   89
mystical space   73–4, 117–18, 141

Nagpur (Madhya Pradesh)   55
Naik, Devi   63, 69, 70, 71, 121, 179
nam   61, 62, 66, 107–8, 110, 123–7, 124, 154, 189
namaz (canonical prayer)   10
Nanakpanth   8, 13, 18, 21, 25, 29, 30, 40, 41, 50, 77, 90, 171, 186, 187, 189
Nao   45
Napier, Charles   33
Naqshbandis   149
    Hindus   13, 125–6, 149
    of Sindh   29
    tariqa   12
Naqshbandiyya   13, 125
Narsain, N. J.   14
Narsain, S. J.   32, 41, 50, 122
Nasir Faqir   14, 88, 109–10, 128
Nathpanthis   8, 64, 79, 107, 179; *see also jogis*
Nausharo Firuz   55
Navani, Parumal   45
Navratri, (festival of goddess Bhavani)   30
nazar (vision/glance)   124
Nebhraj Sahib   102
neo-Hinduism   89
Neo-Vedanta   89, 90–1; *see also* Vedanta
Nimanal Sangam   61, 65, 68–70, 101, 103–4, 119, 129, 159, 191
Nimano Faqir   7, 23, 42, 45, 47, 54, 57–9, 61–2, 65–6, 85, 100, 101–2, 118, 119, 120, 122, 129, 139, 145, 155–6, 159, 188, 189, 191–2

nirguna prem (mystical love)　153
Nirguni Bhakti　75, 76
non-migrant Sindhis　149, 202 n.4
non-Muslims　8
non-poetic Sufism,
　　transmission of　149–56
Nusserwanji, Jamshed　34

objectification of Sufism　30, 34–7, 142
om　36, 123, 155
Oneness of God　54, 74, 78–84, 86–91,
　　96, 125, 148, 150, 165
Oshaq Ali Faqir　109
Osho　142, 202 n.1

Pabuji　30
pag　60
pain (*dard*)　83
Pakistan　2, 3, 5, 14–19, 23, 42, 44, 48,
　　49, 51–3, 55, 59, 60, 64, 66, 79, 99,
　　100, 105, 109, 111, 112, 114, 115,
　　118, 132, 140, 148, 154, 156, 162,
　　163–81, 185, 190
panchayat system　27–8
pandits　40
Panjwani, Ram　55, 78, 131, 141, 142–9,
　　157, 161, 202 n.2
Parsis　34
Parsram, Jethmal　35–7, 42, 142
partition, Sindh　48–50, 51, 53
perfect man (*insal kamil*)　43
Persian language　31, 39
physical mystical space　73, 117–18, 141
pilgrimage to Bijapur　110–11
Pirana (Ahmedabad)　12
Pir Baba Ratannath, Delhi　201 n.6
Pir Data Dastgir *see* al-Jilani, Abd al-Qadir
piri-muridi　60
pirs　10, 14
　　Muslim　14–15, 26
　　power　26
　　of Sindh　26
　　Sufi　23
Pithoro Pir　30, 38, 165–6
Pithoropirpotas　30
poetry (Sufi)　2, 5, 13, 18, 21, 24, 32,
　　36, 46, 65, 68, 72, 73–97, 101, 107,
　　108, 120, 122, 139, 141–2, 144, 146,
　　154–8, 163, 185, 186, 192
　　bhakti　74–7

hindu references in　91–5
Neo-Vedanta in　90–1
Sufi corpus　77–86
Vedanta　74–7
wahdat-e wujud, vernacular
　　ideology of　86–91
pohtal　46
Pollock, Sheldon　5, 8, 10
pothiyyun (Hindu scriptures)　39, 92, 94
Prakash, Moti　148
pranayama yoga　44, 125, 126, 152, 155
prasad　101
Premchand, Lilaram　35
Pritamdas　103
Prophet Muhammad　9, 26, 35,
　　108, 119, 125
puja/pudiya　123, 128, 130–1
puja rooms　101, 131
Puj Nimano Sain Pak Astan　129
Punjab　40, 48–9, 81
Punjabi　5, 39

Qadiriyya　46, 84, 85, 110, 119,
　　125, 126, 187
Qalandar, Bu Ali　108
Qazi Qazan　158
qazi (religious agent)　28
quasi-feudal system　50
Quran　9, 29, 108
qutub　43

Radha (goddess)　119, 120, 121–2
Radhye Shyam　123
rag　83
rahim (grace)　83
Rai, Naval　90
Raikes, Stanley N.　7
Raja Barthari　165
Raja Bharthari　37
Rajasthan　40
Raja Vir　37, 165, 172
Rajputs　27, 29, 30
Ram, Bhagat Kanwar　48
Rama (god)　76, 77, 94, 121, 126, 150
Ramakhrishna　89–90
Rama Pir　30
Ramayana　93, 94, 150
Ramchand　112–14
Ramey, Steven　15–16
rational sciences (*maqallat*)　28

Rauzat al-Shahid (Kashefi) 29
religion
  agents 28
  corpus 39
  knowledge 29
  purity of 11
  sciences *(manqullat)* 28
remembrance *(samaran)* 126
renovator *(mujaddid)* 111
rituals 18–19, 117
  annual fairs 118
  as connecting spaces and
    community 117–40
  daily 118, 127–31
  dhamal at Rochaldas's *darbar* 118
  havan 123
  initiation 123–7
  meditation 118, 123–7
  Sufi paths and 118
  Vedic 123
Rochaldas, Rai 1, 23, 42, 54–5, 65–9, 85,
    114, 118–22, 126, 149
Rohal Faqir 94–5
Rohri 17, 42, 43–4, 47, 48, 55, 65
Rohri dham 65, 71
Roohani Choond Sindhi kalaam
    (Mirchandani) 159–60
Rumi, Jalal al-Din 35, 36, 79, 89, 108,
    127, 146, 157, 198 n.5

Sab ka malik ek hai (there is only one
    God) 173, 181, 201 n.10
Sabzwaris 167
Sachal jyun kafiyun (Panjwani) 202 n.2
Sachal Sarmast 7, 14, 18, 35, 36, 47, 59,
    61, 78, 80–2, 84, 85, 88–9, 91–4, 96,
    118, 119, 123, 129, 130, 136–9, 142,
    143, 145, 147, 148, 153, 155, 185,
    187–8, 191, 200 n.4
Sadh Bela (sanctuary) 18
Sadh Belo 48, 55, 56
saguna prem (physical love) 153
Saguni tradition, Bhakti movement 76
Sai Baba *see* Shirdi Sai Baba; Shri
    Sathya Sai Baba
Sain Lachmandas 105
saints 54
sajjada nashin 198 n.3
  of Daraza 14, 59, 61, 80, 122, 130,
    138, 166, 204 n.1

  of Jahaniyya 60
  of Jhok Sharif 46
  for Muslims 165
  of Tando Jahaniyyan 99
Sakhi 59
Sakhi Darazi 122
Sakhi Kuthiyya 61, 65, 119, 129
Sakhi sabhajhal (Ali Shah) 83, 145, 159
Saksena (Kayasht, subcaste of) 12
samadhi 67–8, 99–100, 104–10, 117
  Dalpat Sufi 104–8
  in Hindu theology 104
  Jogi Sain 100, 107–10, 119
  Kripalani, Molchand 100, 110, 119
  in Sindhicate context 104
samaran (remembrance) 126
sami 64, 78, 81, 82, 94, 147–8
sampradaya 76
Samtani, Dadi Dhan 85, 96, 102,
    114, 135, 150
Sanatana Dharma 36
sanctum sanctorum 68
sandals *(chakriyun)* 106
Sanskrit 28, 39
sants 50, 76, 131
Saraswat Brahmans 27
Sarmast, Sayyid Ali 43
satchidananda 90–1
satgurus (true guides) 35, 152
satsangs 62, 70, 91, 95, 107, 109, 115,
    129–31, 137–9, 149–52, 172, 191
Sayyids 26
scheduled castes 48, 162
script(s)
  Arabic Sindhi 56, 142
  Devanagari 56, 142, 163
  Gurmukhi 41, 81
  Khudawadi 41
  Roman 159–60, 162, 203 n.12
  romanized Sindhi 159–60
scriptures 14, 92
  Hindu 92, 93, 94, 96, 151
  of Islam 29
  of Nanak Shah 131
  pothiyun 94, 177
  Sikh 94
  Vedas 92
Sehwani, Fateh Muhammad 58
Sehwani *panchayat* 167
Sehwani Paro 70

Sehwan Sharif   7, 17, 32, 37, 45, 47, 54,
      58, 62, 66, 68, 84, 100, 105, 109,
      112, 115, 118, 127, 128, 134, 136,
      148, 165–7, 170, 171, 173, 176, 180,
      187, 198 n.3
Sehwan system, Hindus and   166–71
Self   84, 125, 152
Sen, Keshub Chandra   90
shabd   123, 126, 152
Shabd anahat   35
Shackle, Christopher   91
Shah, Abd al-Sattar   107–8
Shah, Bulhe   78, 145, 158
Shah, Darya   143
Shah, Mohsin   110
Shah, Nur Husayn   60–1, 120
Shah, Nur Maḥmad   46
Shah, Paru   55, 143
Shah, Qutub Ali   14, 37, 43–5, 82–5, 88,
      92–4, 102, 117, 120–1, 123–6, 128,
      134–7, 142, 145, 153–4, 159, 185,
      187, 197 n.15
Shah, Rohal   55, 143
Shah, Roshan Ali   134, 154, 159
Shah, Sayyid Rakhiyyal   43, 45, 46, 62,
      88, 124, 125
Shah, Vasan   42–4, 55, 57, 120,
      143, 196 n.13
Shahani, Hiranand   33
shahanshah   57
Shah Bahu   158
Shah jo risalo (al-Latif)   1, 4, 21, 34–5,
      50, 79, 87, 142, 157
Shaikh, Muhammad Bakhsh   166
Sharif, Jhok   14
shaykh   8
shewadaris (attendants)   1
Shia Muslims   18
   figures   12, 108
   iconography   200 n.5
   imam   108, 119
   representation   109
   tradition   12
Shidi   26
Shiites   28
shikara   65, 71
Shikaris (Muslim group)   26
Shikarpur   17, 47, 55, 81
Shikoh, Dara   11
Shirdi Sai Baba   121, 173, 202 n.10

Shiva (god)   30
Shivaite Bhakti   76
Shrimad Bhagavad Gita   150, 153
Shri Sathya Sai Baba   135, 202 n.9
Shri Yoga Vaisishtha   150
Shyam *see* Krishna (god)
sidra al-muntaha   125
Sikhism   30, 36, 95; *see also* Nanakpanth
Sikhs   24, 40–1
Sik ji soghat (Panjwani)   145
silsila Daraza   54, 59, 61, 65, 80, 187, 188,
      189, 190, 192, 197 n.2
Sindh   16–17, 23–4
   British colonization, impact of   4, 17,
      23, 24, 31, 39, 50, 51, 106, 174, 184
   colonial   25–30
   darbar culture   17, 24–5
   episteme of   39
   Hindus of   1, 12, 23–4, 27, 48
   Muslims of   1, 9, 25–6
   mystic doctrine of   36
   Naqshbandis of   29
   partition in   48–50, 51, 53
   pirs of   26
   religious belonging in   25–30
   religious culture of   10, 78, 148
   religious market in   17
   to Sindhicate area   1–4
   social fabric   23–4, 25–30
   socio-economic structures of   17, 24
   Sufi culture of   4–7, 23–5, 36
   Sufi masters   17, 23
   sufism of   4–7, 36
   trans-religious denomination   17
   untouchables in   26, 27, 29–30
Sindhi ain Sindhiyaat (Panjwani)   146
Sindhian culture   40
Sindhicate area   3, 6, 11, 13
   darbar culture in   37
   jogis in   107
   Sindh to   1–4
   Sufism and Hinduism in   14–16
Sindhi Community House, Cricklewood   1
Sindhi Hindus   48
   identity   2, 142, 147
   of India   1, 2, 14, 15, 18, 81, 160
   religion of   15–16
   representations   15
   of Sindh   1, 12
   syncretism of   15–16

Sindhis
  American 21
  devotional literature 40
  diaspora 2–3, 157–60, 195 n.2
  Hindu *panth*s 21
  identity 15, 142, 147
  language 1, 18, 19, 20, 31, 56, 78,
    140, 142, 147, 148, 159, 161, 163,
    190, 203 n.12
  manuscripts 28–9
  Nanakpanthis 40
  poets 10
  religiosity in 24–5
  religious beliefs 24
  religious literature 39
  Sufi devotional literature in 20
  Sufism and Hinduism, encounters
    between 164–6
Sindhi Sufi Literature in Independent India
    (Gajwani) 1
Sindhiyyat 140, 142–3, 146, 148–9,
    160–1, 164
Sindh Sahitiyya Society 35
Sindilo, Abd al-Karim 81
Singh, Guru Gobind 40
Sipahimalani, Dhuru 106
Sipahimalani, Keshavram 106
Siraiki
  language 17, 39, 95, 203 n.11
  poetry 85, 91
Siraiki kalam al-Sufiya
    (Ladkani) 158, 199 n.9
Sita (goddess) 94
Sitala (smallpox goddess) 38
Sita Sindhu Bhavan 144, 146, 148
Slaves of African *see* Shidi
*sloka*s 150
Sobhraj Faqir 47, 166
social sciences, Sufis issue in 7–13
sociotextual community 5
Sohrawardiyya 38, 43, 85, 126,
    187, 204 n.1
Some Moments with the Master
    (Damodar) 120
Sonaros 27
Spain 101
Sri Lanka 93
Stewart, Tony 9
stories *(katha)* 76
Sufi *chowki*s 131

Sufi corpus
  Bhakti 74–7
  classical 77–82, 152
  modern 78, 82–6
  Vedanta 74–7
Sufi Dar 102
Sufi Galaxy 153
Sufi Mandir in Sion, Mumbai 103–4, 110
Sufi math (Sufi religion) 35
Sufis
  affiliation 13, 47, 53, 57, 187
  cults 1, 14, 18, 37, 122, 130, 137,
    160, 174–9
  culture 4–7, 23–5
  darbars (shrine) 18, 24–5, 42,
    57, 59, 82, 96, 97, 99, 102, 104,
    127, 163, 165
  Hindu 14–15, 17–18, 20, 47, 54–9
  Hindu Sindhi 2, 12, 13, 15–16, 20–1,
    111, 188–9
  informal practices 127–31
  legacy 2, 17, 18–21, 30, 85, 108, 116,
    140, 141–61, 162, 164, 166, 173–4,
    180–1, 185, 188, 190–1, 202 n.4
  literature 39–40, 153, 161
  mandir 100, 103–4, 110–11, 115, 173
  masters 8, 14, 17, 23, 38, 42–3, 46, 47,
    54, 57, 59, 85, 88, 99, 105, 107, 110,
    111, 114, 115, 117–19, 122, 141,
    155, 160, 172, 175, 185–7, 189
  *murshid*s 59
  pirs 14–15, 23
  poetry 2, 5, 13, 18, 21, 24, 32, 36, 46,
    65, 68, 72, 73–97, 101, 107, 108,
    120, 122, 139, 141–2, 144, 146,
    154–8, 163, 185, 186, 192
  religion 35
  rituals 18–19, 118
  samadhi as alternative
    structure 104–10
  of Sindh 36
  social marginalization 5
  social sciences, issue in 7–13
  sociocultural communities 6
  traditions 1, 2, 17, 19–20, 47, 105,
    116, 145, 146
Sufi sagora (Premchand and Parsram) 35
Sufism 4–7, 15, 36, 38
  and Bhagti 38
  Bhakti corpus of 74–7

diaspora role in transmission
    of 157–60, 195 n.2
features 10
vs. Hinduism 12–13, 24, 164–6
intelligentsia of 30–4, 196 n.5
Islamic 20
jogi as symbol of 10
networks of transmission 156–7
non-poetic chains for
    transmission of 149–56
objectification of 30, 34–7, 142
representation of 30
in Sindhicate area 14–16
of Sindh in India 1, 141–61
Sindhis encounters 164–6
spirit 146, 148, 157
Vedanta corpus of 74–7
Sufi so jo sachu pachhani (Dalpat) 83, 105
Sufistic chownkies 131, 148
Sufi tomb 165
Sukkur riots 48–9
Sunnis 28
sur asa purbi 83
Surat 44
Surdas 77
Sur Kedaro 79–80
surs 58, 79, 83
Swami Meghraj 81
symbolic mystical space 73
syncretism 11, 16

Tabrizi, Shams 108
Tagore, Rabindranath 142
Tahir, Shaykh 38, 165
Talpur 25, 28, 31, 55
Tando Ahmad Khan dargah 110,
    166, 171–4
Tando Jahaniyya, Hyderabad 14, 47, 82,
    85, 99, 132
Tasawwuf or Theosophy' (Parsram) 36
tawiz (amulets) 113
Tazkira al-awliyya (Attar) 111
tazkiras (hagiographical life narratives of
    Sufi saints) 8, 38
Thakur, Hiro 158
Thakurs 29, 58, 70, 167, 198 n.6, 204 n.7
Thapan, Anita Raina 14–15, 61
Thattah 28
Theosophical Society 17, 24, 31, 33–4,
    36, 51, 142, 144, 184

Tilak, Home Rule League 34
tomb *(maqbaro)* 62
translation 15
Trump, Ernst 50
Tughluq, Muhammad bin 43
Tulsidas 76, 77

Udais temple, Sadh Bela 18
Udasis 40, 196 n.10
Udero Lal 29–30, 38, 41, 165
Ulemas 40
Ulhasnagar (Maharashtra) 1, 2, 55,
    60, 62, 63, 66, 67, 69–70, 72,
    100–1, 115, 122, 129, 131–2, 134,
    136–9, 152, 163, 166–7, 188,
    191, 197 n.17
ulul al-amr 134–5
Umerkot 27
Ummah (Muslim community) 32
unity of being *(wahdat-e wujud)* 74,
    78–84, 86–91, 96, 125, 148,
    149, 150, 165
untouchables 26, 27, 29–30
Upanishad Gyan 35
Urdu 29
urs 44, 46, 110, 131–7, 165, 167–9, 190
    in Arabic 131
    of Jhok Sharif 46
    of Lal Shahbaz Qalandar 45, 68,
        105, 112, 113
    of Muhammad, Sadiq 108
    of Muinuddin Chishti 110
    of Qutub Ali Shah 44
    of Sachal Sarmast 130
Utch (Bahawalpur, Punjab) 43
Utradi 17

Vadodara 47, 59, 101, 119
vahiadaoo (unicity) 36
Vallabhacharya 201 n.4
Valmiki 150
Variyyani, Pritam 158
Varun (Vedic god) 41, 165
Vaswani, J. P. 143
Vaswani, Ranjit Premchand 143
Vaswani, T. L. 34, 143, 152, 160
Vedanta 13, 74–7, 150–2, 198 n.1; *see
    also* Neo-Vedanta
Vedas 81, 92
Vedic god Varun 41, 165

Vedic rituals   123
vernacularization, process of   4, 10, 15, 24, 86, 87, 88, 96, 195 n.5
versi see death anniversary
Vicholi (Sindhi language)   17
Vishnu (God)   125, 150
Vivekananda   32, 89–90
The Voice of Silence (Blavatsky)   35

wahadata (unity)   86
wahdat-e wujud (unity of being)   74, 78–84, 86–91, 96, 125, 148, 149, 150, 165
Waliullah, Shah   29
Weber, Max   6, 14, 62
Western spiritual movements   32
Wisdom of the Upanishad (Besant)   35

worship, categories of   37–8
wujudi   83, 84, 94, 95, 96, 137, 165, 184, 185, 187, 191

Yarhen, festival at Sufi *mandir*   110
yoga   44, 125, 126, 152, 155
   influence   8
   islamization of   8
Yoga Vasishtha   126, 150

Zakariyya, Baha al-Din   38, 165, 175, 179, 181
zakat (alms)   102
zamindar (landowners)   26, 31
Zarathustra   35
zikr   108, 123
Zinda Pir   41
ziyarat   37, 191

www.ingramcontent.com/pod-product-compliance
Lightning Source LLC
Chambersburg PA
CBHW050421280326
41932CB00013BA/1953